GCSE  WEEK

This book is to be
the last date

Author – Jill Duffy

Use this day-by-day listing and the tabs on each page in the book to plan your revision.

D1357621

TALKING ABOUT YOURSELF

The form below, which you might fill in when asking for a French penfriend, gives basic personal details.

⬭ Mes coordonnées

Nom	Je m'appelle <u>Anne Black</u>.
Age	J'ai <u>quinze</u> ans.
Anniversaire	Mon anniversaire est le <u>18 avril.</u>
Description	Je suis <u>assez grande</u>. J'ai les <u>cheveux bruns</u> et les <u>yeux verts.</u>
Domicile	J'habite à <u>Warwick</u>, dans <u>un petit appartement</u>.
Autres informations	J'ai <u>un chat</u> et <u>deux lapins</u>. Je suis <u>sportive et drôle</u>.

Use the words below and on the next page to replace the words underlined in the form, so that they fit your own description.
Revise all of them, as they may appear in exam questions.

Exam hint

In comprehension questions look out for words such as **très** (very) and **assez** (quite), which change the meaning slightly and may make a difference to the mark.

Description

Cheveux		Yeux		Caractère	
longs	long	bleus	blue	drôle	funny
courts	short	verts	green	charmant	charming
frisés	curly	bleu clair	light blue	égoïste	selfish
raides	straight	noisette	hazel	sportif/sportive	sporty
noirs	black	marron	brown	courageux/courageuse	brave
brun foncé	dark brown			généreux/généreuse	generous
blonds	blond			sympa	nice
				timide	shy

Animaux

un lapin	rabbit
une souris	mouse
un cobaye	guinea-pig
un cochon d'Inde	guinea-pig
un cheval	horse
un poney	pony
une gerbille	gerbil
un perroquet	parrot
une perruche	budgerigar

Progress check

Match the questions to the answers.

1 Tu as quel âge?

   a   Oui, deux lapins.

2 A-t-elle des animaux?

   b   Non, elle est petite.

3 Où habites-tu?

   c   J'ai dix-sept ans.

4 Elle est grande?

   d   Il s'appelle Thomas.

5 Comment s'appelle-t-il?

   e   J'habite à Diss dans un bungalow.

THE FAMILY

○ Learn the diagrams below

In the first one, the words for 'my' have been included, as this is how you will often need to use them. Try to work out what they mean before you check the list.

Four generations

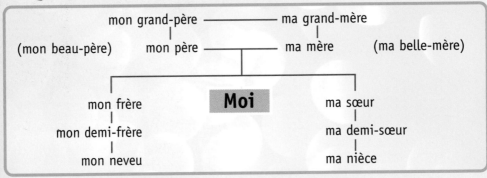

Other family relationships

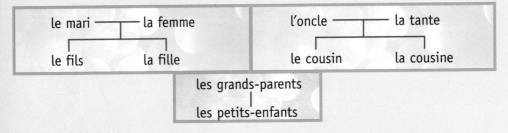

○ Key words

le beau-père	stepfather	la belle-mère	stepmother
le demi-frère	half-brother stepbrother	la demi-sœur	half-sister, stepsister
l'oncle	uncle	la tante	aunt
le mari	husband	la femme	wife
le fils	son	la fille	daughter
le neveu	nephew	la nièce	niece
les grands-parents	grandparents	les petits-enfants	grandchildren

The vocabulary for members of the family is usually learnt at the beginning of the French course, so it is often forgotten.

Some useful adjectives

aîné	older
divorcé	divorced
cadet/cadette	younger
séparé	separated
jumeau/jumelle	twin
unique	only (child)

Exam hints

- Remember to pronounce the 's' on the end of **fils**. It doesn't change its spelling in the plural so may mean 'son' or 'sons'. Check other clues (e.g. *le* or *les*) to be sure.

- **Nièce** is pronounced as 'nyess'.

- The hyphen in the middle of **petits-enfants** is very important. What would it mean if you left it out?

Step 1

Decide which group the verb belongs to: **er**, **ir** or **re**. You can tell from the spelling in the vocabulary list.

Step 2

Learn the three different sets of endings

Step 3

Put the right ending on for the person (see below). There are only six endings to learn for each group. Remember to take off the **er**, **ir** or **re** first.

Table of endings

er	ir	re
je parle	je choisis	j'attends
tu parles	tu choisis	tu attends
il/elle/on parle	il/elle/on choisit	il/elle/on/attend
nous parlons	nous choisissons	nous attendons
vous parlez	vous choisissez	vous attendez
ils/elles parlent	ils/elles choisissent	ils/elles attendent

Key facts

- Most French verbs belong to the first **er** group.

- The **ir** group verbs are the most difficult to spell, particularly in the plural.

- The most common verbs in the **re** group are **vendre** (to sell), **attendre** (to wait) and **perdre** (to lose).

Verbs can be difficult, but they are important. In this section revise the basic rules that apply to most of them.

The present tense describes something that is going on **now**. Some examples are:

- you speak, we choose, he waits
- you are speaking, we are choosing, he is waiting

Examples

Tu parles anglais? Do you speak English?

J'aime écouter de la musique. I like listening to music.

Nous finissons les cours à quatre heures. We finish lessons at 4 o'clock.

Il attend le bus. He is waiting for the bus.

Exam hint

'I do not speak English' is just **Je ne parle pas anglais** and 'Do you speak French?' is just **Tu parles français?** using the present tense. A word for 'do' is not needed.

Progress check

Underline the correct spelling for the verb in each sentence.

1. Ils attends/attendons/attendent le prof.

2. Je choisis/choisit/choisir un croissant.

3. Vous aimons/aimez/aime la musique pop?

4. On vend/vendons/vendent de tout dans un supermarché.

5. Nous retrouve/retrouvez/retrouvons nos amis à la discothèque.

6. Tu ne travaille/travailles/travaillez pas le week-end?

2
3
4
5
6
7

AT HOME

Key facts

- Many French people live in a flat (*un appartement*) in a large block (*un immeuble*).

- Semi-detached houses (*une maison jumelle*) are rare in France.

- Detached houses (*une maison individuelle* or *un pavillon*) often have a cellar (*une cave*) to store wine.

- The word for farmhouse is the same as for farm (*une ferme*).

Revise the words for basic furniture items in each room.

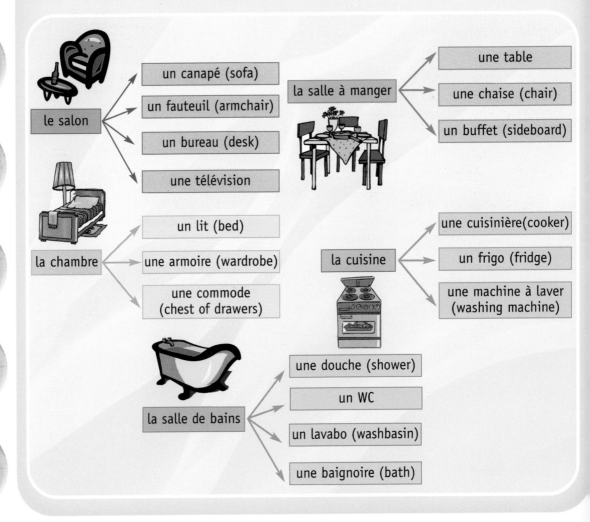

le salon
- un canapé (sofa)
- un fauteuil (armchair)
- un bureau (desk)
- une télévision

la salle à manger
- une table
- une chaise (chair)
- un buffet (sideboard)

la chambre
- un lit (bed)
- une armoire (wardrobe)
- une commode (chest of drawers)

la cuisine
- une cuisinière (cooker)
- un frigo (fridge)
- une machine à laver (washing machine)

la salle de bains
- une douche (shower)
- un WC
- un lavabo (washbasin)
- une baignoire (bath)

This topic is likely to appear in the early questions on your exam papers or may be covered in more detail in the oral test.

Décris ta chambre

When you prepare your answer to this question, you should think about...

- furniture in the room
- colour of walls (**murs**), carpet (**tapis**), curtains (**rideaux**)
- pictures (**tableaux**), photos (**photos**) and posters (**posters** or **affiches**)

Look at the paragraph below. You should be able to adapt the details in italics to fit your own room.

> Dans ma chambre il y a *un lit, une commode, une armoire et un bureau*. Les murs sont *blancs*, le tapis est *vert* et les rideaux sont *rouges*. J'ai *une photo de mon chat* sur le bureau, et aux murs il y a *des posters de mes groupes favoris*.

Now write a similar paragraph to describe your own room.

Progress check

Are these sentences true (**vrai**) or false (**faux**)?

1. Dans un immeuble il y a des appartements.

2. Il n'y a pas beaucoup de maisons jumelles en France.

3. D'habitude on trouve un lit dans la salle à manger.

4. On prend une douche dans la cuisine.

5. On met des bouteilles de vin dans une cave.

6. Si on veut se relaxer on s'assoit dans un fauteuil.

DAY 1

Follow the flow chart to describe your own home.

Now say what there is (or isn't) in your town or village.

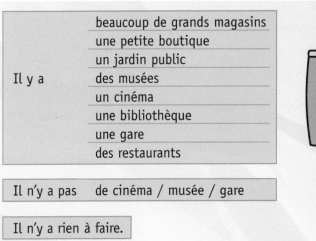

Il y a	beaucoup de grands magasins
	une petite boutique
	un jardin public
	des musées
	un cinéma
	une bibliothèque
	une gare
	des restaurants

Il n'y a pas de cinéma / musée / gare

Il n'y a rien à faire.

Finally, why you like or don't like it.

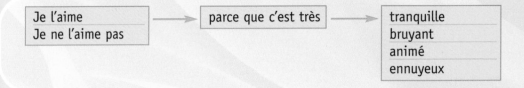

Je l'aime	parce que c'est très	tranquille
Je ne l'aime pas		bruyant
		animé
		ennuyeux

For this topic, describe the position of your house or flat and understand what other people are saying or writing about where they live.

Exam hints

- When **est** means 'east', all three letters are pronounced to rhyme with 'best'.

- Use your common sense; it's more likely that a town will be described as lively (**animé**) or noisy (**bruyant**), and the countryside as quiet (**tranquille**) or boring (**ennuyeux**). If the passage seems to be saying the opposite, perhaps you have missed a negative.

  e.g. **J'aime mon village parce que ce n'est pas bruyant**.

- Recognise the names of a few large towns or cities in France: Paris (s not pronounced), Lyon, Marseille, Bordeaux, Strasbourg and the Channel ports.

Another topic that could be linked with 'Where you live' is the environment. Revise these words:

la poubelle	dustbin
recycler	to recycle
les déchets	waste
réutiliser	to re-use
le verre	glass
gaspiller	to waste
la pollution	pollution
vert	ecological, 'green'

Progress check

Choose the correct sentence from each pair.

1
a) Londres est une grande ville dans le sud de l'Angleterre.
b) Londres est un petit village au bord de la mer.

2
a) D'habitude dans un petit village il y a beaucoup de grands magasins.
b) D'habitude dans un petit village il y a quelques petites boutiques seulement.

3
a) J'aime habiter à la campagne parce qu'il y a trop de bruit.
b) La vie dans une grande ville me plaît parce que j'aime le bruit.

4
a) Il n'y a pas beaucoup de choses à faire dans une grande ville.
b) La vie n'est pas ennuyeuse dans une grande ville.

DAY 1

Verbs are 'irregular' because they have been used so much over the centuries that their form has changed. It follows that they are verbs with very common meanings. The four in the table below are the most important. As you revise them, look across the columns to see the parts that are similar.

avoir (to have)	être (to be)	aller (to go)	faire (to do, to make)
j'ai	je suis	je vais	je fais
tu as	tu es	tu vas	tu fais
il a	il est	il va	il fait
nous avons	nous sommes	nous allons	nous faisons
vous avez	vous êtes	vous allez	vous faites
ils ont	ils sont	ils vont	ils font

Did you notice these points?

- The **tu** part of all four verbs ends in **s**. This is the case for almost every verb except **tu peux** and **tu veux**. It is a frequent error in written French to forget the 's'.

- The **nous** part of three of them ends in **ons**. Être is the only French verb that does not do so in the present tense.

- The **vous** part of two of them ends in **ez**. This is also a firm rule for French verbs, with only three exceptions: **vous êtes**, **vous faites** and **vous dites** (from **dire**, 'to say').

- The **ils** part of all four ends in **ont**. All other French verbs end in **ent**.

Apart from their meanings, why are these verbs so important?

- **avoir** is used in special phrases such as **avoir raison** (to be right), **avoir tort** (to be wrong), **avoir peur** (to be afraid) and **j'ai 16 ans** (I am 16 years old) and also helps to form the perfect tense (see p 72)

- **être** also helps to form the perfect tense of some verbs (see p 78)

- **aller** can be used to talk about the future (see p 67)

- **faire** is used in weather phrases (see p 46)

SPEND 15 MINUTES ON THIS TOPIC

Some verbs do not follow the pattern of page 6. There isn't room here to list them all, but try to learn the ones on these two pages.

The next verb also needs to be carefully learnt:

prendre to take, to have (food and drink) also comprendre and apprendre	
je prends	nous prenons
tu prends	vous prenez
il prend	ils prennent

Learn these sentences, which contain the most useful parts of several other verbs.

boire to drink	D'habitude je bois du coca.
devoir have to, must	Nous devons étudier les maths.
écrire to write	Nous écrivons tous les mois.
lire to read	Je lis des magazines de mode.
ouvrir to open	Ouvre la porte!
partir to leave	Le train part à dix heures.
pouvoir to be able, can	Tu peux venir avec moi.
savoir to know how to	Je sais parler français
sortir to go out	Quand je sors je mets un jean et un T-shirt.
mettre to put, put on	
venir to come	Viens vite!
voir to see	Je vois mon copain tous les samedis.
vouloir to want	Tu veux aller au cinéma?

Progress check

What do these sentences mean? You can work out which verbs are used by comparing them with the list on the left.

1. Je vais prendre une omelette.

2. Viens avec moi.

3. Vous pouvez aller en France avec vos amis.

4. Tu dois rentrer à 11 heures?

5. Elle sait nager.

6. Écris-moi vite.

This is a simple time sequence, which can easily be adapted to fit your own routine. Check how to use the verbs on p 18.

À 7 heures	je me réveille.	
À 7h 15	je me lève	
À 7h20	je me douche.	
À 7h30	je m'habille.	
À 7h50	je prends le petit déjeuner.	
À 8h	je pars pour le collège.	
À 12h30	je mange à la cantine.	
À 16h30	je rentre à la maison.	
À 18h	je mange.	
À 19h	je fais mes devoirs.	
À 21h	je regarde la télé.	
À 22h	je me couche.	

These can be developed if you wish; for example, you could say what you have for breakfast, the clothes you wear, how you travel to school. For further help with these check the appropriate sections later in the book.

Weekend routine is usually different, so be prepared to understand, talk or write about that too. You could either learn a pattern similar to the weekday routine or concentrate on the differences:

- *Que fais-tu d'habitude le week-end?*

- *Le week-end j'aime me relaxer. Le samedi je me réveille plus tard. Je ne porte pas mon uniforme scolaire, bien sûr. Le soir je sors en ville avec mes amis. Quelquefois nous allons au cinéma. Le dimanche j'ai un petit job: je travaille dans un café comme serveur/serveuse.*

You could also practise changing the verbs into the imperfect, perfect or future tenses, in answer to the questions:

- *Que faisais-tu le week-end quand tu étais plus jeune?* (imperfect)

- *Qu'as-tu fait dimanche dernier?* (perfect)

- *Que feras-tu samedi prochain?* (future)

LEISURE TIME

'Free time' in French may be **temps libre** or **loisirs** (leisure), and hobbies are **passe-temps**, **centres d'intérêt** or even **hobbies** (though it is more impressive to use the French word).

Questions about your free time

- Quels sont tes passe-temps/loisirs/hobbies?
- Qu'est-ce que tu aimes faire quand tu as du temps libre?
- Que fais-tu le soir/le week-end?

Look at the sentences below and use some of them as patterns to describe your own interests. You will need to recognise them all to understand comprehension passages.

How to say you like something

- *J'aime lire.*
- *J'aime beaucoup la peinture.*
- *La musique me plaît.*
- *J'adore les jeux d'ordinateur.*
- *Le sport, c'est ma passion.*
- *Je m'intéresse à la photographie.*
- *Je suis fana de football.*

How to say you dislike something

- *Je n'aime pas regarder la télévision.*
- *Je n'aime pas du tout les magazines pour les jeunes.*
- *Je déteste le hockey.*
- *La musique ne m'intéresse pas.*
- *J'ai horreur des jeux vidéo.*

This section deals with likes and dislikes in general. We'll look at some of them in more detail in the next few pages.

15 MINS

There are other ways of saying what you do in your spare time, without using 'liking' verbs.

- *Je fais une collection de peluches.* (soft toys)
- *J'écoute la radio.*
- *Je vais souvent au cinéma.*
- *Je lis beaucoup.*
- *Je joue aux échecs.* (chess)
- *Je joue de la flûte dans un orchestre.*

The last two are very important. **Jouer** means 'to play', but the words following it change depending on whether it's a game or a musical instrument that is being played.

For a game, use the right part of **à** (see p 30)

For a musical instrument, use the right part of **de** (see p 30)

To use the wrong one sounds odd in French (imagine throwing clarinets round a sports field or playing a tune on a football) so try to get it right.

Progress check

Read the paragraph, then answer the question below.

Le week-end Marie aime faire les magasins. Elle achète des livres parce qu'elle adore lire. Quand elle rentre à la maison elle écoute des CD. Elle s'intéresse à la musique classique mais elle a horreur de la musique pop. Le sport ne lui plaît pas du tout. Elle aime le cinéma mais elle n'aime pas aller au théâtre.

List three things that Marie likes and three things that she does not like.

✔ ....

✔ ....

✔ ....

✗ ....

✗ ....

✗ ....

DAY 2

1
4
5
6
7

DAY 2

The verb **laver** means 'to wash', but it has to be followed by a noun: **je lave mes vêtements**. In English we also use 'wash' to mean 'get washed' or 'have a wash'. For that meaning French uses an extra pronoun, which means 'myself', 'yourself', etc. Revise the table below:

person	extra pronoun	verb	meaning
Je	me	lave	wash (myself)
Tu	te	laves	you wash (yourself)
Il	se	lave	he washes (himself)
Nous	nous	lavons	we wash (ourselves)
Vous	vous	lavez	you wash (yourselves)
Ils	se	lavent	they wash (themselves)

- Me, te, se become m', t', s' before a vowel or h
- As usual, elle and on are the same as il
- Don't forget to change the endings on the verbs as well
- Most of these verbs belong to the er group

Il se dépêche.

Nous nous relaxons.

Je m'ennuie.

You will have noticed in the last two sections a number of verbs with an extra word. This section explains what they are and how to use them.

15 MINS

You will recognise verbs of this type in the word lists because they always include **se**. The most useful ones are part of the 'Daily routine' sequence, but there are a few others. Learn the lists below.

Daily routine

se réveiller	to wake up
se lever	to get up
se laver	to wash
s'habiller	to get dressed
se dépêcher	to hurry up
se reposer	to rest
se coucher	to lie down, go to bed

Leisure time

s'amuser	to enjoy oneself
s'intéresser	to be interested
se détendre	to relax
se relaxer	to relax
s'ennuyer	to be bored

Note the accents on **se lever**:

je me lève, tu te lèves, il se lève, nous nous levons, vous vous levez, ils se lèvent

also the spelling of **s'appeler** (to be called):

je m'appelle, tu t'appelles, il s'appelle, nous nous appelons, vous vous appelez, ils s'appellent

Progress check

Fill in the gaps with **me, te, se, nous** or **vous**.

1 Elle ....repose.

2 Nous ....habillons.

3 Tu ....réveilles.

4 Je ....amuse.

5 Vous ....dépêchez.

6 Ils ....ennuient.

DAY 2

SPORTS

These are the main international events that take place in France or in which French players are involved.

Grand Prix automobile	Formula One racing	
Jeux Olympiques (J.O.)	Olympic Games	
Tour de France	Cycle race	
Tournoi des Six Nations	Six Nations Tournament (rugby)	
24 heures du Mans	Le Mans 24 hour road race	

and in various sports

Championnat du Monde	World Championships	
Coupe du Monde	World Cup	
Championnat d'Europe	European championships	
Open	Open Championship	

Apart from the sports that are popular worldwide, there are two that have a particular following in France:

- **boules** (also called **pétanque**) which is a form of bowls played in town parks and village squares

- **cyclisme** (cycling), which attracts huge crowds whenever there is a major race

The French national teams are often called **Les Bleus** or **Les Tricolores**.

Sport is a very popular activity in France. Even if it is not one of your own interests, you need to know some basic facts and vocabulary.

Key words

The French word for most sports is the same as in English (le football, le tennis).

The list below contains some that are different.

l'athlétisme	athletics
le cyclisme	cycling
la gymnastique	gymnastics
la natation	swimming
le patinage	skating
la pêche	fishing
la planche à voile	windsurfing
la voile	sailing
les sports d'hiver	winter sports

Other key words

la course	race
l'équipe	team
la piscine	swimming pool
le stade	stadium
le terrain	pitch, ground

Progress check

Which is the correct answer?

1 On joue aux boules
....
a   dans le supermarché.
b   sur la place du village.
c   à la gare.

2 Dans le Tournoi des Six Nations on joue au ....
a   rugby.
b   football.
c   tennis.

3 On va à la piscine pour faire
....
a   de l'athlétisme.
b   de la natation.
c   de la voile.

4 L'équipe nationale s'appelle
....
a   Les Rouges.
b   Les Verts.
c   Les Bleus.

DAY
2

15 MINS

DAY 2

Talking about TV and radio

The conversation covers these points:

- Whether you prefer TV or radio
- When you listen or watch
- Your favourite programmes and why you like them

- *Tu préfères la radio ou la télé?*
  ⬇
- *Je préfère la télé.*
  ⬇
- **Quand** *est-ce que tu regardes la télé?*
  ⬇
- *Le soir, après huit heures.*
  ⬇
- *Quelle* **sorte** *d'émission aimes-tu?*
  ⬇
- *J'aime les soaps.*
  ⬇
- *Tu as un soap préféré?*

- *Oui, j'aime beaucoup Eastenders.*
  ⬇
- **Pourquoi?**
  ⬇
- *Parce que c'est réaliste.*
  ⬇
- *Ça passe quand, Eastenders?*
  ⬇
- *Trois fois par semaine: le lundi, le mardi et le jeudi.*
  ⬇
- *Et à quelle heure?*
  ⬇
- *Normalement à 7h 30 ou 8h.*

Choose from

quand

le matin
avant d'aller à l'école
après le collège
le week-end

sorte

les séries (serials)
les émissions comiques
la musique
les documentaires
les jeux
les dessins animés (cartoons)
les actualités (news)
les films

pourquoi

intéressant
amusant
relaxant
utile (useful)

This section is in the form of a conversation about TV and radio programmes. Work out what changes you would make if you were answering the questions yourself.

15 MINS

DAY 2

You don't have to wait for the next question in the conversation; for example in answer to *Tu as un soap préféré?* you could say *J'aime Eastenders parce que c'est réaliste.*

You may wish to give more details. Here are some useful words.

le présentateur	presenter
le disc-jockey	DJ
la publicité	advertisement
la chaîne	channel
en direct	'live'

- Many French radio programmes play English and American pop music.
- There are often games shows on TV in late afternoon and early evening.
- Countdown (*Des chiffres et des lettres*) started in France.
- At 9 pm there is usually a choice of films across most TV channels.

Progress check

Look at the description of the programmes, and decide which one

a is funny
b is interesting
c is realistic
d is relaxing
e has a good presenter

1 J'aime l'émission parce que je peux me relaxer.

2 Le présentateur est excellent.

3 C'est une émission très réaliste.

4 Ça m'intéresse beaucoup.

5 C'est amusant.

NOUNS

Nouns are either **masculine** or **feminine**. This is easy when referring to a person, but it is not so easy with other words. It is important to learn whether a noun is masculine or feminine when you learn its meaning.

Study the diagram.

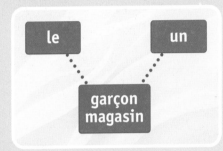

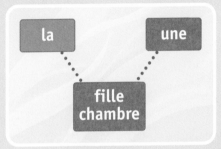

le, la, les mean 'the'

un, une, des mean 'a' or 'some'

Rules

- Use **le** or **un** with a masculine noun.

- Use **la** or **une** with a feminine noun.

- **Le** and **la** usually change to **l'** before **a**, **e** , **i**, **o**, **u**, and **h**.

- Use **les** or **des** with any plural noun.

DAY 2

24

Nouns (names of people and things) are divided into two categories in French, masculine and feminine. Revise the basic rules.

10 MINS

Nouns also have to be made plural in French. (This does not change the pronunciation, so it's only in written French that it is really important.)

- To make a noun plural, add **s**:
  le parent, les parents

- If it already ends in s or x, leave it as it is: **le fils, les fils**

- If it ends in **eu** or **au**, add **x**:
  le gâteau, les gâteaux

- If it ends in **al**, change it to **aux**:
  le journal, les journaux

Both halves of the next four nouns are made plural.

grand-parent	grands-parents
petit-fils	petits-fils
petite-fille	petites-filles
monsieur	messieurs
madame	mesdames

Don't forget

la pomme de terre, les pommes de terre
(potato, potatoes – 'apples of the earth')

le piano

la maison

la chaise

DAY 3

● A conversation in a small shop

This conversation might take place in any of the small specialist shops still found in France. Learn it and practise substituting other items for the words in brackets.

- Bonjour, madame. Vous désirez?
- Je voudrais (deux éclairs au chocolat).
- Voilà, madame. Et avec ça?
- Je prendrai aussi (une tarte aux pommes).
- Bon. Vous voulez autre chose?
- Non merci, c'est tout. C'est combien?
- Ça fait 5,80€
- Voilà.
- Payez à la caisse, s'il vous plaît, madame

Key words and phrases

À la banque

Je voudrais changer un chèque de voyage.	I'd like to change a travellers'cheque.
Je voudrais changer 60 livres en euros.	I'd like to change £60 into euros.
Voici mon passeport.	Here's my passport.

À la poste

Trois timbres pour l'Angleterre.	Three stamps for England
C'est combien pour envoyer une carte postale?	How much is it to send a postcard?

Dans les grands magasins

Le magasin ouvre/ferme à quelle heure?	What time does the shop open/close?
Avez-vous des pulls en coton?	Do you have any cotton sweaters?
Je n'aime pas la couleur.	I don't like the colour.
C'est quelle taille?	What size is it?
Je peux l'essayer?	Can I try it on?
Il y a un trou dedans.	There's a hole in it.

The next few pages deal with the process of shopping, from changing money right through to buying souvenirs.

On achète des souvenirs

Je cherche un cadeau pour ma mère.	I'm looking for a present for my mother.
Où est le rayon de musique?	Where is the music department?
Ils sont en promotion.	They are on special offer.
Je prends le CD de MC Solaar.	I'll take the CD by MC Solaar.
C'est pour offrir?	Is it a present? (It could be gift-wrapped)

Progress check

In these sentences the words in red are wrong. What should they be?

1. On peut changer de l'argent à la **boulangerie**.

2. Pour changer un chèque de voyage il faut montrer son **billet**.

3. En France les prix sont en **francs**.

4. Dans les magasins on doit souvent payer à la **porte**.

5. On peut demander à **refuser** des vêtements.

6. Les CD se vendent au **livre** de musique.

7. Avant de partir on achète des **timbres** pour la famille.

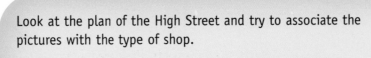

SHOPPING 2

Look at the plan of the High Street and try to associate the pictures with the type of shop.

La rue principale

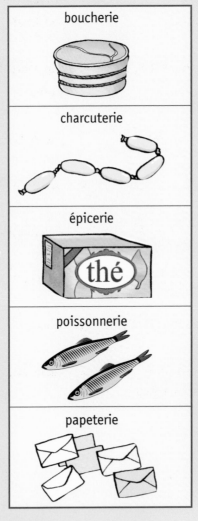

boucherie

charcuterie

épicerie

poissonnerie

papeterie

pharmacie

Poste

pâtisserie

confiserie

boulangerie

Note also these two:

la librairie	bookshop
la bibliothèque	library

- Hypermarchés are also called grandes surfaces.

- Grands magasins are department stores such as Monoprix and Galeries Lafayette.

- Boutiques are small individual shops of any type, not clothes shops.

- Some types of shop are combined: a boulangerie sells bread, a pâtisserie sells cakes, and a boulangerie-pâtisserie sells both bread and cakes.

- Marchés (markets) are held in many towns and villages and often include live produce such as chickens.

- A centre commercial (shopping mall) often in a zone piétonne (pedestrianised area) is found in many town centres.

- Soldes means 'Sales'.

Progress check

Match the phrases to their meanings.

1. soldes
2. en promotion
3. Vous désirez?
4. payez à la caisse
5. et avec ça?
6. C'est tout.
7. grands magasins
8. centre commercial

a. What would you like?
b. department stores
c. pay at the till
d. anything else?
e. shopping mall
f. on special offer
g. sales
h. That's all.

DAY
3

A means 'to'. There is no problem when it is followed by a name:
à Marie, à Paris.

De means 'of'. Again, no problem when it is followed by a name:
de Pierre, de Londres.

Look at the flow chart below to see what happens when 'to' and 'of' are followed by 'the'. Think about the noun.

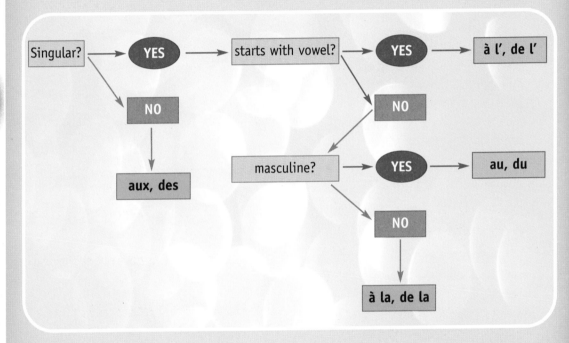

Examples

singular noun starting with vowel or **h**	**à l'appartement, de l'école**
masculine singular starting with any other letter	**au salon, du chat**
feminine singular starting with any other letter	**à la chambre, de la campagne**
any plural noun	**aux Etats-Unis, aux enfants, des filles**

Key points

- To say 'Peter's friend' you must say 'the friend of Peter': **l'ami de Pierre**

- **Du, de la, de l'** and **des** can also mean 'some': **du café**, **des chocolats**

- After a negative (not) **du, de la, de l'** and **des** change to **de (d')**: **je n'ai pas de chocolats, il n'y a plus de beurre.**

- **Beaucoup** (a lot) is followed by **de or d'** only: **beaucoup de personnes, beaucoup d'amis.** The same applies to most other expressions of quantity.

- Some towns have **Le** in their name: **Le Havre, Le Mans.** These follow the same rules. **Au Havre** means 'to Le Havre', **Du Mans** means 'of (or from) Le Mans'

Progress check

Fill in the gaps with the right words.

1. Nous allons .... Lyon.

2. Je vais acheter .... vêtements.

3. Il faut manger beaucoup .... fruits.

4. La voix .... prof est très forte.

5. Il va ...... appartement

6. On joue .... boules.

7. Le frère .... Anne a dix-sept ans.

8. Pour prendre le train il faut aller .... gare.

ARRANGING TO MEET

Check that you know what these phrases mean.

Invitation

Tu es libre samedi soir?
Tu veux sortir avec moi?
Tu veux aller au cinéma?
Si on allait au café?
Allons à la discothèque!
On pourrait peut-être aller au stade?
On y va?

Acceptance

Oui, je veux bien.
Peut-être.
Bonne idée.
D'accord.
Pourquoi pas?

Refusal

Désolé, je ne peux pas.
Je ne suis pas libre.
Ce n'est pas possible.

Place

Rendez-vous   devant le cinéma
          au café
          chez moi

This is one of the most useful topics as you may wish to go out with friends on an exchange visit to France.

Time

À sept heures et demie
À huit heures
À neuf heures et quart

Confirmation

À bientôt!
À tout à l'heure!
À demain!
À ce soir!

Progress check

Using the words on this page, find the French for...

1 Are you free this evening?

2 Shall we go to the disco?

3 Yes, I'd love to.

4 See you outside the café.

5 See you soon.

6 Sorry, I can't.

7 Shall we go?

DAY
3

Practise choosing food and drink from a menu and paying for it.

Here are two sample conversations. The first might take place in a café, where there will probably be a restricted menu, particularly at lunchtime. The second might take place in a restaurant, and involves three courses from the set menu (Table d'hôte).

– Garçon!

– Oui, mademoiselle. Qu'est-ce que vous voulez prendre?

– Il y a un plat du jour?

– Oui, mademoiselle, steak-frites.

– Je n'aime pas ça. Je prendrai une omelette au fromage s'il vous plaît.

– D'accord, mademoiselle. Vous voulez boire quelque chose?

– Un jus d'orange s'il vous plaît.

– Bien, mademoiselle.

(later…)

– L'addition, s'il vous plaît.

– Voilà, mademoiselle. Payez à la caisse.

– Merci. Au revoir.

– Au revoir mademoiselle.

– Comme entrée, je prends la soupe à l'oignon.

– D'accord, monsieur. Et comme plat principal?

– Le coq au vin, s'il vous plaît. Qu'est-ce qu'il y a comme légumes?

– Pommes dauphine ou frites, carottes et petits pois, monsieur.

– Alors, pommes dauphine et carottes s'il vous plaît.

– Bien monsieur. Et comme boisson?

– Une demi-bouteille de vin rouge et une carafe d'eau, s'il vous plaît.

(later…)

– Vous voulez prendre un dessert, monsieur?

– Oui, je vais prendre une glace au chocolat.

– D'accord, monsieur. C'est tout?

– Oui. Voulez-vous apporter l'addition, s'il vous plaît?

– Voilà, monsieur.

– Merci. Le service est compris?

– Ah oui, monsieur.

CAFÉ DUFY
~·~·~·~

Omelettes variées

Croque-monsieur

Plat du jour mercredi
17 août :

Steak-frites

Restaurant
Tante Elisabeth

Menu à 18 €

Entrée
Soupe à l'oignon
Œuf mayonnaise

Plat principal
Steak au poivre
Coq au vin
Spaghettis bolognaise

Dessert
Tarte au citron
Glaces variées

> There is usually a selection of tisanes (herbal teas) such as **tilleul** (lime blossom) and **menthe**.

In a restaurant the Table d'hôte (set) menu is always cheaper than the A la carte (free choice) menu.

Key facts

- If you order **'un café'** you will automatically receive a small black coffee. For white coffee you have to specify **café crème**.

- Sitting outside on the **terrasse** is the best way to enjoy a French café, but may incur an extra charge.

- The food menu in a café usually includes items such as omelettes, **croque-monsieur** (toasted ham and cheese sandwich) and **steak-frites or poisson-frites**

- Popular non-alcoholic cold drinks include mineral waters such as Perrier (fizzy) and Evian (still), **jus de fruits**, **citron pressé** and **diabolo menthe** (mint cordial).

Progress check

Look at the menus.

Use the sample conversations to order...

1. a toasted cheese and ham sandwich and apple juice

2. the *plat du jour* and mint cordial

3. a ham omelette and white coffee

4. Egg mayonnaise, spaghetti bolognaise, lemon tart and black coffee

5. onion soup, steak, a strawberry ice cream and mineral water

ADJECTIVES 1

You have already revised nouns, so you should have the two ideas of **gender** (masculine or feminine) and **number** (singular or plural) in your mind. Remember this important fact:

> **Adjectives 'agree' with the noun they describe.**

So make them feminine to go with a feminine noun, and plural to go with a plural noun. How?

- Add **e** for feminine
- Add **s** for plural
- Add **es** for feminine plural

Examples

un livre intéressant	une émission intéressante
un grand magasin	des grands magasins
la chemise noire	les chemises noires

Exceptions

- If it already ends in **e**, don't add another to make it feminine:

  (unless it is é: l'enfant fatigué, la mère fatiguée)

le pull rouge, la jupe rouge

- If it already ends in **s** or **x** don't add another to make it plural:

le cahier gris, les cahiers gris

This is an item of language that can really make a difference to your written French if you can master it.

Most adjectives come **after** the noun they describe, but a few common ones come before it. They include:

grand	petit
bon	mauvais
jeune	méchant
joli	gros

cher (dear) may come before or after the noun depending on its exact shade of meaning.

mon cher ami	beloved
un livre cher	expensive

When you are speaking French you may need to change the sound of the adjective when it is feminine.

petit	t not pronounced	un petit café
petite	t pronounced (it is no longer the last letter)	une petite boutique

Adjectives agree with their nouns

une fille contente

des garçons tristes

DAY 3

○ **Traverser la Manche**

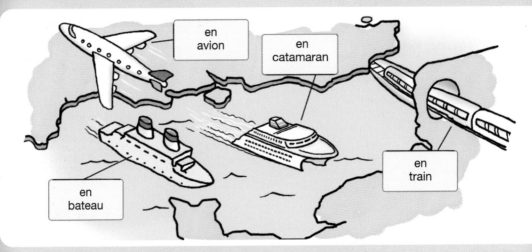

The paragraph in French below sums up the ways of crossing the Channel as shown in the diagram. Check that you understand it.

On peut traverser la Manche en avion, en bateau ou en catamaran. On peut aussi aller sous la Manche par le train avec ou sans la voiture. Quand on arrive il faut passer par la Douane.

These are the current Channel crossing routes by ferry : Dover – Calais, Folkestone – Calais, Newhaven – Dieppe, Poole – Cherbourg, Portsmouth – Cherbourg, Portsmouth – Le Havre, Portsmouth – Caen, Plymouth – Roscoff.

The main airport in Paris is Charles-de-Gaulle at Roissy. Regional airports include Nice, Marseille, Lyon, Toulouse, Bordeaux, Strasbourg and Nantes.

Eurotunnel opened in 1994. Passengers without vehicles travel by the Eurostar train.

There are several different methods of transport you need to know about. First we'll consider crossing the Channel.

Key words

voyager	to travel
le trajet	journey
le guichet	ticket office
le billet	ticket
le départ	departure

l'aéroport	airport
le décollage	take-off
l'atterrissage	landing
la sécurité	safety
le pirate de l'air	hijacker

débarquer	to disembark
la carte d'embarquement	boarding card
Douvres	Dover

l'autoroute	motorway
le péage	toll
tomber en panne	to break down
l'aire de repos	motorway rest area

Progress check

Match the signs to their English meaning.

1. Douane   **a** security check

2. Guichet   **b** toll

3. Aire de repos   **c** customs

4. Péage   **d** rest area

5. Contrôle de sécurité   **e** ticket office

○ Public transport

en train, en bus, en car (coach) **en métro** (underground), **le tramway**

Asking where to go

Où est   la gare?
l'arrêt d'autobus/de tramway?
la gare routière
la station de métro?

Asking for a timetable

Avez-vous un horaire, s'il vous plaît ?

Buying tickets

Un aller simple pour Caen, s'il vous plaît.
Un aller-retour première classe pour Dijon

Understanding about arrivals and departures

Il part/arrive à quelle heure?
C'est quel quai?
C'est direct?
Le train en provenance de Paris (from Paris)
Le train à destination de Paris (to Paris)
Descendez ici.
Il y a un retard. (delay)

○ Private transport

en auto, en voiture, à vélo (bike),
à vélomoteur (moped) **à pied** (on foot)

We'll look now at moving around in town. Many of the phrases are the same for each method of transport so you only need to learn them once.

Asking where to go

Où est le parking le plus proche?
le garage?
la station-service?
Il y a une station-service près d'ici?

Problems with parking and with the vehicle

Je peux stationner/me garer ici?
La voiture ne marche pas.
Il y a un pneu crevé. (puncture)

Revise this conversation, which is useful if you are travelling in France with friends or family as well as for exams! It's set in a self-service petrol station.

– *Faites le plein d'essence, s'il vous plaît.*

– *C'est libre-service, monsieur.*
  Vous devez faire le plein vous-même.
  Vous désirez sans-plomb ou gazole?

– *Non, super seulement. Et je veux vérifier la pression des pneus.*

– *D'accord. La pompe est là-bas à droite, et pour la pression des pneus allez à gauche.*

– *Merci. Je paie à la caisse?*

– *Oui monsieur.*

Progress check

Are these sentences true **(vrai)** or false **(faux)**?

1 Le car, ça veut dire 'car' en anglais.

2 Si on veut prendre le bus, on va à l'arrêt.

3 Si un train est 'direct', il n'est pas nécessaire de changer.

4 Un train 'à destination de Paris' vient de Paris.

5 S'il y a un retard, il faut attendre.

6 Le sans-plomb est une sorte d'essence.

1
2
3
DAY
4
5
6
7

For the adjectives in the first two boxes, check that you know what the masculine singular and plural spellings would be.

Groups

Masculine singular ending	Feminine singular ending	Examples
er	ère	mon cher ami/ma chère amie
eux	euse	le camion dangereux/la route dangereuse
ic	ique	le jardin public/une réunion publique
if	ive	un garçon sportif/une fille sportive
il	ille	un homme gentil/une femme gentille

Masculine singular ending	Masculine plural ending	Example
al	aux	le magasin principal/ les magasins principaux

Individuals

Masculine singular	Feminine singular	Examples
blanc	blanche	le livre blanc/la Maison Blanche
bon	bonne	un bon repas/une bonne décision
favori	favorite	mon film favori/ma chanson favorite
gros	grosse	le gros homme/la grosse dame
long	longue	un long voyage/une longue journée

Masculine singular	Masculine plural	Example
tout	tous	tout le monde
		tous les jours

Not all adjectives fit the patterns you revised on p 36. These are the most important of the ones that are different.

Some adjectives have an extra spelling to make them easier to pronounce. Look across the columns at the similarities of the first three in the table:

masc. singular	beau	nouveau	vieux	ce
(before vowel or h)	bel	nouvel	vieil	cet
feminine singular	belle	nouvelle	vieille	cette
masculine plural	beaux	nouveaux	vieux	ces
feminine plural	belles	nouvelles	vieilles	ces
meaning	beautiful/ handsome	new	old	this/ that

Exam hints

There is no such word as 'cettes'.

To make a distinction between 'this' and 'that', particularly if you want to contrast two things, add **-ci** or **-là** to the noun: **ce livre-ci** (this book), **ces livres-là** (those books)

Progress check

Choose the right answer.

1. des gâteaux délicieux/délicieuses

2. la semaine dernier/dernière

3. le jardin public/publique

4. des cheveux longs/longues

5. un bon/bonne résultat

6. un nouveau/nouvel/nouvelle ami

7. ma vieux/vieil/vieille tante

8. cette/ces bananes

DAY
4

This is the neatest way to ask for directions:

Essential verbs

> **Pour aller
> (au château), s'il vous
> plaît?**
>
> The simpler
> **Où est...?** or
> **Où se trouve...?**
> can also be used.

aller	go
prendre	take
tourner	turn
traverser	cross
continuer	carry on
descendre	go down
monter	go up

It's also helpful to recognise the French for first, second and third: **première**, **deuxième**, **troisième** and the words for...

on the left	à gauche
on the right	à droite (the **t** is pronounced)
straight on	tout droit (the **t** is not pronounced)
in front of	devant
behind	derrière
opposite	en face de
near	près de
not far from	pas loin de
next to	à côté de
at the end of	au bout de

In comprehension questions these may be linked with arrows as shown.

Some 'landmark' words and phrases are also important:

le rond-point

les feux

la place

le coin

This is another extremely useful topic and one that is best linked to travel and transport.

Examples

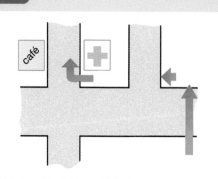

Cross the road and turn left, then take the second road on the right. The chemist's is opposite the café.

Traversez la rue, puis tournez à gauche et prenez la deuxième rue à droite. La pharmacie est en face du café.

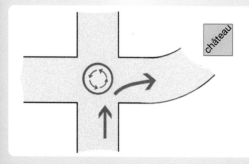

Go straight on until the roundabout, turn right and go up the road in front of you. The castle is at the end of the road.

Allez tout droit jusqu'au rond-point, tournez à droite et montez la rue devant vous. Le château est au bout de cette rue.

Progress check

What directions are given?

1. Tournez à gauche, continuez tout droit et le café est en face.

2. Descendez la rue jusqu'au bout, puis tournez à droite.

3. Traversez la place et prenez la première rue à gauche.

4. Continuez tout droit jusqu'aux feux.

5. Le théâtre n'est pas loin. C'est en face du cinéma dans la rue principale.

DAY 4

WEATHER

- *Quel temps fait-il?*
- *Quel temps faisait-il?*
- *Quel temps fera-t-il?*
- *Quel temps a-t-il fait?*

Il fait	beau mauvais	It's	fine unpleasant
Il fera	chaud froid	It will be	hot cold
Il faisait	du vent du soleil	It was	windy sunny
Il a fait	du brouillard	It was	foggy

Il pleut	it is raining	Le soleil brille	the sun is shining
pleuvra	it will rain	brillera	the sun will shine
pleuvait	it was raining	brillait	the sun was shining
a plu	it rained	a brillé	the sun shone
neige	it is snowing		
neigera	it will snow		
neigeait	it was snowing		
a neigé	it snowed		

Le temps est	orageux	The weather is	stormy
sera	pluvieux	will be	rainy
était	nuageux	was	cloudy
a été	couvert	was	overcast
	variable		changeable

Il y a	des éclaircies	There are	clear periods
Il y aura	des averses	There will be	showers
Il y avait	des éclairs	There was/were	lightning
Il y a eu	un orage	There was/were	a storm

This topic is useful for all four-skills, and should be linked with the section on Holidays. Revise the present, future and past tenses, particularly of *faire*.

15 MINS

Choose the tense carefully.

Description of the weather **at the moment** should be in the PRESENT tense:

Il fait beau, le soleil brille et il fait très chaud.

The weather **forecast** should be in the FUTURE tense:

Il fera du brouillard dans le nord, le temps sera nuageux dans la région parisienne et il y aura des averses dans le Midi.

Description of how the weather was **in the past** should be in the IMPERFECT tense:

Il pleuvait et il faisait assez froid.

To say what the weather was like on **one particular occasion**, such as 'yesterday' or 'last Sunday', the PERFECT tense (passé composé] should be used:

Hier il a fait froid.

Progress check

With the help of the pictures and the clues in the rest of the sentence, complete these weather sentences.

1 Quand nous étions en vacances il

....

2 Demain le temps

....

3 D'habitude quand on va en Provence il

....

4 Mardi dernier il

....

5 Il ....
et nous faisions du ski tous les jours.

6 La semaine prochaine il y

....

1

2

3

DAY 4

5

6

7

IMPERFECT TENSE

How to form the imperfect tense

Start with the nous part of the present tense
parlons, finissons, attendons, prenons, écrivons, lisons

⬇

take off the ons
parl, finiss, attend, pren, écriv, lis

⬇

add these endings
ais, ais, ait, ions, iez, aient

⬇

je parlais, tu finissais, il attendait, nous prenions,
vous écriviez, ils lisaient

The only exception is **être**, which goes like this:

j'étais
tu étais
il était
nous étions
vous étiez
ils étaient

Examples

Nous buvions du vin.

Elle travaillait toujours très bien.

J'attendais à l'arrêt d'autobus.

Normalement tu choisissais un éclair.

Il avait l'air sympa.

This is the easiest of the tenses in French so it's worth trying to learn it and use it.

10 MINS

The imperfect tense is used for...

- description (places, people and character) in the past

Le château était très vieux.

Le soleil brillait et les oiseaux chantaient.

Jean avait les yeux bleus.

Ils étaient très timides.

- unfinished action in the past (was/were doing)

Je travaillais dans la cuisine (quand tu as téléphoné).

Nous roulions à 90 km/h.

- regular action in the past (used to do)

Tous les matins elle se levait à 7h.

> **Sometimes a word or phrase such as d'habitude or normalement (usually), chaque semaine (every week), tous les mercredis (every Wednesday) or le dimanche (on Sundays) can tell you that the imperfect tense is needed.**

Progress check

Choose a suitable verb from the list to fill in the gaps:

avait, étaient, finissions, preniez, se couchait, voulais

1. D'habitude il .... à 22h30.

2. Vous .... toujours une tasse de thé.

3. Les fleurs .... très belles.

4. Quand elle était jeune elle .... les cheveux bruns.

5. Généralement nous .... les devoirs avant 8h.

6. Je .... devenir ingénieur.

15 MINS

The Tourist office in France used to be known as the **Syndicat d'Initiative**, but is now more often called **l'Office de Tourisme**. There is an **Office de Tourisme** in most towns and also in many villages, where it may be part of another building. It can be identified by the internationally-recognised *i* sign.

The sort of information that you would be expected to ask about or understand is listed below.

Attractions in the area

Qu'est-ce qu'il y a à voir dans la région?
Qu'est-ce qu'on peut faire dans la région?

Accommodation

Pouvez-vous me donner une liste des hôtels/gîtes/terrains de camping?

Finding your way around

Avez-vous une carte de la région/un plan de la ville, s'il vous plaît?
Pour aller à l'auberge de jeunesse, s'il vous plaît?
Y a-t-il un restaurant près d'ici?

Timetables

Je voudrais un horaire pour les trains entre Caen et Paris, s'il vous plaît.

DAY 5

Exam hint

This is a very likely topic for a letter: you may be asked to write to the tourist office requesting information about the area. Some of the phrases on the previous page can be used as they are, but for others you may have to change them to a more polite form. Check with the letter-writing section on p 82.

Key words

un dépliant	leaflet
une brochure	brochure
des renseignements	information
des excursions en car	coach trips
un spectacle	show
Son et Lumière	Sound and Light
des monuments intéressants	interesting monuments
le stade	sports stadium
la randonnée	long walk, hike
envoyer	to send

Progress check

Here are some answers to questions that might be asked in a tourist office. Which questions? (There may be more than one possibility.)

1　Traversez la place de l'église et l'AJ est juste en face.

2　Oui, monsieur, la voilà.

3　Il y a un beau château et des musées intéressants.

4　Oui, le restaurant Tante Elisabeth est là-bas, à côté du cinéma.

5　Il y a toutes sortes d'activités sportives.

6　Oui, beaucoup. Le car part de l'hôtel de ville. Voici un horaire.

15 MINS

Revise these aspects:

- Where you go/went
- Who you go/went with
- What sort of accommodation you choose/chose
- What you like to do/what you did/what you will do

Where

Je vais	à Bournemouth
Je suis allé(e)	au pays de Galles
J'irai	en France

Note: use **à** with towns and islands, **en** with most countries, which are feminine (but a few are masculine, like Wales above: use **au** for these).

With

Avec	ma famille
	mes amis
	mon copain/ma copine

What sort of accommodation

Nous allons	dans une auberge de jeunesse.
Nous prendrons	la tente.
Nous avons loué	un gîte.
Nous avons logé	chez mes cousins.
Nous louerons	une caravane.
Nous allons séjourner	dans un hôtel.

This topic could be tested in the past, present or future tenses.

There are several verbs you can use, such as **aller**, **prendre**, **loger**, **louer** (to hire), **avoir** or **séjourner** as above, but NOT **rester** which means to remain, not to stay in the holiday sense.

What you like to do

J'aime	me bronzer.
	faire les magasins.
	nager dans la mer.
	aller en boîte. (nightclub)
	visiter les monuments célèbres.
	faire des randonnées.

What you did

Je me suis	bronzée.
J'ai fait	les magasins.
J'ai	nagé dans la mer.
Je suis allé(e)	en boîte de nuit.
J'ai visité	les monuments célèbres.
J'ai fait	des randonnées.

What you will do

Je me	bronzerai.
Je ferai	les magasins.
Je	nagerai dans la mer.
J'irai	en boîte.
Je visiterai	les monuments célèbres.
Je ferai	des randonnées.

Progress check

a

b

c

Which phrase fits each picture?

1. Je me suis bronzé.

2. Je visiterai les monuments.

3. J'aime faire des randonnées.

The negative sandwich

There are two parts of the negative in French: *ne* (or *n'* before a vowel, **h** or **y**) and *pas*. **Ne** goes before the verb, and **pas** after it. Think of the verb as the filling in the sandwich, and **ne** and **pas** as the two slices of bread.

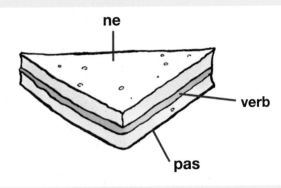

> *Je n'aime pas les maths.*
> *Anne ne veut pas aller au théâtre.*

There are four other useful negative phrases, which work in the same way.

ne jamais	never
ne personne	no-one
ne plus	no longer
ne rien	nothing

A good way to remember what they mean is to learn each one in a sentence that means something to you personally, such as:

> *Une végétarienne ne mange jamais de viande.*
> *On ne rencontre personne à la campagne.*
> *David Beckham ne joue plus pour Manchester United.*
> *Je ne fais rien quand je suis en vacances.*

Saying 'not' is easy in French, but take care with the word order.

10 MINS

Note

After these negatives, change **du/de l'/de la/des** to **de**, as in the first example on the previous page.

- 'No-one' and 'nothing' can come first in the sentence. When this happens, put **personne** or **rien** first, followed immediately by **ne**:

  Personne ne doit jouer au golf quand le temps est orageux.

  Rien n'est plus intéressant que le français.

- They can also be the only word in the sentence.

  Qui veut faire des cours supplémentaires? – Personne!

  Qu'as-tu mangé? – Rien!

Ne...que

- This means 'only':

  Il n'y a que trois groupes que j'aime.

- Watch out for it in comprehension passages, but when you are speaking or writing French it is probably safer to use **seulement**.

  Il y a seulement trois groupes que j'aime.

Progress check

Give the French for:

1. We never go to school on Sundays.

2. – What do you want to drink?
   – Nothing.

3. There isn't anyone in the café.

4. My parents don't like Beyoncé.

5. I'm no longer going out with François.

Compare three booking letters, which refer to the facilities offered in a hotel, a campsite and a youth hostel. Follow the diagrams, then check them with the sample letters:

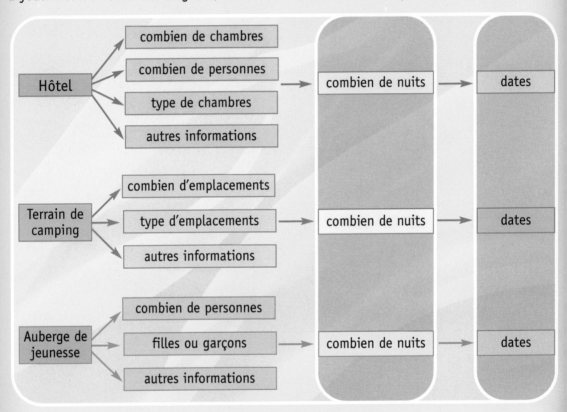

Je voudrais réserver _deux chambres_ pour _quatre personnes_. Nous voulons _une chambre à deux lits_ _avec une douche_ et _vue_ _sur la mer_, et _une_ _chambre avec un grand_ _lit_ et _salle de bains au_ _premier étage_. C'est pour _six nuits_, du _22 au 27_ _juillet_.

Je voudrais réserver _deux_ _emplacements_, _un pour_ _une tente_ et _un pour une_ _caravane_. Nous voulons être _près du bloc_ _sanitaire_, _sous les arbres_ si possible. C'est pour _dix_ _nuits_, du _22 juillet au 1er_ _août_.

Je voudrais réserver _quatre places_, pour _deux_ _garçons et deux filles_. Nous avons des sacs de couchage, mais _nous_ _voulons louer des draps_. C'est pour _quatre nuits_, du _22 au 25 juillet_.

Much of the material for the three types of holiday in this section is similar, so you can save time on revision.

15 MINS

You may also have to understand or ask questions:

- *Pouvez-vous m'envoyer le tarif, s'il vous plaît?*
- *Est-ce qu'il y a un terrain de jeux/un restaurant/une piscine?*
- *Il y a des activités sportives?*
- *Voulez-vous confirmer la réservation, s'il vous plaît?*
- *Vous avez vos cartes d'adhérent?* (membership cards)
- *Où sont les dortoirs?*
- *L'auberge ferme à quelle heure?*

Progress check

Change the underlined words in the booking letters on the previous page to give the following information:

1. Hotel: three rooms (one single with shower, one twin and one double with bath), on the second floor, for five people for seven nights from 21st to 27th May.

2. Campsite: one pitch for a tent, near the swimming pool, for three weeks from 21st June to 11th July.

3. Youth hostel: six places, four girls and two boys, need to hire sleeping-bags, three nights from 4th to 6th September.

Writing the date was probably one of the first things you did in French, so you may think you don't need to revise days and months. Not true. Mistakes are often made, but could easily be avoided. Pronunciation and spelling can also be a problem. In the lists below concentrate on the letters in **bold** (spelling) or <u>underlined</u> (pronunciation).

Les mois de l'année

janvier
fé**v**rier
mar<u>s</u> (pronounce s)
avril
mai
juin
jui**ll**et
aoû<u>t</u> (pronounce t)
septemb**r**e
octob**r**e
novemb**r**e
décemb**r**e

Les jours de la semaine

lundi
mardi
me**r**credi
j**e**udi
vend**r**edi
samedi
dimanche

Les saisons

au printemps
en été
en auto<u>mn</u>e pronounce **n** not **m**
en hiv<u>er</u> pronounce as 'air'

A few special dates in France

le 1ᵉʳ janvier	le jour de l'an
le 6 janvier	la fête des Rois
le 1ᵉʳ avril	poisson d'avril!
le 14 juillet	la fête nationale
le 11 novembre	l'Armistice
le 25 décembre	la fête de Noël

Key facts

- Except for the 1st of the month (**1er**), dates just have the number, e.g. **le 3 avril**.

- No capital letters for months or days unless it's the first word in the sentence.

- 'On Saturday' is just **samedi**, NOT **sur samedi**.

- 'On Mondays' meaning 'every Monday' is **le lundi**.

- There are many bank holidays, mainly for religious festivals, in France.

- Most people take three or four weeks off in July or August. School holidays last for two months in the summer: from the beginning of July to the beginning of September.

Progress check

Match the dates to the holidays.

1. le 14 juillet   **a**   la Saint-Valentin

2. le onze novembre   **b**   la fête de Noël

3. le 1er août   **c**   la fête nationale

4. le 25 décembre   **d**   l'Armistice

5. le 1er janvier   **e**   poisson d'avril

6. le 14 février   **f**   le jour de l'an

7. le 1er avril   **g**   départ en vacances

There are several ways of asking questions in French: fortunately the most common way is also the easiest. Look at these two sentences:

Tu aimes la musique.

Tu aimes la musique?

- Simply by adding a question mark you have made the statement of fact (you like music) into a question 'Do you like music?' It couldn't be easier; but you **must** remember to put in the question mark. In speaking, just make your voice go up at the end. Read the two sentences aloud, to hear the difference.

- Another way is to put the phrase **est-ce que** 'is it that...?' at the beginning of the sentence. Spell it carefully if you are writing it.

Est-ce que tu aimes la musique?

- A third way is to turn round the person and verb:

Aimes-tu la musique?

- This way is often used with question words:

Quelle sorte de musique aimes-tu?

- Use whichever method you feel most comfortable with. If you decide to use the third way, take care with word order if the sentence is negative; **aimes-tu** counts as one word when making your sandwich:

N'aimes-tu pas la musique?

- Remember that the question form of *il y a* is *y a-t-il?*

Revise these question words. Be particularly careful not to confuse **qui** and **où**.

combien   how much? how many?
-    *Combien de personnes y a-t-il dans le groupe?*
-    *Il y en a vingt.*

Exam papers usually require you to answer questions. In French you have to be able to ask them as well.

15 MINS

comment   how?
- *Comment vas-tu voyager?*
- *En avion.*

comment   what...like?
- *Comment est-il?*
- *Il est grand.*

où   where?
- *Où vas-tu?*
- *À la discothèque.*

pourquoi   why?
- *Pourquoi sors-tu avec Paul?*
- *Parce qu'il est sympa.*

quand   when?
- *Quand travailles-tu au restaurant?*
- *Le week-end.*

que what?
- *Que fais-tu le soir?*
- *J'écoute la radio.*

qui who?
- *Qui veut faire la vaisselle?*
- *Moi!*

quel, quelle (+ noun)   what? which?
- *Quelles chaussures préfères-tu?*
- *Les noires.*

Exam hint

Qui and **que** are also used to mean 'who' and 'which' or 'that' when they are not questions:

- *Le garçon qui joue de la guitare est mon copain.*

- *Le groupe que je préfère s'appelle Super Furry Animals.*

Progress check

Fill in the gaps with the correct question word.

1. ....viens-tu au collège?
   – À pied.

2. ....ne manges-tu pas les saucisses?
   – Je suis végétarien.

3. ....est le garçon aux cheveux bruns?
   – C'est mon frère.

4. ....vont-elles arriver?
   – Samedi prochain.

5. ....de cours y a-t-il par jour?
   – Il y en a cinq.

6. ....vas-tu en vacances cette année?
   – En Espagne.

DAY 5

SCHOOL 1

Follow the chart to describe your school, or to understand the description of another school. Change the words to fit your own facts.

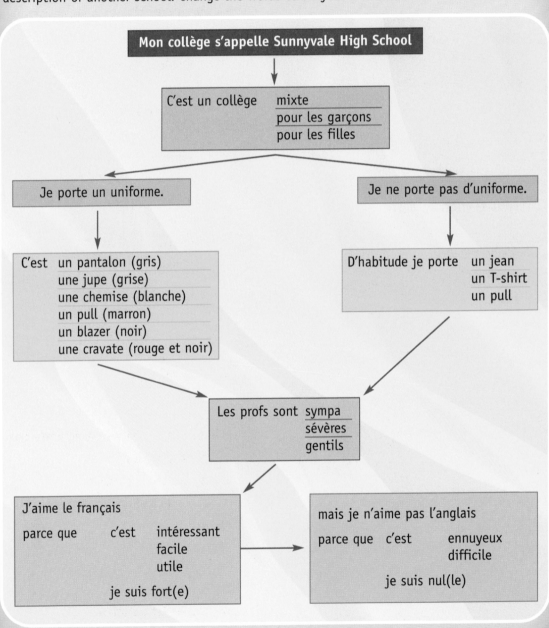

Mon collège s'appelle Sunnyvale High School

C'est un collège   mixte
                   pour les garçons
                   pour les filles

Je porte un uniforme.

Je ne porte pas d'uniforme.

C'est   un pantalon (gris)
        une jupe (grise)
        une chemise (blanche)
        un pull (marron)
        un blazer (noir)
        une cravate (rouge et noir)

D'habitude je porte   un jean
                      un T-shirt
                      un pull

Les profs sont   sympa
                 sévères
                 gentils

J'aime le français

parce que   c'est   intéressant
                          facile
                          utile

         je suis fort(e)

mais je n'aime pas l'anglais

parce que   c'est   ennuyeux
                        difficile

        je suis nul(le)

This first section about school is concerned with general points.

> Uniform is not usually worn in French schools.

> Ages can vary within a class as French students have to repeat a year if they don't do well enough.

Key words and phrases

le bulletin	report
la journée scolaire	school day
les cours	lessons
la cantine	school dining-room, canteen
demi-pensionnaire	pupil who has lunch at school
apprendre	to learn
passer un examen	to take an exam
réussir	to pass, succeed
être reçu	to pass
échouer	to fail
rater	to fail
redoubler	to repeat the year

Progress check

Choose the answer that completes each sentence correctly.

1. Si on est demi-pensionnaire, on prend
   - a le petit déjeuner à l'école.
   - b le déjeuner à l'école.
   - c le dîner à l'école.

   J'aime le dessin parce que c'est
   - a ennuyeux.
   - b difficile.
   - c intéressant.

3. Si on ne réussit pas aux examens, on doit
   - a redoubler.
   - b être reçu.
   - c rater.

4. D'habitude en France on ne porte pas
   - a d'uniforme à l'école.
   - b de pantalon à l'école.
   - c de vêtements à l'école.

5. Les profs envoient un bulletin aux parents
   - a tous les jours.
   - b toutes les semaines.
   - c tous les trois mois.

Look at the French timetable below and see whether you can remember what the subjects are. Then check the subject groups below to see whether you were right. The timetable includes most subjects, so is not typical for a pupil who has chosen his/her options.

	LUNDI	MARDI	MERCREDI	JEUDI	VENDREDI	SAMEDI
8h30-9h30	maths	français	géographie	histoire	anglais	EPS
9h30-10h30	EPS	biologie	chimie	technologie	physique	maths
RÉCRÉATION						
10h40-11h35	dessin	permanence	sciences	géographie	musique	anglais
11h35-12h25	instruction civique	anglais	maths	latin	dessin	
DÉJEUNER						
14h15-15h15	français	espagnol		maths	espagnol	
RÉCRÉATION						
15h25-16h25	allemand	histoire		français	maths	

Langues	Sciences	Lettres	Arts	Autres
français	physique	histoire	dessin	EPS
anglais	chimie	géographie	musique	instruction civique
allemand	biologie			technologie
espagnol	maths			
latin				

- Although le week-end anglais is being piloted in some schools in France, most still have part of Wednesday off and go to school on Saturday mornings.

- The school day starts earlier and ends later than in the UK, with a long lunch break.

- Pupils can opt for a vocation-based curriculum from age 14.

- School years are numbered differently; the English year 11 is 2e seconde, followed by première (year 12) and terminale (year 13).

As well as the school subjects, you should also revise these key words.

l'emploi du temps	timetable
la matière	subject
la langue vivante	modern language
permanence	private study period
EPS (éducation physique et sportive)	PE
la pause-déjeuner	lunch break
étranger	foreign

Progress check

Look at the timetable again, then correct the deliberate mistake in each of these sentences.

1. Il y a trois cours de langues étrangères le vendredi.

2. Les cours de dessin sont après la pause-déjeuner.

3. Le cours de musique est entre les cours de physique et de géographie.

4. Les cours finissent à 15h25.

5. La chimie est une langue vivante.

How to form the future tense

There are two simple steps (three for re verbs):

Take the infinitive (the 'title' part of the verb, as it is spelt in word lists)

For re verbs, take off the e

Add these endings: ai, as, a, ons, ez, ont

Examples

(entrer) j'entrerai   (choisir) tu choisiras   (écrire) vous écrirez
(jouer) elles joueront   (sortir) nous sortirons   (prendre) il prendra

The endings are always the same, but there are some verbs that don't follow the rule for the first step. They are verbs that are often needed, so revise them carefully. The first four are the most important (and the most difficult!).

avoir	j'aurai	I will have
être	je serai	I will be
aller	j'irai	I will go
faire	je ferai	I will do, I will make
devoir	je devrai	I will have to
envoyer	j'enverrai	I will send
pouvoir	je pourrai	I will be able
recevoir	je recevrai	I will receive
savoir	je saurai	I will know how to
venir	je viendrai	I will come
voir	je verrai	I will see
vouloir	je voudrai	I will want

DAY 6

Examples

Cette année nous irons en France.

Tu reviendras la semaine prochaine?

Il fera froid demain.

Vous verrez le château juste en face.

The future tense means 'will' (or 'shall'). There is another way to talk about the future, so if you find these verbs difficult to learn, try this instead:

- Use the present tense of the verb **aller**

- Add the verb you need in its infinitive form.

This means 'I am going to ...' which is just about the same as

'I will...'

Examples

Elle va revenir la semaine prochaine

Il va faire froid demain

Je vais envoyer une carte postale

Ils vont voir la Tour Eiffel

Progress check

What is the correct spelling of the future tense of the verb in brackets?

1 Je ne (pouvoir) pas aller à la piscine.

2 Elle (être) en retard.

3 Mon frère (avoir) douze ans en avril.

4 Tu (recevoir) ma lettre demain.

5 Vous (aller) chez vos amis?

6 Nous (revenir) vite.

7 Je (parler) couramment le français.

8 Ils (boire) du café.

FUTURE PLANS

Revise these possible career paths. All of them could be introduced by one of these phrases (as well as the future tense):

J'ai l'intention de...	I plan to...
J'espère...	I hope to...
Je voudrais...	I would like to...
J'aimerais...	I would like to...
Mon ambition, c'est	My ambition is...

As the English phrases suggest, all are followed by a verb in the infinitive form. You should also be able to give further details:

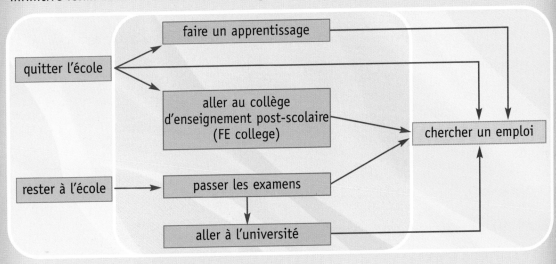

Où?	Dans une petite compagnie de fabrication; dans un grand magasin; dans un garage; dans une grande ville
Formation (training)	il y aura une période de formation de six semaines/trois mois/deux ans.
Genre d'emploi?	vendeur/vendeuse; mécanicien/mécanicienne; professeur; médecin; secrétaire; employé(e) de bureau; ouvrier/ouvrière d'usine (factory worker)
Raisons?	travailler en équipe; avoir des responsabilités; aider les gens; gagner beaucoup d'argent.

DAY 6

1 2 3 4 5 6 7

This section also revises some other ways to talk about the future.

Link this topic with School (p 64) so that you can say which subjects you will be studying if you are staying on to do A levels, and with Work experience (p 70) so that you can describe the job you may decide to do.

Key words and phrases

le poste	job, position
le métier	job, profession
le salaire	wages, salary
le stage	course, placement
le travail	work
les diplômes	qualifications
la licence	degree
devenir	to become
étudier	to study
bien payé	well paid
mal payé	badly paid
au chômage	unemployed

J'ai l'intention de devenir journaliste.

Je serai chef de cuisine.

J'aimerais être chauffeur de taxi.

WORK EXPERIENCE

The paragraphs below describe a particular session of work experience in each category. Check that you understand them and then change the underlined words and phrases to fit in with your own circumstances.

A

J'ai un petit job pour gagner de l'argent de poche. Je travaille _le samedi_ _dans un supermarché_, où je suis _caissière_. _Quand les clients ont fait leurs achats, ils apportent le chariot à ma caisse, et je dois prendre leur argent ou les détails de leur carte de crédit *._

Mes horaires de travail sont de _8h30 à 17h00_. Je gagne l'équivalent de _6€_ de l'heure. Avec l'argent j'achète _des vêtements, des CD et des magazines_.

B

Pour mon stage en entreprise j'ai travaillé _dans un bureau_ pendant _deux semaines_. Le travail était _très varié_. J'ai dû (I had to) _faire des photocopies, classer des papiers, aider les autres employés et préparer du thé et du café *._ Une fois j'ai eu l'occasion _d'utiliser l'ordinateur_.

Les horaires de travail étaient _de 9h à 16h_. Le matin je prenais _l'autobus_ _à l'arrêt près de chez moi_ _à 8h30_. Je mangeais _à la cantine_ _à midi_, et je rentrais chez moi _à 16h45_. J'ai aimé _le travail_, mais à la fin de chaque journée j'étais _fatigué._

* Describe the details of your job here.

Work experience may refer to a job you have at weekends or in the holidays, or to a one or two-week period taken out of school as part of your studies.

10 MINS

Key words

le stage en enterprise	work experience
le bureau	office
la compagnie	company
l'entreprise	company
l'usine	factory

l'employé(e)	employee
le caissier/la caissière	cashier
le garçon de café	waiter
le serveur/la serveuse	waiter, waitress
le vendeur/la vendeuse	salesman/woman

l'ordinateur	computer
la photocopieuse	photocopier

classer	to file
ranger	to tidy up
utiliser	to use

ennuyeux	boring
intéressant	interesting
monotone	monotonous
varié	varied

Progress check

Answer these questions. They refer to the paragraphs on the previous page.

A

1. Which day of the week does she work?

2. What details might she have to take?

3. What does she buy with the money she earns?

B

4. Where did he work?

5. For how long?

6. What did he have to do?

7. How did he get to work?

8. How did he feel at the end of each day?

2

3

4

5

DAY 6

7

The perfect tense describes an action that has already happened:
'I wrote', 'he has seen'. There are two parts to it: follow these steps carefully to learn how to form it for the majority of verbs.

○ How to form the perfect tense

● Start with the right 'person' **je**, **tu**, **il**, etc. of **avoir**

● Add the words that mean 'spoken', 'finished', 'seen', etc.
(This is called the 'past participle'.)

Look at the tables below for help with this.

These are the three regular verb groups. The ending is in bold type:

er	parler	parl**é**
ir	finir	fin**i**
re	vendre	vend**u**

Other important verbs:

avoir	eu	had
devoir	dû	had to
dire	dit	said
écrire	écrit	wrote, written
être	été	been
faire	fait	did, made
lire	lu	read
mettre	mis	put, put on
ouvrir	ouvert	opened
pouvoir	pu	could
prendre	pris	took, taken
recevoir	reçu	received
voir	vu	seen
vouloir	voulu	wanted

Examples

J'ai fait mes devoirs.

Tu as mis ton pull?

Il a écrit une lettre.

Elle a ouvert la porte.

Nous avons parlé en français.

Vous avez fini votre travail.

Ils ont perdu leurs tennis.

Elles ont pris un verre ensemble.

In the last section one paragraph included verbs in the past tense. Here's your chance to revise it.

15 MINS

- The second part of the verb (vendu, eu, voulu etc.) does not change its spelling.

- Take care with the 'negative sandwich': ne and pas sandwich avoir only, not the whole verb. Learn an example and then use the same pattern for any verb:

  Je n'ai pas reçu la lettre.

- For questions, choose your favourite method as before:

  Il a été en retard?

  Est-ce qu'il a été en retard?

  A-t-il été en retard?

  (The extra t, also used with elle and on, makes it easier to say.)

Exam hint

To see the difference between this tense and the imperfect tense, read the examples on p 49 and compare them with the sentences in this section.

Progress check

How would you say or write the following?

1 I saw a good film.

2 He put on his trainers.

3 She opened the letter.

4 We couldn't close the window.

5 They played football.

6 Have you lost your pen?

7 She has chosen her A level subjects.

HEALTH PROBLEMS

Explaining what is wrong

Je suis malade	I'm ill
Je suis enrhumé(e)	I have a cold
ça ne va pas du tout	I don't feel at all well
J'ai mal à la tête	I have a headache
à la gorge	a sore throat
au ventre	stomach ache
au dos	backache
aux dents	toothache
Ma jambe me fait mal	My leg hurts
C'est douloureux	It's painful
J'ai vomi	I've been sick

Asking for help

Pouvez-vous me conseiller quelque chose?	Can you recommend something?
Pouvez-vous me donner une ordonnance?	Can you give me a prescription?
C'est grave?	Is it serious?

Diagnosis and treatment

C'est enflé		It's swollen
Vous avez de la fièvre		You have a temperature
On va	faire une radio	We'll do an X-ray
	mettre un pansement	We'll put a bandage on
Il faut	vous reposer	You must rest
	prendre ces comprimés	take these tablets
	boire beaucoup d'eau	drink lots of water
	suivre un régime	go on a diet
	arrêter de fumer	stop smoking
Prenez	des aspirines	Take some aspirin
	un sirop	cough medicine
	une tisane	a herbal tea
	des pastilles	some cough sweets

This topic could be tested in the context of doctor, chemist or dentist, but the words you need are similar in each case.

15 MINS

- Tisanes are popular in France for treating minor health problems. One of the best known is menthe (mint) for stomach upsets.

- To claim back the cost of medicine you must send the price label (la vignette) which is on the packet or bottle.

- The word piqûre means both 'injection' and 'sting' (It is easy to understand why!) so take care when you hear or see it.

Other words and phrases to learn

le rendez-vous	appointment
le cabinet	surgery
le médecin	doctor
la grippe	flu
un coup de soleil	sunstroke
ça va mieux	it's better

It is also helpful to revise the parts of the body, so that you can explain which bit of you is hurting. In the last resort, though, in an oral exam (or on holiday in France) you could simply point to the painful bit and say ça me fait mal, là 'it hurts just there'.

Progress check

Complete the conversation in the chemist's shop as shown:

1 Qu'est-ce qui ne va pas?

   – I have a sore throat and a headache.

2 Depuis quand?

   – For two days

3 Vous êtes enrhumée, mademoiselle.

   – Can you recommend something?

4 Prenez des aspirines et des pastilles pour la gorge.

   – OK. If it's not better after the weekend, shall I go to the doctor's?

5 Bonne idée.

   – Thank you.

1 2 3 4 5 6 DAY 7

The basic information you are likely to have to deal with is the same for all types of accident.

- What happened
- Where
- How many people are injured

Look at the diagrams below and make sure you understand the descriptions that follow each one.

Il y a eu un accident au coin de la rue Napoléon et la rue Gambetta. Une voiture a heurté un camion. Il y a deux blessés: le chauffeur de la voiture s'est cassé la jambe, et le passager a mal au bras.

Il y a eu un accident dans le jardin public. Un garçon grimpait dans un arbre, et il est tombé. Il s'est fait mal à la tête et il s'est coupé au bras.

Il y a eu un accident dans la cuisine. Ma mère s'est brûlé la main.

This topic may include road accidents, falls, and accidents in the home.

Key words and phrases

les services d'urgence	emergency services
le secours	help
au secours	help!
appelez une ambulance	call an ambulance
appelez police-secours	dial 112
la chute	fall
un blessé	casualty, injured person
téléphoner	to telephone
blesser	to injure
brûler	to burn
casser	to break
couper	to cut
faire mal à	to hurt
grimper	to climb
tomber	to fall
heurter	to hit (a car)

You will also find some useful information in the section on Telephone calls.

Progress check

Read the accident descriptions on the previous page again, and decide whether these sentences are true, false, or the information is not given.

1. The road accident took place at a street corner.

2. A lorry and a car were involved.

3. The lorry driver was injured.

4. A boy fell out of a tree in his garden.

5. He cut his arm.

6. It was very windy at the time.

7. The accident in the kitchen involved boiling water.

8. The mother burnt her arm.

PERFECT TENSE
– ÊTRE VERBS

- Start with the right person **je, tu, il, elle, nous, vous, ils, elles** of **être**
- Add the word that means 'went', 'came', etc.
- Make this word **agree** (like an adjective) with the person

Look at the diagrams below to see the verbs that use **être**.

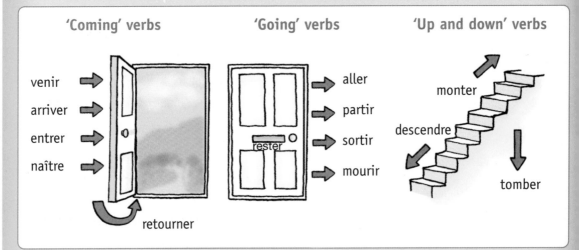

'Coming' verbs

venir
arriver
entrer
naître

retourner

'Going' verbs

aller
partir
sortir
mourir

rester

'Up and down' verbs

monter
descendre
tomber

Here are the verbs again, with the correct spelling (before agreement) of their perfect tense:

Arriver	arrivé	partir	parti
Descendre	descendu	monter	monté
Venir	venu	aller	allé
Entrer	entré	sortir	sorti
Naître	né	mourir	mort
Tomber	tombé	rester	resté

(The ADVENT verbs and their opposites) plus:

retourner	retourné

Some verbs use *être* instead of *avoir* to make the perfect tense. Most of them are verbs involving movement.

Examples

Je suis allé au cinéma.
(or *Je suis allée au cinéma* if you are a girl)

Nous sommes partis à huit heures.

Ils sont sortis ensemble.

Napoléon est mort en 1821.

Les filles sont entrées dans le café.

Julie et Manon ne sont pas venues.

Céline Dion est née en 1968.

Tout le monde est arrivé à neuf heures.

Laura est partie avant moi.

Exam hint

'Reflexive' verbs also use **être**:

- *Je me suis levée à 7h.*
- *Il ne s'est pas rasé ce matin!*

Progress check

Underline the correct spelling.

1. Jean, tu es venu/venue trop tard!

2. Nous sommes arrivé/arrivés de bonne heure.

3. Vous êtes tombé/tombée/tombés/tombées, madame?

4. Il est sorti/sortie tout seul.

5. Tout le monde est entré/sont entrés dans la cantine.

6. Je ne suis jamais retourné/retournés aux Etats-Unis.

7. Les filles sont déjà partis/parties.

8. Paul et David sont allés/allées en vacances.

9. Ma sœur est né/née en 1988.

10. Ils sont descendue/descendus très vite.

LOST AND FOUND

The Lost Property Office in France is called the 'Found Property Office' **Bureau des Objets Trouvés**.

Be prepared to give or understand details of:

- What is lost **l'objet**
- What it looks like **description**
- When **quand**
- Where **où**

J'ai perdu...　　　　　　　　　　**J'ai laissé...** (left)

objet
mon porte-monnaie
mon portefeuille
mon sac
mon appareil
mon passeport
ma montre
mes clés

quand
hier soir
ce matin
entre dix heures et midi
cet après-midi
avant 7h

description
taille (size)	grand/petit/moyen
couleur	brun/noir/rouge
forme (shape)	rond (round)
	carré (square)
matière (material)	en cuir (leather)
	en or (gold)
	en argent (silver)
	en plastique (plastic)
marque (make)	un Kodak

où
dans la rue
dans le métro
à la piscine

If you have revised the other sections in this book you will already know most of what you need for this topic. Here are some more details to help you.

When a loss or theft is reported, other questions may be asked (depending on the information that has already been given)

C'est marqué à votre nom?
Is your name on it?

C'est neuf?
Is it new?

Quelle est la valeur?
How much is it worth?

Qu'est-ce qu'il y avait dedans?
What was in it?

Quel numéro?
Which number (bus)

Quelle ligne?
Which line? (underground)

Comment est-ce qu'on peut vous contacter?
How can we contact you?

Progress check

Use the details below to complete the table in French.

objet	quand	où	description
a porte-feuille	....	Rue St-Jean	....
b	vers 11h	....	Kodak
c sac	cet après-midi	....	....
d	hier matin	....	petite, ronde
e stylo	....	au café	....

a this morning, black leather

b camera, underground

c in the street, navy plastic

d watch, swimming pool

e yesterday evening, gold

Letters are of two types

Informal: to a pen-friend, writing about yourself, your interests, school etc.

Formal: booking accommodation, applying for a job, asking for information, reporting a loss etc.

Informal letters

These will probably be written in the *tu* part of the verb (used for a friend or relative).

Follow this pattern:

Start	*Salut!* *Cher Pierre, Chère Anne*
Main body of letter	*J'ai reçu ta lettre...* *Merci pour ta lettre...*
Start to close	*Je dois terminer ma lettre* *Ecris-moi bientôt*
End	*Amitiés* *Bisous* (use carefully; it means 'love and kisses')

Formal letters

These must be written in the *vous* part of the verb (the polite form used to one person as well as the plural).

Start	*Monsieur/Madame* (Dear Sir/Dear Madam) *Messieurs* (Dear Sirs)
Main body of letter	*Je serais très reconnaissant(e)* (grateful) *si vous pouviez m'envoyer...* *Pourriez-vous me dire...* *Je voudrais vous demander....*
Ending	*Je vous prie d'agréer, Monsieur/Madame/Messieurs, l'expression de mes sentiments distingués* (Yours faithfully)

- **serais** (would be), **pourriez** (would be able) and **voudrais** (would like) are in the conditional tense. This is a combination of the 'stem' of the future tense and the endings of the imperfect tense).

We have covered most of the topics that could be the subject of letters and phone calls. Now revise using them in a formal or informal framework.

Telephone calls

- Dial 15 for ambulance, 17 for police, 18 for the fire service **pompiers**.

- French telephone numbers are usually given in pairs; 491632 would be **quarante-neuf, seize, trente-deux**.

- To answer a phone call, say **Allô?**

Key words and phrases

le (téléphone) portable	mobile phone
Qui est à l'appareil?	Who's speaking?
C'est John à l'appareil.	It's John speaking.
Je voudrais parler à...	I want to speak to...
Je voudrais réserver une table.	I'd like to book a table.
occupé	engaged
Ne quittez pas	hold the line
laisser un message	to leave a message
prendre un message	to take a message
Je vais rappeler plus tard.	I'll ring back later.
Je ne vous entends pas.	I can't hear you.
en PCV	reverse-charge call
composer	to dial
décrocher	to pick up the phone
raccrocher	to hang up/put down the phone
la télécarte	phone card

Progress check

What do these phrases mean?

1. Écris-moi bientôt

2. Merci pour ta lettre

3. Monsieur,

4. Je voudrais vous demander...

5. Je serais très reconnaissant

6. Je vous prie d'agréer l'expression de mes sentiments distingués

7. Qui est à l'appareil?

8. Ne quittez pas

9. Voulez-vous laisser un message?

10. Je vais rappeler plus tard

My, your, his, her, our, their

These words are *adjectives* just as much as words like 'big', 'red' and 'interesting' because they tell us something extra about the noun. So the same rules must be used as those that apply to all adjectives (see p 36); they must *agree with the noun they describe*.

No one really likes learning tables of words, but this one is an exception; it has a good rhythm and the sound is fun, particularly at the end. It's best to learn it in columns across rather than down.

masc. sing.	fem. sing.	plural	meaning
mon	ma	mes	my
ton	ta	tes	your (with tu)
son	sa	ses	his, her
notre	notre	nos	our
votre	votre	vos	your (with vous)
leur	leur	leurs	their

Examples

Il aime sa mère.	(**sa** is describing 'mother', who is feminine)
Elles lavent leur voiture.	(only one car)
J'ai perdu mon livre.	(**livre** is masculine singular)
Tu finiras tes devoirs.	(**devoirs** is plural)
Vous faisiez votre travail.	(**travail** is singular)

In the last few pages you have seen examples using the words for 'my', 'your' etc. In this section you will revise how to use them.

Me and mine

If you want to say 'it's mine' you can say **c'est à moi**. Here, **moi** means 'me', so you are really saying 'it belongs to me'. The full list for each 'person' is:

moi	me	nous	us
toi	you	vous	you
lui	him	eux	them
elle	her	elles	them

These same words are also used with **prepositions** (words like 'with', 'without', 'for', 'in', 'on', 'after', 'behind' etc.).

Check that you understand these phrases:

chez moi	at my house, at home
après toi	after you
sans lui	without him
devant elle	in front of her
derrière nous	behind us
pour vous	for you
avec eux	with them
avant elles	before them

TIME AND NUMBERS

◯ Time

Look at the clock face to revise times. The words inside the circle are the hours, and the numbers outside the circle are the minutes before or after each hour. The figures in brackets give the equivalent in the 24 hour clock: it's usually the hours from 16 to 22 that cause problems.

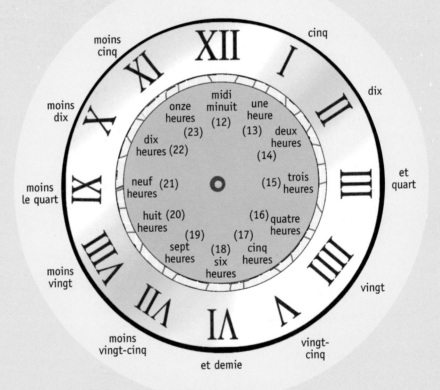

You will also need to know these phrases:

du matin	in the morning
de l'après-midi	in the afternoon
du soir	in the evening

Link this topic with Daily routine, Arranging to meet and School.

Numbers

It's very important to understand numbers when you hear them. When you write them down it will probably be enough to put them in figures, particularly in the case of large numbers.

Some are easy to confuse. Make sure you don't get these mixed up:

deux 2, **douze** 12

trois 3, **treize** 13

quatre 4, **quatorze** 14

cinq 5, **quinze** 15

six 6, **seize** 16

vingt-quatre 24, **quatre-vingts** 80

Remember that to say 70 the French use **soixante-dix** (literally 'sixty ten'): 71 to 79 are 'sixty-eleven' **soixante et onze** to 'sixty-nineteen' **soixante dix-neuf**.

80 is 'four twenties', and 90 'four twenties ten', so 82 is **quatre-vingt-deux**, 94 is **quatre-vingt-quatorze**.

100 is **cent**, 1000 is **mille**.

the decimal 'point' is a comma (**virgule**).

Progress check

Choose the logical time or number from the list to complete each sentence.

Quatorze virgule dix; vingt heures; midi; huit heures et demie du matin; trente-trois, soixante-cinq, quarante-neuf; vingt-deux heures.

1 Les cours commencent à

....

2 Rendez-vous devant le cinéma ce soir à

....

3 D'habitude je me couche vers

....

4 Ça coûte

.... €

5 Mon numéro est

....

6 La pause-déjeuner est à

....

Adverbs

An adverb is a word that tells you *how* something is done; it *adds* something to the *verb*.

In English many adverbs end in **ly**: slowly, fortunately, quickly, exactly. In French the equivalent of **ly** is **ment**, usually added to the feminine form of the adjective.

> **Examples**
>
> lentement, heureusement, rapidement, exactement

There are a few exceptions; the most important are:

Vraiment really, **vite** quickly (an alternative to **rapidement**), **mieux** better, **bien** well, **mal** badly, **évidemment** evidently.

Comparison

The important words to learn are:

plus...que	more...than
moins...que	less...than
aussi...que	as...as
le/la/les plus...de	the most...of
le/la/les moins...de	the least...of

> **There is no French equivalent of er in English: 'taller' is 'more tall'.**

When comparing adjectives, always make the adjective agree with the first person or thing mentioned.

Anne est plus grande que Paul.
Les garçons sont moins élégants que les filles.
Pierre est le plus intelligent des enfants.

No problems of agreement with adverbs:

Shania Twain chante mieux que Gareth Gates.

This section covers several assorted items that are useful to know.

The infinitive

You have probably noticed examples of a verb being used in its infinitive form. This happens when it follows another verb (in any tense), such as **aller**, **aimer**, **vouloir**, **pouvoir**, **devoir**, **savoir**, **espérer**:

J'aimerais sortir avec toi.	I'd like to go out with you.
Tu veux venir au cinéma?	Do you want to come to the cinema?
Elle est allée voir la Tour Eiffel.	She went (or has gone) to see the Eiffel Tower.

Sometimes you have to use **à** or **de** as well. As a general rule, verbs needing **à** often have the idea of starting:

aider à   *apprendre à*
commencer à   *encourager à*

and those needing **de** have the idea of stopping:

arrêter de   *cesser de*
oublier de   *refuser de*

But they don't all fit neatly into these categories. Learn these two:

réussir à   *essayer de*

Je vais commencer à faire mon travail.
Elle a arrêté de fumer.
Nous essayerons d'écrire en français.

Progress check

Underline the correct answer.

1 Nous travaillons *bon/bien*.

2 *Malheureusement/malheureux* elle a perdu ses clés.

3 Simone est moins *âgé/âgée* que Michel.

4 L'équipe de Lille a joué plus *mal/mauvais* que l'équipe de Marseille.

5 Je voudrais *achète/acheter* une carte postale.

6 On apprend *à/de* parler français.

7 Ils ont essayé *à/de* vendre leurs billets.

ANSWERS

Talking about yourself
1 c 2 a 3 e 4 b 5 d

Present tense
1 attendent
2 choisis
3 aimez
4 vend
5 retrouvons
6 travailles

At home
1 vrai
2 vrai
3 faux
4 faux
5 vrai
6 vrai

Where you live
1 a 2 b 3 b 4 b

Irregular verbs
1 I'm going to have an omelette.
2 Come with me.
3 You can go to France with your friends.
4 Do you have to go home at 11 o'clock?
5 She knows how to swim./She can swim.
6 Write to me soon.

Leisure time
Marie likes: (any three) shopping, reading, listening to CDs, classical music, cinema
She doesn't like: pop music, sport, going to the theatre

Reflexive verbs
1 se 2 nous 3 te 4 m' 5 vous 6 s'

Sports
1 b 2 a 3 b 4 c

TV and radio
1 d 2 e 3 c 4 b 5 a

Shopping 1
1 banque
2 passeport
3 euros
4 caisse
5 essayer
6 rayon
7 cadeaux/souvenirs

Shopping 2
1 g 2 f 3 a 4 c 5 d 6 h 7 b 8 e

A* and *de
1 à
2 des
3 de
4 du
5 à l'
6 aux
7 d'
8 à la

Arranging to meet

1 Tu es libre ce soir?
2 On va en boîte?/Allons en boîte?
3 Oui, je veux bien.
4 Rendez-vous devant le café
5 à bientôt
6 Désolé(e), je ne peux pas.
7 On y va?

Eating out

'Ordering' sentences should be:
1 Je prendrai un croque-monsieur.
  Un jus de pomme, s'il vous plaît.
2 Je prendrai le plat du jour.
  Un diabolo-menthe, s'il vous plaît.
3 Je prendrai une omelette au jambon.
  Un café crème, s'il vous plaît.
4 Je prends l'œuf mayonnaise.
  Les spaghettis bolognaise, s'il vous plaît.
  Je vais prendre une tarte au citron.
  Un café (noir).
5 Je prends la soupe à l'oignon.
  Le steak au poivre, s'il vous plaît.
  Je vais prendre une glace à la fraise.
  Une eau minérale. (or order a specific one
  such as Perrier, Evian or Vittel)

Travel and Transport – getting there

1 c   2 e   3 d   4 b   5 a

Travel and transport – getting around

1 faux
2 vrai
3 vrai
4 faux
5 vrai
6 vrai

Adjectives 2

1 délicieux
2 dernière
3 public
4 longs
5 bon
6 nouvel
7 vieille
8 ces

Finding the way

1 Turn left, go straight on and the café is opposite.
2 Go down to the end of the road, then turn right.
3 Cross the square and take the first street on the left.
4 Go straight on to the traffic lights.
5 The theatre isn't far. It's opposite the cinema in the High St.

Weather

1 faisait du soleil
2 sera pluvieux
3 fait chaud
4 a fait du vent
5 neigeait
6 aura des averses

Imperfect tense

1 se couchait
2 preniez
3 étaient
4 avait
5 finissions
6 voulais

Tourist office

1 Pour aller à l'auberge de jeunesse, s'il vous plaît?
   Où est/se trouve l'auberge de jeunesse, s'il vous plaît?
2 Avez-vous une carte de la région s'il vous plaît?
3 Qu'est-ce qu'il y a à voir dans la région?
4 Y a-t-il un restaurant près d'ici?
5 Qu'est-ce qu'il y a à faire dans la région?
   Est-ce qu'on peut faire du sport dans la région?
6 Est-ce qu'il y a des excursions en car?

Holidays

1 b   2 c   3 a

Negatives

1 Nous n'allons jamais à l'école/au collège le dimanche
2 Qu'est-ce que tu veux boire? – Rien.
3 Il n'y a personne dans le café.
4 Mes parents n'aiment pas Beyoncé.
5 Je ne sors plus avec François.

Holiday accommodation

1 Je voudrais réserver trois chambres, pour cinq personnes. Nous voulons une chambre pour une personne avec une douche, une chambre à deux lits et une chambre avec un grand lit et salle de bains au deuxième étage. C'est pour sept nuits, du 21 au 27 mai.
2 Je voudrais réserver un emplacement pour une tente. Nous voulons être près de la piscine. C'est pour trois semaines, du 21 juin au 11 juillet.
3 Je voudrais réserver six places, pour quatre filles et deux garçons. Nous voulons louer des sacs de couchage. C'est pour trois nuits, du 4 au 6 septembre.

Days and dates

1 c   2 d   3 g   4 b   5 f   6 a   7 e

Asking questions

1 Comment
2 Pourquoi
3 Qui
4 Quand
5 Combien
6 Où

School 1

1 b   2 c   3 a   4 a   5 c

School 2

1 deux (not trois)
2 avant (not après)
3 dessin (not géographie)
4 16.25 (not 15.25)
5 science (not langue vivante)

Future tense

1 pourrai
2 sera
3 aura
4 recevras
5 irez
6 reviendrons
7 parlerai
8 boiront.

Work experience

A
1 Saturday
2 credit card
3 clothes, CDs, magazines

B
4 Office
5 two weeks
6 photocopying, filing papers, helping other staff, getting tea and coffee
7 bus
8 tired

Perfect tense

1 J'ai vu un bon film
2 Il a mis ses tennis/baskets
3 Elle a ouvert la lettre
4 Nous n'avons pas pu fermer la fenêtre
5 Ils ont joué au football
6 As-tu perdu ton stylo/ton bic?
7 Elle a choisi ses matières pour les examens de niveau avancé.

Health problems

1 J'ai mal à la gorge et à la tête.
2 (Depuis) deux jours.
3 Pouvez-vous me conseiller quelque chose?
4 Si ça ne va pas mieux après le week-end, je dois aller chez le médecin?
5 Merci beaucoup.

Accidents and emergencies

1 true
2 true
3 false
4 false
5 true
6 not given
7 not given
8 false

Perfect tense – être verbs

1 venu
2 arrivés
3 tombée
4 sorti
5 est entré
6 retourné
7 parties
8 allés
9 née
10 descendus

Lost and found

a ce matin, cuir noir

b appareil (photo), métro

c dans la rue, bleu marine, plastique

d montre, piscine

e hier soir, en or

Letters and telephone calls

1 Write soon

2 Thank you for your letter

3 Dear Sir

4 I'd like to ask you

5 I'd be very grateful

6 Yours faithfully

7 Who's speaking?

8 Hold the line

9 Do you want to leave a message?

10 I'll ring back later

Time and numbers

1 huit heures et demie du matin

2 vingt heures

3 vingt-deux heures

4 quatorze virgule dix

5 trente-trois, soixante-cinq, quarante-neuf

6 midi

Other useful grammar

1 bien

2 malheureusement

3 âgée

4 mal

5 acheter

6 à

7 de

NOTES

THE BOOK OF
AYURVEDA

An interactive guide to using Indian healing for personal wellbeing

JUDITH H MORRISON

CLASSICS

An Hachette UK Company
www.hachette.co.uk

First published in 1995 by Gaia Books Ltd
This edition published by Octopus Publishing Group Ltd
Endeavour House, 189 Shaftesbury Avenue
London WC2H 8JY
www.octopusbooks.co.uk

ISBN 978-1-85675-334-0

A CIP catalogue record for this book is available from the
British Library.

Printed and bound in China
10 9 8 7 6 5 4 3 2 1

Editorial acknowledgements for the first edition:
Pip Morgan, Fiona Trent, Eleanor Lines, Sara Mathews,
Tilney Kirkbride, Joss Pearson and Patrick Nugent

Commissioning Editor: Liz Dean
Art Directors: Jonathan Christie, Mark Kan
Designer: Penny Stock
Photographer: Adrian Pope (pp.98–103)

To A.D.M.

"Words do not create facts, they either describe them
or distort them. The fact is always non-verbal." Sri
Nisgadatta Maharaj in *I am That*.

It is my sincere hope that through this book you will
glimpse the depth, beauty and potential of Ayurveda.
I apologize for any distortion of the teachings due to
my interpretation and trust that in pursuing your
interest in Ayurveda you will use your discrimination
to find genuine and compassionate teachers.

I would like to give thanks:
For the bounty of the universe which has given
me many gifts, including the privilege of studying
with teachers who are part of the living tradition of
Ayurveda
To my parents
To my teachers, Dr. Vasant Lad and
  Dr. Robert Svoboda
To my brother
To all the Staff and Friends at the Ayurvedic Institute,
  Albuquerque, for their love, encouragement,
  and support
To Anne Wyatt and Hart De Fouw for the benefit of
  their exceptional though different skills, without
  which I would never have written a book
To Dr. Vasant Lad and the Ayurvedic Press for
  contributing the Food Guidelines
To Will Foster for his help with the Sanskrit Sutras
To Duncan Hulin of the Devon School of Yoga for
  his help with the exercise sequence
To Barbara and Jack Savage, Angela Hope-Murray,
  Richard Barton, Pauline Dunn, and Eileen Pettit
  for their loving support and practical help.

Judith Morrison

CONTENTS

FOREWORD

We live in the Age of Information, an age in which we are literally being inundated with information of all kinds. But if a little knowledge can be a dangerous thing, it can also be risky to have too much, unless you have a reliable way to organize it. This is particularly true in the realm of health and disease, for today we have a bewildering array of effective but often contradictory therapies from which to choose. Though advocates of each therapy maintain the superiority of their approach, it is clear that one remedy is good for some people sometimes, but none is appropriate in all cases at all times, because all people are not the same.

It is because living beings are so diverse that Ayurveda was developed as a medical system which can be carefully tailored to individual requirements. Ayurvedic theory has been used to organize all the many types of knowledge and varieties of therapies which have developed in India over the past 5000 years or more, and can do the same for today's therapeutic techniques. Ayurveda's theories of health and disease are also sufficiently common-sensical that they can be understood by almost anyone. Ayurveda teaches self-knowledge and self-discovery; it encourages people to learn who they are, why they stay healthy and why they get sick, and how they can change their lives so that they can maximize their healthy enjoyment of living.

Because Ayurvedic wisdom is not dependent on any particular time or space, anyone from any country can benefit from Ayurveda, so long as its concepts are properly translated into the appropriate idiom. Judith Morrison, the author of this volume, has studied Ayurveda extensively at the Ayurvedic Institute in New Mexico, USA, and both Dr. Vasant Lad and I greatly appreciate her contribution to this enormous work of translation. Read what she has written, try it out in your own life, and you will have personal experience of what Ayurveda can do for you.

Dr. Robert E. Svoboda, *Ayurvedic Physician*

The Value of Ayurveda

The increasing pace of our working lives and the amount of information that is transmitted rapidly around the world is changing our lifestyles, often to the detriment of our physical, mental, and spiritual health. You can use Ayurveda to restore balance to your life by looking at the qualities you experience through your diet, work, leisure activities, and relationships — and how these interact with your unique constitution.

INTRODUCTION

Common knowledge tells us that a strong constitution brings good health. We all know someone whose health seems robust. Not because they keep fit, eat the right foods, and avoid excess toxins. But because they were born with a strength that equips them to cope with the stresses of modern life, and to restore an inherent equilibrium to their health. How most of us wish we could be like that: eat and do what we like, and not suffer the consequences!

But what is this constitution? Ayurveda stresses that we are all born with an individual constitution that is unique: an integral part of our being, a fixed point which is our personal baseline for health, a health equilibrium which we restore if we wish but which results in illness if we do not.

Ayurveda is a very comprehensive medical system which has been practised for generations in India as well as other countries, such as Sri Lanka. Based on the fundamental principles of life observed in deep meditations by ancient seers, Ayurveda is growing in popularity in the West. The lifestyle guidance in this book has been distilled from the vast body of Ayurvedic teachings, and is designed to help us live and eat in a way that prevents illness.

Ayurveda is a science of life which focusses on the subtle energies in all things – not only in living and inorganic things, but also in our thoughts, emotions, and actions. Each person's constitution is based on a particular relationship of three fundamental and vital energies, or doshas. Known by their Sanskrit names of vata, pitta, and kapha, these doshas are at the heart of Ayurveda. Not only do they determine your capacity for health but they also govern the way you respond to the world around you.

To understand Ayurveda and to think Ayurvedically, you need to familiarize yourself with the way the energies of vata, pitta, and kapha manifest themselves in your everyday life. These manifestations can be described in terms of the way we experience them. This book introduces you to the basic principles of Ayurveda, and helps you identify the characteristics, or qualities, of the doshas through a variety of common adjectives you already know, e.g. hot or cold, light or heavy, wet or dry.

This book shows you how to assess the balance of the three doshas in your constitution, and how to decide which dosha predominates. In other words, you can discover whether you are a vata type, a pitta type, or a kapha type. But remember, everything is relative in Ayurveda – these types are the starting points for understanding your health.

How is your Constitution Determined?

The state of your parents' doshas at the time you were conceived is primarily responsible for your constitution. This is because the qualities your parents experience in life continuously affect the doshas in every cell of their bodies, including the sperm or ovum.

Let us look at a simple example. Imagine a father-to-be who has a pitta constitution and a pressurized, intellectual job in which he is very ambitious. His current doshic state has even higher pitta than his constitutional balance. The mother-to-be has a kapha constitution and works part time in an undemanding job. She is often bored in the evening waiting for her partner to come home, so she spends her time nibbling and dozing in front of the television. Her kapha energy will be in excess.

All three doshas will be in the baby's constitution, but one, or maybe two, will predominate. If, at the time of conception, the pitta in the father's sperm is stronger than the kapha in the mother's ovum, the baby will have a pitta constitution, with kapha secondary. If the kapha from the ovum dominates, the baby will be kapha, with pitta secondary. If kapha and pitta are of equal strength, the baby will have a pitta–kapha constitution.

In the same way, the state of your doshas and those of your partner will determine the constitution of your offspring. If you and your partner wish to conceive a child, your aim should be to give the baby a well balanced constitution. Factors during pregnancy, such as the mother's diet as well as her physical and emotional health, and the circumstances surrounding the birth experience, can have a secondary influence on the baby's constitution.

The Three Ages of Life

During the cycle of birth to death, we evolve through three different ages, each related to the functions of the doshic energy that predominates in that age. Childhood is the kapha age. The body grows and has a constant demand for nourishment to develop strong tissues. Ailments related to disturbances of kapha are more common in childhood.

The pitta age begins at puberty and lasts through the middle years. Many problems, such as acne, experienced by teenagers can be related to pitta, as this dosha increases in the

MEANING OF AYURVEDA

Ayurveda is a Sanskrit word which literally means "science of life". "Ayur" means life and "Veda" means science, or knowledge.

body. During the pitta age, the body needs to be maintained in a stable state, and conditions due to excess pitta, such as acid indigestion, are more likely.

The vata age begins at about 55 years or with the menopause in women. Metabolism begins to slow down and the tissues are not replenished so readily. Often, a dryness in the body precedes more obvious degeneration of the tissues. The correct diet and a regular oil massage can help keep the body supple.

Making Changes

Every day, the ratio of the three doshas within us is altered by whatever we do – eat heavy food, fly on a plane, sit in front of the television for hours, drink lots of coffee in the morning, or stay up all night. So long as the disturbances to our everyday equilibrium are small and not habitual, and so long as we take steps to restore the balance of our constitution, we should remain in health. Once you have a good idea of the doshic nature of your constitution, you can then go on to establish whether or not your lifestyle is helping you stay healthy.

If the relationship between your vata, pitta, and kapha is disturbed then you will need to take steps to redress the balance and restore the integrity of your constitution. The books contains many charts, lists, and a handful of case studies, or Ayurvedic profiles, to help you establish the details of your lifestyle and to guide you on the changes you may need to make.

In Ayurveda, ill health is related to disturbances of vata, pitta, and kapha in the body. To a trained practitioner, the qualities of the signs and symptoms in the body indicate which dosha is disturbed. For example, excessive dryness in the body is frequently associated with a disturbance of vata, excessive hotness with a disturbance of pitta, and excessive heaviness with a disturbance of kapha. Whatever the signs and symptoms, you will need to adjust your lifestyle and modify some of your habits in order to restore your wellbeing and health.

AGE AND THE DOSHAS

Although one (or perhaps two) of the doshas predominate in your constitution, you will experience a relative increase: in kapha, during childhood; in pitta, during your middle years; in vata after the menopause and during old age.

But how do you adjust your lifestyle? First, you have to discover which dosha is disturbed, and decide what in your lifestyle and diet is causing the disturbance. Then, with your knowledge of qualities uppermost in your mind, select the steps you need to take to restore balance to your doshas. Two crucial principles to remember when planning these changes are: "like increases like" and "opposite qualities decrease". Thus, if your vata dosha is increased and needs to be pacified, do not do things or eat foods that increase vata; instead, select those things and eat those foods that are antagonistic to vata.

Balance and moderation are part of life and health. For example, habitually eating hot spicy food causes the heat in your body and mind to increase. Depending on your constitution and other circumstances in your life, if this heat becomes excessive it could contribute to the disease process – the first signs may have "hot" qualities, such as an itchy rash or an unhelpful, critical attitude of mind. But if you have a "cold" constitution, hot spicy food may help maintain your balance.

As you begin to think Ayurvedically you will understand your uniqueness, your individual requirements in daily life for good health, and how your needs change according to your age, the seasons, and your living circumstances. By understanding the basic principles of Ayurveda you will know how and when to act and what to eat to maintain your health and vitality, and enjoy life up to your constitutional capacity.

GOOD MEDICINE

According to Ayurveda, everything can be a medicine, or a poison, depending on how it is used. Moreover, Ayurveda acknowledges that no treatment or remedy is appropriate for all people or in all circumstances. The art of good medicine is two-fold: to understand the patient and their situation; and to know how and when to act to assist nature in bringing appropriate healing to the patient.

Caution:

The guidelines and information provided in this book are not intended to be a substitute for qualified medical advice.

Hot, Spicy Foods

By understanding your current doshic balance, you will know if hot, spicy foods can beneficially be included in your diet.

PART ONE

UNDERSTANDING
AYURVEDA

1. THE ORIGINS OF AYURVEDA

व्याधयी हि समुत्पन्नाः सर्वप्राणिभयङ्कराः ।
तद्ब्रूहि मे शमीपायं यथावदमरप्रभी ॥
तस्मै प्रीवाच भगवानायुवेदं शतक्रतुः ।
पदैरल्पैर्मतिं बुद्ध्वा विपुलां परमषर्ये ॥

"Diseases causing fear in all living things have appeared, so, O Lord
of god, tell me the proper measures for (their) amelioration."
Then Lord Indra, having observed the wide intelligence of the
great sage, delivered to him Ayurveda in a few words.
(*Charaka Samhita* Chapter 1: 18)

Ayurveda is a traditional healing system of India, with origins firmly rooted in the culture of the Indian subcontinent. Some 5000 or more years ago, the great *rishis*, or seers of ancient India, observed the fundamentals of life and organized them into a system. Ayurveda was their gift to us, an oral tradition passed down from generation to generation.

A few treatises on Ayurveda date from around 1000 BC. The best-known is *Charaka Samhita*, which concentrates on internal medicine. Many of today's Ayurvedic physicians use *Astanga Hrdayam*, a more concise compilation written over 1000 years ago from the earlier texts. Later texts include modifications derived from the medical systems of invading cultures.

Ayurvedic teachings were recorded as *sutras*, succinct poetical verses in Sanskrit, containing the essence of a topic and acting as aides-memoire for the students. The students memorized entire texts, which their *guru*, or teacher, then brought alive by expounding on the deeper knowledge contained within the verses. Parts of these texts are available in translation from Sanskrit, but without a teacher they are not readily accessible to Western minds.

Sanskrit, the ancient language of India, reflects the philosophy behind Ayurveda and the depth within it. Sanskrit has a wealth of words for aspects within and beyond consciousness. We lose some of the depths of meaning when we translate the Sanskrit words into Western languages, which cannot deal effectively with all Ayurveda's concepts. Only when concepts, ideas, and inventions enter a culture are words and language developed for them.

The Sanskrit Language

Sanskrit is a beautiful, powerful, resonating language, with a structure and richness not found within most modern languages. The logic and beauty within Sanskrit reflect the two levels needed to appreciate Ayurveda fully: the outer knowledge passed on from teachers and books, and the inner knowledge or intuition gained through experience, by applying what we learn to our daily lives.

पृथिव्यादीनि तत्त्वानि पुरुषान्तानि पञ्चसु ।

क्रमात् कादिषु वर्गेषु मकारान्तेषु सुव्रते ॥

वाय्वग्निसलिलेन्द्राणां धारणानां चतुष्टयम् ।

तदूर्ध्व शादि विरव्यातं पुरस्ताद् ब्रह्मपञ्चकम् ॥

अमूला तत्क्रमाज्झेया क्षान्ता सृष्टिरुदाहृता ।

सर्वेषामेव मन्त्राणां विद्यानां च यशस्विनि ॥

इयं यीनिः समारव्याता सर्वतन्त्रेषु सर्वदा ।

THE PHILOSOPHY OF MANIFESTATION

No philosophy has had greater influence on Ayurveda than Sankhya's philosophy of creation, or manifestation. To use Ayurveda in your life, you do not have to accept, or even understand, this philosophy. But if you keep an open mind toward it, you will gain a deeper insight into the ways Ayurveda can benefit your health.

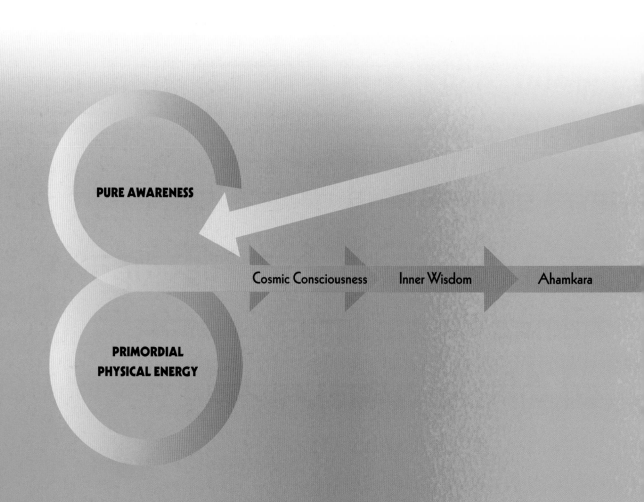

PURE AWARENESS

PRIMORDIAL
PHYSICAL ENERGY

Cosmic Consciousness   Inner Wisdom   Ahamkara

According to Sankhya, behind creation there is a state of pure existence or awareness, which is beyond time and space, has no beginning or end, and no qualities. Within pure existence there arises a desire to experience itself, which results in disequilibrium and causes the manifestation of primordial physical energy.

This energy is the creative force of action, a source of form that has qualities. Matter and energy are closely related: when energy takes form, we tend to think of it in terms of matter rather than energy. The primordial physical energy is imponderable and cannot be described in words. The most subtle of all energies, it is modified until ultimately our familiar mental and physical world manifests itself.

Pure existence and primordial energy unite for the dance of creation to happen. Pure existence is simply "observing" this dance. Primordial energy and all that flows from it cannot exist except in pure existence or awareness. These concepts of awareness are central to Ayurveda's philosophy and, ultimately, to maintaining health in human beings.

The Energy of Creation

The energy of the dance of creation arises out of pure awareness or existence, the unlimted energy of the universe; this energy is love.

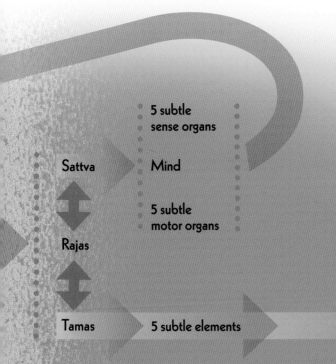

Sattva
Rajas
Tamas

5 subtle sense organs
Mind
5 subtle motor organs
5 subtle elements
5 dense elements

Inner Wisdom

Primordial energy gives rise to cosmic consciousness or intelligence, which is the universal order that pervades all life. Your individual intelligence, which is different from your everyday intellectual mind, is derived from and is part of this cosmic consciousness. It is your inner wisdom: the part of your individuality that cannot be swayed by the demands of daily life or by *ahamkara*, your sense of "I-ness".

Ahamkara is a Sanskrit word with no easy translation; it is a concept that is not fully formed in the West. Sometimes, the word "ego" is equated to ahamkara, but this is misleading, since ahamkara embraces much more. In essence, it is that part of "me" that knows which parts of universal creation are "me". It is my unique vibration to which all physical parts of "me" resonate. "I" am not separate from any part of creation, but "I" have an identity that differentiates and defines the boundaries of "me". All parts of creation have ahamkara, not only human beings.

Elements and Organs

There are five sense organs and five motor organs in the physical body, each has a counterpart in the subtle body. Each of these 10 organs and the five modes of stimuli which correspond to the subtle elements have an affinity to one of the five dense elements (see p. 23).

CONNECTING ELEMENTS WITH ORGANS

Dense Element	Subtle Element	Sense Organ	Motor Organ	Function
Ether	Sound	Ears	Vocal chords	Speaking
Air	Touch	Skin	Hands	Grasping
Fire	Sight	Eyes	Feet	Moving
Water	Taste	Tongue	Genitals	Procreating
Earth	Smell	Nose	Anus	Excreting

Subjective and Objective Worlds

The next part of the philosophy of creation is often difficult for the Western mind to accept, for the concepts are outside what is familiar to most of us, and there is no easy logic to follow.

There arises from ahamkara a two-fold creation: *sattva*, comprising the subjective world, which is able to perceive and manipulate matter; and *tamas*, the objective world of the five elements. *Rajas*, which is the force or energy of movement, brings together parts of both the subjective and objective worlds.

The subjective world comprises the subtle body, which is the mind and the potential for the five sense organs to hear, feel, see, taste, and smell, and for the five organs of action to speak, grasp, move, procreate, and excrete. Your mind and subtle organs are the bridge between your body and your ahamkara and inner wisdom.

This subtle body, together with ahamkara and inner wisdom, is considered the essential nature of humans. Sankhya's philosophy says that there are eight dispositions or fundamental strivings within humans, which are also part of the innermost nature. These are virtue, vice, knowledge, ignorance, non-attachment, attachment, power, and impotence. Until the ultimate knowledge is obtained these strivings are the reason for ordinary existence and suffering. It is this essential, or innermost, nature that "occupies" the physical body.

On a subtle level, the objective world of tamas is sound, touch, vision, taste, and smell – the five subtle elements. These elements give rise to the dense elements – ether, air, fire, water, and earth – from which all matter of the physical world is derived. Even at the stage of the dense elements, the philosophy of creation is still dealing with aspects of existence that are beyond our physical realms. The essential point of this philosophy is that we are first and foremost spirit experiencing existence.

CREATION IS NOW

Sankhya's philosophy of creation is described in stages to aid understanding. In reality, creation, or manifestation, is now and in the present, without past or future. This concept is difficult to comprehend with our everyday mind.

THE GREAT ELEMENTS

In Ayurveda, everything is composed of the five dense elements (known as the *great* elements) – ether, air, fire, water, and earth. They represent five states, or qualities of energy or matter. Western science cannot see or measure them, but we know them through the qualities of the energy and matter we experience daily in our physical, mental, and emotional lives.

The elements are everywhere and always together in all things, in an infinite variety of proportions. Although each element has a range of attributes, only some are evident in any particular situation. This variety of proportions and attributes allows for the enormous diversity of life. The five elements are part of the dynamic dance of creation: they are constantly changing and interacting. A change in one element affects the others.

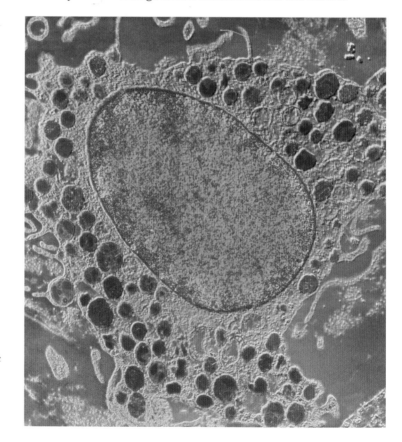

The Elements in Life

All the elements are present in the cell membrane, but the earth element predominates, giving structure to the cell. The water element predominates in the cytoplasm, the liquid in the cell. The metabolic processes regulating the cell are governed mainly by the fire element. The air element predominates in the gases in the cell. The space occupied by the cell represents the ether element.

AIR

The air element is gaseousness, and has airy qualities. It is light, clear, dry, and dispersing.

ETHER

Ether is so subtle that we rarely think about it. It is equated to size or space.

FIRE

Fire is the power of change and transformation. It has the qualities of heat, dryness, and upward movement.

WATER

Water is liquid, cool, and flows downward. It has no shape of its own.

EARTH

Earth is substantial, with the qualities of heaviness, hardness, and only a little downward movement.

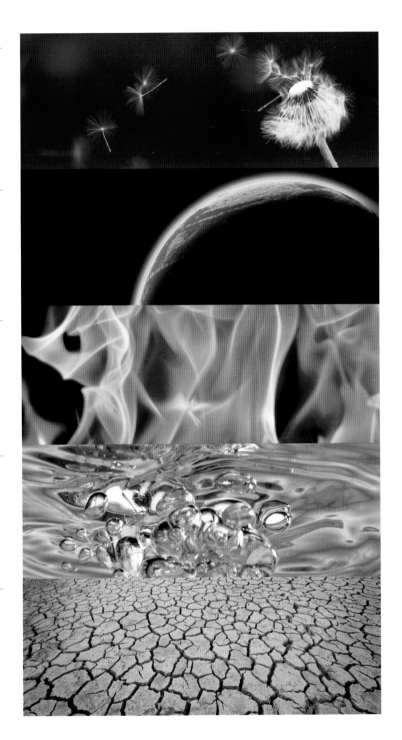

THE FUNDEMENTAL QUALITIES

Ayurveda is a science of qualities. Although we naturally experience them daily, few in the West are trained to think in terms of qualities and to use our qualitative experiences in an analytical way. To use Ayurveda you need to be able to read qualities in yourself, and in the world around you.

In Ayurveda, subtle and insignificant matters have an influence on a situation. Its philosophy starts at the most subtle level with awareness and then consciousness, which is progressively projected until we can perceive it, with our senses, in its manifested form.

These subtle and dense levels interrelate and affect each other through the mind.

Qualitative and quantitative methods of description and analysis do not compete with each other – they are just different models for reality. The secret is to know when, and for what, each is appropriate. Many illnesses are most easily described in terms of experiences and feelings. Fatigue, for example, is hard to define clearly, but may be described with reference to the qualities experienced. In Ayurveda, qualitative descriptions determine what beneficial measures can be taken to restore health.

Elements and Qualities

In Ayurveda, everything in our world is made up of a combination of the five great elements, which manifest differing aspects and intensities of their qualities. Here, the great elements are related to the fundamental qualities listed by *Charaka Samhita*.

QUALITIES OF THE GREAT ELEMENTS

Ether	Air	Fire	Water	Earth
Minuteness	Lightness	Hotness	Coldness	Heaviness
	Mobility	Lightness	Liquidity	Solidity
	Roughness	Sharpness	Softness	Stability
		Liquidity	Smoothness	

According to *Charaka Samhita*, we experience everything through 10 pairs of fundamental qualities. Each pair represents the extremes of a continuum (see right). The relationship between a pair of qualities is the basis of two of Ayurveda's fundamental rules. First, that like increases like; second, that a quality is decreased by its opposite quality.

No absolutes exist in the qualitative model, only relativity. Hot is only hot relative to something cooler. To make a qualitative assessment of anything, always take the context and previous circumstances into account. Relationships or interactions between different qualities are also important. One quality can have a different effect on two substances. For example, heat adds a dry quality to bread, but a liquid quality to butter. As you learn to see people in terms of their qualities, it will become clear why each individual is unique, and reacts to stimuli and events in very different ways.

A PAIR OF QUALITIES

Each pair of qualities, such as hot and cold, represents the extremes of a continuum. If you take food out of the refrigerator it will be cold. Put it in the freezer and it will become colder – more cold quality has been added. Put it in the oven, adding some hot quality, and the food will become less cold. Leave it in the oven long enough and its temperature will have moved from the cold half of the continuum to the hot half.

The Ten Pairs of Qualities

The traditional text, *Charaka Samhita*, lists 20 qualities organized into 10 pairs. Each pair represents two extremes of a continuum and are relative to each other. The two qualities in a pair influence each other.

Heaviness — Lightness
Coldness — Hotness
Unctuousness — Roughness
Dullness — Sharpness
Stability — Mobility
Softness — Hardness
Non-sliminess — Sliminess
Smoothness — Coarseness
Minuteness — Grossness
Solidity — Liquidity

2. THE THREE VITAL ENERGIES

वायुः पित्तं कफश्चेति त्रयी दोषाः समासतः ॥
विकृताविकृता देहं घ्नन्ति ते वर्तयन्ति च ।

Vayu (vata), pitta, and kapha are the three doshas, in brief; they destroy and support
(sustain, maintain) the body when they are abnormal and normal respectively.
(*Astanga Hrdayam* Chapter 1: 6)

The rishis understood the world in terms of the five great elements. In creating Ayurveda as a healing system, the rishis described these elements in a more simplified form as three vital energies, or doshas. Each dosha is a combination of two elements. The three doshas are responsible for all the physiological and psychological processes in your body and mind. They are dynamic forces that determine growth and decay. Each of your physical characteristics, mental capacities, and emotional tendencies can be described in terms of the three doshas.

The Sanskrit names for the three doshas are vata, pitta, and kapha. These do not translate easily from Sanskrit. You aim should be gradually to learn to recognize the effects of the doshas in your body and your daily life. The doshas, like the elements, cannot be detected with our senses, but their qualities can. They have the qualities of their two constituent elements, both individually and in combination. Hence, vata has qualities of air and ether, plus qualities from a combination of the two.

Vata, pitta, and kapha have specific functions in the body but they do not work in isolation. Full health and wellbeing is only possible when the doshas work harmoniously together. It is important to realize that the three doshas in your being change constantly, due to the doshic qualities of your lifestyle and environment, such as time and season (see pp. 150–1).

When you can recognize the qualities of the doshas in your body and the doshic qualities in your daily life, you will be able to use Ayurveda to maintain them in a healthy balance for you. By learning to distinguish any imbalances, you can use Ayurveda to restore equilibrium to your doshas and so regain full health (see Chapter 4).

The Three Doshas

Each dosha is a combination of two elements, one of which predominates over the other. Often, the three doshas — vata, pitta, and kapha (VPK, for short) — are referred to as the air, fire, and water humours respectively.

VATA

Vata is a combination of the air and ether elements, with air predominating.

PITTA

Pitta is primarily the fire element, with water as the secondary element.

KAPHA

Kapha is a combination of the water and earth elements, with water as the primary element.

THE QUALITIES OF VPK

In using Ayurveda it is important to have awareness of the qualities you experience and relate these to the qualities of the doshas. The many nuances in the qualities in your life will be overwhelming, so look initially for broad principles associated with each dosha. For example, the qualities of a windy day sum up vata. The wind is erratic, moves in gusts, dries the washing, and cools you. It is not seen, but its effects are. Heat relates to pitta. A fire gives heat and radiance, and moves upward. Heat melts and penetrates. The two elements of kapha are more equally balanced; the dosha is connected to wet, heavy, or solid qualities. Mud is a useful simile. It is cold and soft, heavy and dense; it might slide slowly downward.

The key words that describe the qualities associated with the doshas are shown on the chart below. Once you have built up a broad picture of qualities for each dosha you can start to think about yourself in doshic terms. You will then be ready to decide what qualities to add or reduce in order to keep your doshas working harmoniously.

When learning about Ayurveda you should first isolate the concepts of vata, pitta, and kapha to understand their range of qualities, and only then try to apply the qualities to the

KEY QUALITIES OF VPK

VATA (Air and Ether)	PITTA (Fire and Water)	KAPHA (Water and Earth)
Light	Light	Heavy
Cold	Hot	Cold
Dry	Oily	Oily
Rough	Sharp	Slow
Subtle	Liquid	Slimy
Mobile	Sour	Dense
Clear	Pungent	Soft
Dispersing		Static
Erratic		Sweet
Astringent		

Key Words

You will probably grasp the idea of VPK more quickly if you commit this list of key words to memory. Copy the list and display it prominently. Remember that qualities are a continuum — they are always relative rather than absolute, and are experienced in a context, not in isolation.

complexities of the human mind and body. The qualities of VPK are listed separately for convenience (see pp. 28, 30–1), but VPK are not separate energies but different aspects of the same energy. They are always present together in an infinite variety of combinations. As your understanding increases you will appreciate how their qualities overlap and interrelate.

Your body and all your daily experiences are comprised not of one but many qualities. As you learn to think qualitatively, look for the main qualities of your feelings and of situations around you as well as in the physical characteristics of yourself and those around you. As you gain in confidence and experience in reading qualities, you will eventually become skilled in distinguishing the subtleties in the qualities you observe.

Qualities of Trees

The qualities of vata, pitta, and kapha are all around us. If you go for a walk through the woods, see if you can see these qualities in different kinds of trees.

The Oak

The oak is a kapha tree; large, sturdy, with a massive trunk, thick bark, and big branches that give a full, rounded silhouette. It is slow growing, taking perhaps 100 years to reach maturity.

The Holly Tree

The holly tree displays pitta qualities: smooth, light grey bark and sharp, spiked leaves.

The Birch

The birch has vata qualities: the tall, thin trunk sways as the wind blows through its flimsy branches, and the bark peels off like dry skin. It grows rapidly to its prime in less than 50 years, but then soon fades.

QUALITIES OF VATA, PITTA & KAPHA

This list divides up some of the words we commonly use to describe circumstances in our lives, and assigns them to the key qualities of each dosha.

Vata Qualities

DRY barren brittle crisp husky non-slimy parched shrivelled wrinkled

ERRATIC changeable fidgety fitful inconstant irregular kinky spasmodic

DISPERSING dissipating evaporating scattering spreading sprawling

ROUGH bumpy coarse gritty harsh husky irregular jagged ragged scaly scratchy

CLEAR empty obvious transparent

SUBTLE discreet hidden imperceptible minute sensitive veiled

LIGHT flimsy fluffy fragile skinny thin

MOBILE active animated changeable fluid lively moving running swift travelling

COLD bitter bleak chilled cool freezing glassy icy

Pitta Qualities

OILY buttery fat greasy sebaceous slippery smooth unctuous

SHARP cutting enquiring inquisitive keen penetrating perceptive piercing pointed quick shrill strong

LIQUID flowing fluid structureless wet

LIGHT bright fair fire glowing pale radiant

HOT burning eager fiery inflamed passionate raging scorching sharp spicy sweltering

Kapha Qualities

COLD bitter bleak chilled cool freezing glassy icy

HEAVY chubby dense gross lethargic listless massive obese stodgy

OILY buttery fat greasy sebaceous slippery smooth unctuous

SLOW dense dull inert lacklustre lingering sleepy slothful tardy torpid

SLIMY clammy mucusy oily runny slippery smooth soft

DENSE dull firm heavy obtuse opaque slow solid thick

SOFT comfortable creamy cushioning flabby mushy receptive sinking into

STATIC calm immobile still

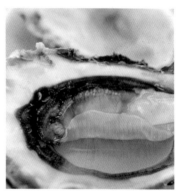

SHARED AND OPPOSING QUALITIES

Each dosha shares a quality with another dosha; the third has the opposite quality. For example, vata and pitta both have a light quality; kapha is heavy. Slight differences exist in the nature of shared qualities. Vata's lightness relates to weight, pitta's to radiance as well as weight. Similarly, both vata and kapha are cold, but vata is dry cold while kapha is wet cold. Vata is not as cold as kapha – for example, a dry, cold climate does not *feel* as cold as a wet, cold climate. Pitta is slightly oily, whereas kapha can be profusely so.

Antagonistic Qualities and Balance

Each dosha has an inherent quality to regulate and balance itself. This ability comes from the antagonistic qualities that arise from the dosha's constituent elements. In vata, for example, one quality of the predominant air element is dispersing but the extent of its dispersal is determined by the space (ether). Too much fire in pitta can evaporate water and have a drying effect; yet too much water quenches fire. In kapha, an increase in liquid quality makes for a runnier substance, but a relative overabundance of earth element makes a substance more solid.

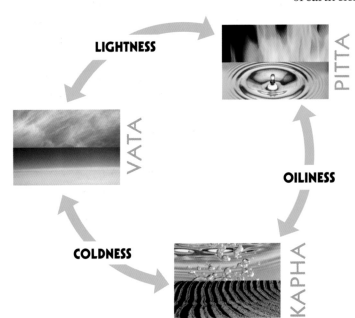

LIGHTNESS

PITTA

VATA

OILINESS

COLDNESS

KAPHA

Shared Qualities

Pitta and kapha share the quality of oiliness and vata has the opposite, dry quality. Vata and kapha share the quality of coldness, whereas pitta is hot. Vata and pitta share the quality of lightness whereas kapha is heavy. An excess of vata, pitta, or kapha energy in the body is often associated with symptoms that have dry, hot, or heavy qualities respectively.

VPK AND YOUR CONSTITUTION

Ayurveda is a science of the individual. You are unique, in that only you display the doshas in your way. The ratio of the doshas in your constitution (see p. 9), and the qualities expressed by it, are as unique to every individual as fingerprints. This ratio is the baseline against which you can compare the current levels of your doshas; and it reflects characteristic tendencies and susceptibility to illness.

Although VPK qualities combine in the individual in an infinite number of ways, Ayurveda describes three types of constitution. In mono-types, one dosha predominates: they have either a vata, pitta, or kapha constitution. In duo-types, two doshas have equal strength: they have either vata–pitta, pitta–kapha, or vata–kapha constitutions. In the third type, the three doshas have equal strength. This is rare. When the doshas are well combined, individuals experience excellent health under most circumstances. But if the doshas are poorly combined the individual, however much care he or she takes, suffers illness most of the time.

The uniqueness of an individual arises for two reasons. First, nobody shares exactly the same ratio of vata, pitta, and kapha. Second, no two people manifest the qualities of their doshas in an identical way. You and your friend may both be mono-types, with vata predominating in your constitution, but there will be differences in the qualities of the vata and also of pitta and kapha that manifest in you both.

Knowing your constitution (see pp. 38–41) is the first step to anticipating the sort of imbalances that can make you ill and the sort of illnesses you are likely to suffer from. Equally, the knowledge enables you to adjust your life to keep your doshas "balanced", which means maintaining the same ratio of doshas as your constitution. When you have achieved this, you may be able to obtain a better balance which will give you increased vitality. As a rule of thumb, the strongest dosha in your constitution has the greatest tendency to increase, so you will be most susceptible to illnesses associated with an increase of that dosha.

CONSTITUTIONAL CHARACTERISTICS

To use Ayurveda to maintain wellness and vitality, you need to know what your constitution is – the original combination of vata, pitta, and kapha in your body. Ideally, you should ascertain this from an expert Ayurvedic physician, who will have been trained in Ayurvedic pulse diagnosis. Your constitution can also be assessed by accurate observation.

However, as yet there are few people in the West who have had sufficient training to assess constitution accurately.

Generally, vata characteristics tend to be extreme, irregular, small, light in weight, or dry. Pitta ones will be average or medium, but sharp, quick, and light. Large, heavy, or slow qualities are connected with kapha.

Different Faces

Study the faces around you — family, friends, colleagues, acquaintances. Try to assign their characteristics to V, P, or K, using the descriptions here. Remember, nobody has a face that is completely one dosha or another; everyone is a combination of doshas. Remember, too, that in assessing constitutions all characteristics are taken into account (see pp. 38–41).

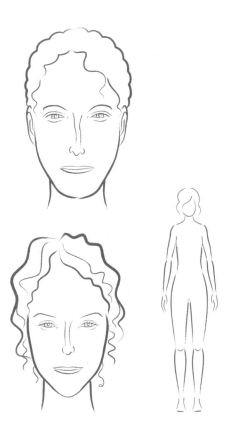

VATA

Vata skin is thin, dry, darkish, and cool, and vata hair is thin, dark, coarse, and either kinky or curly. The face is long and angular, often with an underdeveloped chin. The neck is thin and scrawny. The vata nose is small and narrow, and may be long, crooked, or asymmetrical. Vata eyes are small, narrow, or sunken, dark brown or grey in colour, with a dull lustre. The vata mouth is small, with thin, narrow, or tight lips. Teeth are irregular, protruding, or broken, set in receding gums.

PITTA

Pitta skin is fair, soft, lustrous, and warm, and tends to burn easily in the sun. The skin has freckles, many moles, and a tendency to rashes. Pitta hair is fine and soft, either fair or reddish. The face is heart-shaped, often with a pointed chin. The neck is average and in proportion. The nose is neat, pointed, and average in size. Pitta eyes are average in size, either light blue, light grey, or hazel in colour, with an intense lustre. The pitta mouth is medium with average lips. Teeth are medium-sized and yellowish.

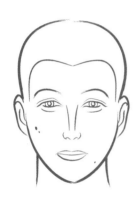

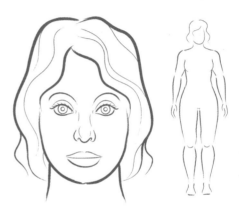

KAPHA

Kapha skin is thick, oily, pale, white, and cold. Kapha hair is plentiful, thick, wavy, lustrous, and generally brown. The face is large, rounded, and full. The neck is solid, with a tree-trunk quality. The kapha nose is large and rounded. Kapha eyes are attractive and large, blue or light brown in colour. The kapha mouth is large with big, full lips. Teeth are big and white, and set in strong gums.

THE DOSHAS AND THE MIND

In Ayurveda, the mind also has a constitution and generally there is a close correlation with your physical constitution. Emotions, too, can be classified into VPK. Individuals have a natural tendency toward certain emotional traits, which will be influenced by their constitution (see also p. 78 and Chapter 7).

As a rule, you will feel positive emotions more readily when your doshas are balanced.

THE GIFT OF LOVE

Love is unconditional and universal. It cannot be affected by physical, emotional, or mental states, though your ability to receive and give love can be.

Positive States

This list classifies our positive mental and emotional states according to VPK. Your current doshic balance will affect how you think and feel at present. Use this list in conjunction with the qualities on pp. 30–1.

PITTA

Ambition – Concentration – Confidence – Courage – Enthusiasm for knowledge – Happiness – Intelligence

A pitta constitution generally means you have a very alert, focussed mind. You grasp information quickly and manipulate it to your advantage. Your memory is good for information you consider useful for furthering your aims, but not so good at remembering birthdays and anniversaries.

VATA

Creativity – Enthusiasm – Freedom – Generosity – Joy – Vitality

If you have a vata constitution, you are likely to be artistic and creative with a good imagination, though you may find it hard to put your ideas into practice, as new ideas continually catch your imagination. Your memory may not be very good.

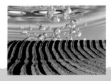

KAPHA

Caring – Centredness – Compassion – Contentment – Faith – Fulfilment – Groundedness – Patience – Sense of being nourished – Stability – Support – Tenderness

If kapha predominates in your constitution, you will have a steady and reliable mind. You may take time to learn, but will remember what you have learnt. There can sometimes be an element of dullness with a kapha mind; it is usually content not to seek fresh mental stimulation.

FUNCTIONS OF VPK

Vata, pitta, and kapha have specific functions in the body and mind. Vata is mobile, and is involved in all movements, large and small. Pitta is hot; its chief function is the metabolic transformations in the body and assimilation of mental experiences. Kapha is the body's supply system and also provides lubricating fluids such as mucus.

VATA

Stimulation of nerves

Transmission of sensory stimuli

Initiation of motor functions

Creation of impulses

Creation of reflexes

Maintenance of consciousness through prana, the life force

Inspiration and expiration

Heart beats

Circulation of blood, oxygen, nutrients, thoughts

Stimulation of digestive juices

Peristalsis

Normal elimination

Normal transformation of tissues

Ejaculation

Delivery of fetus from womb

Stimulation of tears

Expression of emotion

Enthusiasm

Creativity

PITTA

All transformations within the mind and body

Digestion, absorption, and assimilation of food

Maintenance of body temperature

Creation of hunger and thirst

Lustre of eyes and skin

Vision

Comprehension of sensory stimuli

Assimilation of thoughts

Recognition

Discrimination

Intellect, comprehension, and reasoning capacity

Confidence

Cheerfulness

KAPHA

Protection, e.g. mucous lining of stomach

Unctuousness

Lubrication, e.g. synovial fluid in joints

Binding, firmness, heaviness in the body

Softness in the body

Distribution of heat

Strength and stamina

Longevity of cells and thus the person

Sleep

Long-term memory

Groundedness and security

Compassion

Absence of greed

CONSTITUTIONAL ASSESSMENT

The charts on the next three pages are designed to help you assess your constitution. Look at the entries in the left hand column and then assess whether you are vata, pitta, or kapha for that particular characteristic. If the concepts of vata, pitta, and kapha are new to you, repeat the assessment as your understanding of the doshas increases in order to get a more accurate result.

Be honest and observant; judge how you are, not how you would like to be. Look for trends that endure. For example, if your weight has been average for 40 years but has increased recently, the gain is likely to be due to lifestyle rather than constitution. Make the assessments in relation to your ethnic background. Ask a friend who knows you well to check your assessments. Take time to reflect on the questions but not for so long that too many details sway your judgment. Rely on the answer that comes to you after honest consideration.

No one is purely vata, pitta, or kapha. To get an accurate assessment you may need to assess secondary influences. For example, a sharp pointed nose will be pitta, but if it is slightly larger than average then there will be a secondary kapha influence.

Guidelines for Filling in the Charts

Photocopy the following pages to fill in the charts.

For each entry place a tick over the doshic description that describes you as you are or have been for most of your life.
If you fall equally between two descriptions, tick both.

If you detect a strong secondary influence mark it with a cross.

Leave any items that you do not know, e.g. fertility.

There are no right or wrong answers. Use the information as a guide to help you understand your unique combination of the doshas.

Take your time to consider the qualities in the assessment. Treat it as a learning exercise. Before you start, look at the questions in relation to people around you. This will help you to see the doshas and enable you to recognize your own qualities. You will also begin to realize that the descriptions are all relative — you may even see yourself in a different way once you notice the qualities in others.

Assessing the Ticks and Crosses

Everyone has vata, pitta, and kapha in their constitution, so you should have ticks in all three columns and crosses in some.

When you have finished the assessment, add up the total number of ticks and crosses for each column in each of the four assessments (physical build, physical characteristics, etc.). The dosha with the highest number of ticks should be your constitutional type.

If the highest two doshas are very close, look at the number of crosses under each. The one with substantially more crosses than the other might be your constitutional type; or else you have a duo-type of constitution (see p. 33).

If the totals for all three are very close, and no one column has substantially more crosses, then put greater emphasis on your answers under physical build and characteristics as these are the most stable and least affected by lifestyle changes. Repeat the assessment when you are more experienced in reading qualities — an equal ratio of the doshas is rare.

PHSICAL BUILD

	V	P	K
Size at birth	Small	Average	Large
Height	Exceptionally short or tall (bean-pole)	Medium	Tall and sturdy, or short and stocky
Weight	Light. Difficulty putting on weight	Moderate. No problem gaining or losing weight	Heavy. Finds it hard to lose weight
Frame/bone structure	Light, delicate. Hips/shoulders narrow	Medium	Large. Broad shoulders/big hips.
Joints	Prominent, dry, knobbly	Normal. Well proportioned	Big. Well formed and lubricated
Musculature	Slight. Prominent tendons	Medium. Firm	Plentiful. Solid
Ticks	**Total**	**Total**	**Total**
Crosses	**Total**	**Total**	**Total**

PHYSICAL CHARACTERISTICS

	V	P	K
Skin	Thin, dry, darkish. Cool	Fair, soft, lustrous, warm. Freckles. Many moles	Thick, oily, pale or white. Cold
Hair	Thin, dark, coarse, kinky or curly	Fine, soft, fair, or reddish	Plentiful, thick, wavy, lustrous, generally brown
Shape of face	Long, angular. Chin often underdeveloped	Heart-shaped. Chin often pointed	Large, rounded, full
Neck	Thin. Very long or very short	Average. In proportion	Solid, tree-trunk quality
Nose	May be crooked, small, or narrow	Neat, pointed, average in size	Large, rounded
Eyes — size	Small, narrow, or sunken	Average	Large, prominent
Eyes — colour	Dark brown or grey	Light blue or grey, hazel	Blue or light brown
Eyes — lustre	Dull	Intense	Attractive
Teeth	Irregular, protruding. Receding gums	Medium size, yellowish	White, big. Strong gums
Mouth	Small. Receding gums	Medium	Large
Lips	Thin, narrow, tight	Average	Big, full
Ticks	**Total**	**Total**	**Total**
Crosses	**Total**	**Total**	**Total**

PHYSIOLOGICAL FUNCTIONS

	V	P	K
Sweat	Minimal	Profuse, especially when hot. Strong fleshy or sour smell	Moderate, but present even when not exercising
Temperature preferences	Craves warmth	Loves coolness	Dislikes cold
Sleep	Light, fitful	Sound but short	Deep, likes plenty
Stools and elimination	Irregular, constipated. Hard, dry stools	Regular. Loose stools	Slow elimination, plentiful and heavy
Activity level	Always doing many things, fidgets	Moderate	Lackadaisical
Endurance	Expends energy quickly, and sinks until recovered	Manages energy well	Good stamina
Sexual arousal	Intense; quickly expended. Fantasizes	Strong; desires and actions matched	Slow; then passion maintained
Fertility	Low	Average	Good
Speech	Fast talking	Sharp, clear, precise	Slow, maybe laboured
Ticks	**Total**	**Total**	**Total**
Crosses	**Total**	**Total**	**Total**

PSYCHOLOGICAL ASPECTS

	V	P	K
Thinking	Superficial with many ideas. More thoughts than deeds	Precise, logical. Good planner and gets plans carried out	Calm, slow, cannot be rushed. Good organizer
Memory	Poor long-term	Good, quick	Good long-term, takes time to learn
Deep beliefs	Changes these frequently, according to latest mood	Extremely strong convictions that may govern behaviour	Deep steady beliefs that are not easily changed
Emotional tendencies	Fearful, anxious, insecure	Angry, judgmental	Greedy, possessive
Work	Creative	Intellectual	Caring
Lifestyle	Erratic	Busy, but plans to achieve much	Steady and regular. Maybe stuck in a rut
Ticks	**Total**	**Total**	**Total**
Crosses	**Total**	**Total**	**Total**

PART TWO

THE BODY
IN HEALTH AND DISEASE

3. THE BODY IN HEALTH

दीषधातुमला मूलं सदा देहस्य .... ।

Doshas, dhatus (tissues) and malas (waste products) are the roots
(causes, chief constituents, supports) of the body always (throughout the span of life).
(*Astanga Hrdayam* Chapter 11: 1)

Ayurveda says we each reflect every aspect of creation. Like a hologram, each part potentially contains the knowledge of the whole, the smaller being reproduced in the image of the greater. The universe is the macrocosm, and nested within are human beings, or microcosms.

According to Sankhya's philosophy (see pp. 18–21), all matter, including our bodies, consists of the five great elements. The physical structure and functions of the body are also understood in terms of the three doshas (see p. 37), as are aspects of our emotional and mental processes.

In health, the doshas work together to produce strong, healthy tissues and good powers of digestion, assimilation, and elimination. When the doshas are in balance the mind and body will be in harmony, producing emotional stability and good mental faculties.

The key to using Ayurveda is knowing how vata, pitta, and kapha work in the body, and how they are affected by influences from both inside and outside the body. These influences include the state of your metabolism, what you eat and do each day, how you think and feel, and the climate and environment in which you live and work. Understanding and recognizing vata, pitta, and kapha's roles in the healthy body will help you understand how they are involved in disease and ill health.

Ayurveda primarily describes the functions and sequences of refinements of tissues in the body. It also describes a subtle system of energy channels, or *nadis*, similar to the meridians in Chinese medicine.

VPK in the Body

You need to consider two main aspects of the doshas when looking at the body in health. First and foremost is the unique balance of the doshas in your body – your constitution (see pp. 38–41). Second is the range of each dosha's normal functions (see p. 37) and the areas of the body with which the doshas have a special affinity (see pp. 46–7).

As you examine the functions of vata, pitta, and kapha in the body, refer back to the list of the doshas' qualities on pages 30–1; this will help you see the way Ayurveda is organized. You may find that a number of paradoxes and ambiguities arise. But if you keep an open, enquiring mind you allow opportunities for insights.

At this stage, do not be tempted to draw conclusions about your health. You will need to let your understanding deepen first, as you learn to think from the Ayurvedic perspective. As with any new skill you need to start with the broad principles and cannot expect to know everything immediately. The skill comes with practice, as does judging which factors are most important for you and your body. You are already familiar with your body, and can learn to relate how you feel physically and emotionally to the qualities of the doshas. Reading your body through qualities requires clear observation and experience. You need to understand the qualities in the whole context of your spirit, mind, body, and environment. You should not draw conclusions from one factor alone.

Elements in the Body

Vata (air/ether) is mainly concerned with movement, and the space in which it happens. Pitta (fire/water) is linked to metabolism and its secretions. Kapha (water/earth) gives the body structure and solidity.

Classifying parts of the body into VPK seems to contain ambiguities. Don't dismiss these for they are a reflection of the different levels of understanding in Ayurveda. For example, bones can be related to the earth element as they give structure and support to the body. But on page 47, you will see that they are a subsidiary site of vata. This is because bones are porous and the spaces in them are related to ether, one of the vata elements.

ETHER	All cavities, e.g. abdominal cavity
AIR	Movement, breath
FIRE	Enzymes, hormones
WATER	Liquid tissues, e.g. lymph
EARTH	Solid tissues

SEATS OF
VATA, PITTA & KAPHA

As different aspects of one energy the doshas are always together. However, each dosha is associated with particular parts of the body, places where its force tends to predominate. First and foremost, each dosha has a main place, or seat, in a part of the gastrointestinal tract.

One major role of the seat is to accommodate the small daily changes in the dosha without significantly disturbing the body's functioning. The small "excesses" of a dosha (see pp. 62–3) are held in its seat and expelled from the body via the gastrointestinal tract. But accumulation of excessive dosha in its "seat" is part of the early stage of the disease process (see pp. 68–9).

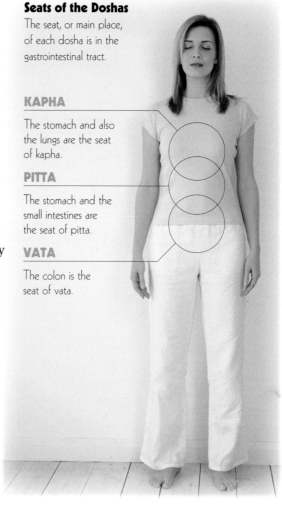

Seats of the Doshas
The seat, or main place, of each dosha is in the gastrointestinal tract.

KAPHA

The stomach and also the lungs are the seat of kapha.

PITTA

The stomach and the small intestines are the seat of pitta.

VATA

The colon is the seat of vata.

SUBSIDIARY SITES

In addition to its seat, each dosha has a special affinity with subsidiary sites (see below), which are closely related to its functions (see p. 37). For example, a subsidiary site of vata, which is responsible for the movement of the body, is the nervous system. The gallbladder and thus bile are linked with pitta and digestion. One function of kapha is lubrication, which is related to the synovial fluid in joints.

KAPHA

Mucous membranes
Plasma and lymph
Cytoplasm (in cells)
White matter (in brain)
Joints (synovial membrane and fluid)
Subcutaneous fat
Mouth
Nose
All secretions, e.g. mucus, saliva

PITTA

Liver
Spleen
Gall bladder
Blood
Sweat
Eyes
Endocrine glands, e.g. pituitary

VATA

Pelvic cavity
Lower back
Thighs
Bones
Ears
Skin
Nervous system
Cavities, e.g. ear canal

AGNI

In Ayurveda, *agni* encompasses changes or refinements in the body and mind from the dense to the more subtle. Such changes include the digestion and absorption of food in the gastrointestinal tract and cellular transformations, as well as the assimilation of sensory perceptions and mental and emotional experiences. As such, agni covers whole sequences of chemical interactions and changes in the body and mind. Your "digestive" abilities on all levels are related to the strength of your agni.

Agni and pitta are closely connected. Agni and pitta are both hot and light but the other qualities of agni are subtle and dry. According to Dr. Vasant Lad in his book *Ayurveda: The Science of Self-Healing*, "Pitta contains heat energy, which helps digestion. This heat energy is agni." The strength of the body to resist disease and also your physical strength are the outcome of this heat-energy, which determines the metabolic processes of the body.

Balanced agni is vital for health. Ayurveda regards disturbances to agni as one of the chief causes of disease (see pp. 76–7). You must take your power to digest food into account when deciding what is the correct diet for you (see Chapter 6).

Ayurveda describes various agnis in the body and mind according to the conversion or transformation made. The main agni is the gastric fire, responsible for digesting the food we eat and turning it into substances that the body can absorb. This agni correlates with the hydrochloric acid in the stomach and the digestive enzymes and juices secreted into the stomach, duodenum, and small intestines. If your digestive agni is low, your digestive capacity will be impaired: you may experience pain, discomfort or a feeling of heaviness after eating, gases, gurglings, constipation, or loose stools (see pp. 76–7).

THE DIGESTIVE PROCESS

Good digestion is vital for health. To achieve it, you need to understand your digestion and eat according to your agni, i.e. digestive capacity. The alternative – indigestion or incomplete digestion – leads to *ama* (see p. 77) and the disturbance of one or more of the doshas. According to Ayurveda, this is a root cause of illness.

Often, we only think about our digestive organs when we experience discomfort. Digestion is your body's means of "cooking", or transforming food into a form that can be absorbed. If you digest your food fully, it will be absorbed and assimilated by the body and used to build strong, healthy tissues (see pp. 56–7).

Your digestive ability is related to the strength of your agni. Poor digestion leads to malabsorption and the absorption of undigested or incompatible products that result in ama, clogged channels, inferior tissues, and disturbed doshas. One indication of malabsorption is teeth indentations on the sides of the tongue.

Digestion within the body starts in the mouth. Food stimulates your taste buds and your smell receptors. These perceptions, via the brain, influence how much and which digestive juices (agni) are secreted in the stomach and small intestines. The breakdown of the food begins with chewing, which mixes it with saliva. The more juice-like each mouthful is when swallowed the better: the particles are smaller, thereby increasing the food's surface area, which allows the digestive fluids to act upon them more effectively. This first stage of digestion is related to kapha and food that is well masticated is associated with the sweet taste (see pp. 52–5).

Your stomach mixes food with digestive enzymes and hydrochloric acid, which is capable of burning – the "fire" of digestion. This is the beginning of the pitta activity of transforming what was external into an integral part of you. The length of time food remains in the stomach depends on the individual and the nature and amount of food eaten.

Pain during Digestion

The stages of the digestive process are related to vata, pitta, and kapha. If you experience discomfort or pain during digestion, note how long after eating the pain arrives. Pain soon after eating, whilst the food is still in the stomach, indicates imbalanced kapha. Pain two to four hours after eating may involve a pitta problem. Flatulence or discomfort some time after eating is a sign of disturbed vata. Remember not to read single signs or symptoms in isolation.

For example, melons pass through the stomach more quickly than cereals. Consequently, if you eat melons at the same meals as cereals, the cereals may not be properly digested. In the intestines, bile and other digestive enzymes continue the process, transforming the food and preparing it for absorption. If absorption is impaired you do not obtain all the nutrients, nor any supplements, from your food. However, a simple, easily digestible diet facilitates absorption. The digestion in the stomach and small intestines is associated with pitta and the sour and salt tastes (see pp. 52–5). This corresponds with the release of enzymes and bile salts. At a later stage of digestion, in the ileum, the predominant taste is pungent.

The colon continues the absorption process, particularly of water, calcium, and other minerals. According to Ayurveda, the colon absorbs prana, the life force, which we obtain from breath and food. Prana from food supplies the body's long-term reservoir of this vital life force. If you habitually eat foods with insufficient prana – for example, food that is stale or over-processed – or if your colon's ability to absorb prana is impaired (e.g. by flatulence or clogged channels), then your vitality may be low and this may lead to fatigue. The final stages of digestion are associated with vata and the bitter and astringent tastes.

Regular and complete elimination of faeces (see pp. 126–7) is the last part of the digestive process, preparing the system for further supplies of nutrients.

Agni

The literal translation of agni is fire, and fire transforms completely that which it consumes.

Digestive Requirements

Fruit should not be eaten with foods that have different digestive requirements. For example, you should avoid eating melons with other foods because the fruit passes through the stomach more quickly.

THE THREE STAGES
OF DIGESTION

Ayurveda describes the digestion of food in three stages related to the effects on the body. These are "tastes", or the immediate effect; "energetics", or medium-term effect; and the "post-digestive", or long-term, effect.

In Ayurveda, "taste" has an extended meaning and does not just refer to the perceptions on the tongue. Ayurveda says there are six tastes: sweet, sour, salty, pungent, bitter, and astringent (see pp. 54–5). The six tastes also include the effects substances and experiences have within the body and are also related to the five great elements (see chart opposite). When first encountered, you may find this way of looking at food and digestion difficult to comprehend. As your understanding of Ayurveda deepens you will see the relationship between the subtle aspects, through the elements, doshas, and tastes, of digestion and food to your physical, mental, and emotional wellbeing.

The immediate effect of putting food or drink into your mouth is the sensory stimulation of taste on your tongue. The perception of taste is within the eater, not the food. Your perception of taste will be affected by what you habitually eat, your doshic preferences, the tastes your body needs, and what you have recently consumed. Coffee, for example, is bitter and makes other foods more palatable.

It is sometimes drunk with very sweet foods to reduce their sweetness.

The "energetics" of food influence the digestive process, either enhancing it or slowing it (and also the body) down. Energetics are either heating or cooling. Foods with heating energetics are more easily digested, generally increasing pitta and pacifying kapha and vata. Foods with cooling energetics give rise to slower, heavier digestion and they tend to decrease pitta and increase kapha and vata.

The general rule is that sour, salty, and pungent foods are heating and, except in excess, will aid digestion. Sweet, bitter, and astringent tastes are cooling and slow down digestion. There are exceptions – for example, honey is sweet but heating.

"Post-digestive" effects (PDE) are the long-term effects that substances have on the body. They can be either anabolic (increasing tissues and thus weight) or catabolic (breaking down or depleting tissues). There are three categories of PDE – sweet, sour, and pungent (these refer to the effects on the body, see pp. 54–5, not the taste on the tongue). Foods with sweet and salty tastes have sweet PDE, which increases tissues. Sour-tasting foods are sour in PDE, while pungent, bitter, and astringent tastes have pungent PDE. Sour and pungent PDE reduce or dry up body tissue.

Tastes and Elements

There are six tastes (see pp. 54–5), each a combination of two elements. Tastes either increase or reduce the doshas, digestion, and the body tissues. For example, the sweet taste (earth/water) increases kapha, slows digestion, and increases weight.

CONNECTING TASTES WITH ELEMENTS

Taste	Great elements	Effect on dosha			Energetics	PDE
		Vata	Kapha	Pitta		
Sweet	Earth & water	P	I	P	C	Sweet
Sour	Fire & earth	P	I	I	H	Sour
Salty	Water & fire	P	I	I	H	Sweet
Pungent	Fire & air	I	P	I	H	Pungent
Bitter	Air & ether	I	P	P	C	Pungent
Astringent	Air & earth	I	P	P	C	Pungent

P = pacifies I = increases C = cooling H = heating

Special Actions

Some substances, mainly herbs and substances used in Ayurvedic medicine, do not comply with the rules about tastes, energetics, and PDE; they have their own special actions, or prabhav in Sanskrit, which are known through long usage. The versatility of Ayurvedic herbology comes from the detailed knowledge of these rules and prabhav of substances.

ACTIONS OF THE
SIX TASTES

Sour Taste

Increases P and K

Stimulates agni

Good for heart and digestion

Encourages inactive vata energy in
the pelvic cavity to move downward,
aiding elimination

Sets teeth on edge, increases salivation

Excess use may cause looseness or
flabbiness, loss of strength, giddiness,
itching, irritation, a whitish yellow pallor,
herpetiform lesions, swellings, thirst,
fever and diseases arising from excess
pitta or kapha

Sweet Taste

Mitigates P and V

Produces greater strength in the tissues

Valuable for the aged, wounded,
emaciated, and children

Universally liked, often adheres to the
inside of the mouth, and gives feelings
of pleasure, contentment, and comfort

Good for complexion, hair, senses, ojas

Increases breast milk

Unites broken parts such as bones

Prolongs life and helps life activities

Excess use may produce diseases
arising from fat and excess kapha, e.g.
obesity, dyspepsia, unconsciousness,
diabetes, enlargement of neck glands,
or malignant tumours

Salt Taste

Increases P and K

Clears obstructions of the channels
and pores

Increases digestive activity and salivation

Lubricates and causes sweating

Penetrates the tissues

Improves taste

Excess use may cause baldness, greying
of the hair, wrinkles, thirst, skin diseases,
blood disorders, herpetiform lesions,
loss of body strength

The Sanskrit text, *Astanga Hrdayam*, describes the characteristics of the six tastes and the problems that might be experienced from habitual over-consumption of foods of a particular taste. Most foods are a combination of two or more of these tastes, e.g. coffee is bitter and pungent.

Bitter Taste

Mitigates P and K

Not liked by itself

Dries up moisture from fat, muscles, faeces, urine

Cleans the mouth, destroys taste perception

Bitter herbs and spices include fenugreek seeds

Said to cure anorexia, worms, bacteria, parasites, thirst, skin diseases, loss of consciousness, fever, nausea, burning sensations

Excess use increases vata, causing diseases of vata origin and depletion of the tissues

Astringent Taste

Increases V

Mitigates increased P and K

Cleans the blood

Causes healing of ulcers

Dries up moisture and fat

Absorbs water, causing constipation and dryness

Hinders digestion of undigested food

Diminishes taste perception and causes a choking sensation

Astringent foods include unripe bananas, pomegranates, chick peas

Excess use causes stasis of foods without digestion, flatulence, pain in the cardiac region, emaciation, loss of virility, obstruction of channels, and constipation

Pungent Taste

Increases V and P, mitigates K

Increases hunger, is digestive, and improves taste

Causes irritation, brings secretions from the eyes, nose, mouth, and gives burning feeling in the mouth

Pungent foods include onion, garlic, and chillies

Dries up the moisture of food

Breaks up hard masses, dilates the channels

Excess use may cause thirst, depletion of reproductive tissue and strength, fainting, contracture, tremors, pain in the waist and back, and other disorders due to excess vata or pitta

THE SEVEN TISSUES

The tissues are the body's structure. Ayurveda classifies them by the way they are produced, as a series of transformations and refinements within the body. There are seven tissue types, with primary and secondary "by-products". Broadly, the types are: plasma and lymph; blood; muscle; fat; bone; bone marrow and nerve tissue; and reproductive tissue. These terms are not entirely accurate, since they do not correspond exactly to the original Sanskrit. The blood tissue, for instance, includes blood vessels and all tissues connected with the blood system.

The by-products are tissues or substances that are either used in the body, or expelled by it once they have served their purpose. In assessing the health of each tissue type the amount and quality of the by-products are taken into account, since they give information about the tissues and the doshas. Light menstrual flow, for example, will indicate to an Ayurvedic practitioner that the first tissue type (plasma and lymph) may be affected by excess vata. Each tissue type has its own agni (see p. 48), which equates to the enzymes and other secretions needed to create the tissue.

The Tissue Transformation Sequence

An analogy to explain the manner in which the tissues are produced is a series of seven related factories (see opposite), each generating one of the tissue types and the "raw materials" for the next factory.

Under this arrangement, the product of the seventh factory is the most refined, as its raw materials have already undergone a number of processes. Many days go by after the first factory receives its raw materials before the seventh factory can complete its product. Each factory is dependent on the previous ones. If the processing is not right in one factory the amount or the quality of its products will be affected, which will affect the functioning of the other factories further down the line. Later factories will be affected if earlier ones produce insufficient raw materials or the channels are clogged by over-production.

It is a system that requires co-operation and balance for efficient operations. The first factory produces plasma and lymphatic tissue, and the raw material for blood tissues from the results of the digestion of food. The seventh factory produces reproductive tissue and raw ojas (see opposite).

Producing Tissues

Imagine each "factory" has a product, or tissue type. Each manufacturing process (the metabolic functions of tissue agnis) has by-products — one becomes the raw material for the next factory. Primary by-products are tissues or substances used in their own right (they are not processed further). Secondary by-products are thrown out, although they still have a function.

OJAS

Ancient texts say there are eight drops of ojas in the heart. A subtle substance on the border between mind and body, it maintains life and is closely related to immunity. The West has no concept of ojas; it literally means vitality or bodily strength. Illness arises from the low production or depletion of ojas. According to *Charaka Samhita*, causes of diminution of ojas include excessive exercise, fasting, loss of blood and semen, anxiety, fear, grief and injuries. Excessive sexual activity reduces ojas in both sexes. Diminished ojas reduces the body's immunity. It also makes you fearful, emaciated, causes disorders of the sense organs, and impairs mental abilities.

TISSUE TRANSFORMATION SEQUENCE

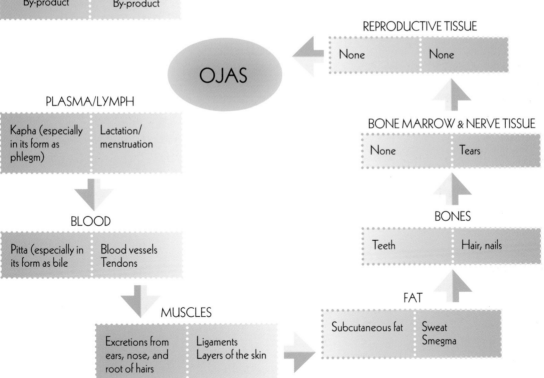

MAIN TISSUE

Secondary By-product	Primary By-product

REPRODUCTIVE TISSUE

None	None

OJAS

PLASMA/LYMPH

Kapha (especially in its form as phlegm)	Lactation/ menstruation

BONE MARROW & NERVE TISSUE

None	Tears

BLOOD

Pitta (especially in its form as bile	Blood vessels Tendons

BONES

Teeth	Hair, nails

MUSCLES

Excretions from ears, nose, and root of hairs	Ligaments Layers of the skin

FAT

Subcutaneous fat	Sweat Smegma

CHANNELS

A constant flow of nutrients, tissues, and waste products moves into, around, and out of the body. Ayurveda describes many channels of circulation from the large (e.g. the gastrointestinal tract) to the small (e.g. capillaries) and more subtle ones (e.g. biochemical pathways, nerve stimuli, and nadis – like meridians) and doshas. In health, these channels have functional integrity and permit proper flows on all levels. Habitually suppressing natural urges (see pp. 66–7) disturbs the health of the channels and may result in changes in the flow through them (e.g. constipation), obstructions, or deviations of the channels.

TYPES OF CHANNEL
Channels of intake of nutrients

Prana channel	Respiratory system
Water channel	Palate, pancreas, kidney
Food channel	Oesophagus to large intestine

Channels of tissue nutrition

One channel for each of the seven tissue types

Channels of elimination

Urine channel	Kidney and bladder
Faeces channel	Colon and rectum
Sweat channel	Fat and hair follicles

The mind is also regarded as a channel that pervades all parts of the body

The Channels

In Ayurveda, there are 13 principal channels in the body, concerned with the consumption of air, liquids, and food, the metabolic changes of these into tissues, and elimination from the body (see left column). The main parts of the channels of intake and elimination are listed in the right-hand column.

RELATIONSHIP OF ORGANS TO CHANNELS

Channels of intake of nutrients

Organ	Channel
Bladder	Urine
Brain	Nerve, but different parts connected to channels which they stimulate or monitor
Breasts	Lymph (milk is a by-product of lymph tissue production)
Gall bladder	Blood (stores bile, a waste of blood tissue production)
Genitals	Reproductive
Heart	Lymph, blood, prana, and the channel of the mind, as it is regarded by some as the seat of consciousness
Kidney	Water, fat, urine
Large intestine	Prana, faeces
Liver	Blood
Lungs	Prana
Pancreas	Water
Small intestine	Food
Spleen	Blood
Stomach	Food

WASTES

The body expels three waste products: urine, sweat, and faeces. These substances also have important physiological functions as part of a well-balanced, healthy system. Urine helps with the water balance, sweat keeps the skin moist and supple, and the faeces give support to the colon and body.

The condition of the waste products can indicate doshic imbalances or digestive problems. Healthy stools should be: well-formed; soft but not sticky; banana-shaped; able to float (stools that sink indicate ama); free of undigested food (its presence indicates low

agni); neither too dark (which may indicate a vata imbalance) nor too yellowish (which may indicate a pitta imbalance); not containing mucus (mucus indicates that kapha may be disturbed); without an unpleasant odour (odour is an indication of ama).

Organs and Channels

The organs of the body are related to the channels and the seven tissue types of which they are formed. Ayurveda lays stress on the functions of the tissue type as a whole. Thus an organ may be related in more than one channel.

4. THE DISEASE
PROCESS

विकारजातं विविधं त्रीन् गुणान्नातिवर्तते ॥
तथा स्वधातुवैषम्यनिमित्तमपि सर्वदा ।
विकारजातं त्रीन्दीषान् .... ॥

All the different kinds of diseases cannot be apart from (devoid of) the doshas. Even so, those caused by (arising from) the abnormalities of the dhatus (tissues), cannot be without the (involvement) of the doshas.

(Astanga Hrdayam Chapter 12: 32–34 ½)

What does Ayurveda mean by good health? Your three doshas are balanced according to the unique constitution; you have balanced agni – that is, your powers of digestion and metabolism are good; your seven tissue types have functional integrity; you have proper elimination of the three wastes; you have clear perceptions; a balanced mind; and a contented soul. Because all aspects of your being are interdependent, problems in one area may cause repercussions elsewhere.

We live in a dynamic world. We cannot be isolated from experiences. Everything in our daily life – from the food we eat, the colour of the clothes we wear, our jobs, the people we meet and the nature of our interactions with them, our attitudes and emotions, the seasons and the time of day – has qualities that can be classified as vata, pitta, and kapha. Whether you give attention to these qualities or not they will affect your doshas. If the effect is minimal, and your doshas are in balance, you are unlikely to notice any change in your health. This is because your body will naturally accommodate small change in the doshas through their seats (see p. 46).

Problems begin when your body's ability to cope with excess qualities has been over-extended, or when your mind does not accept experiences, or when you need more time to adjust to changes. At this point, you should take active steps to restore the natural harmony of your being.

Ayurveda's concept of the disease process is logical. The doshas are energy. The right amount of the right kind of energy at the right time produces the right results. Too much or too little energy, or the wrong type, or at the wrong time, or in the wrong place, and your system will suffer adversely.

Generally, a diet and lifestyle inappropriate to your constitution will cause your doshic levels to increase slowly. However, if you suffer traumas, such as bereavement, accidents, sudden life changes, surgery, or become a victim of crime, these levels can change dramatically. The effect of such doshic changes depends on the state of your doshas, mind, and body.

Your doshic balance can be disturbed by depleted agni and by the production and/or accumulation of toxins in the body. By understanding the qualities of various signs in the mind and body you will learn about any doshic imbalances that you are experiencing. But first you need to understand your constitutional balance (see pp. 38–41) – this is your baseline against which you can assess any imbalance.

VPK and the Seasons

Each dosha is naturally increased during the season that has similar qualities (see also p. 150). You should take care to keep your predominant dosha pacified during its season. In addition, your doshas may be more easily disturbed at the junctions between seasons.

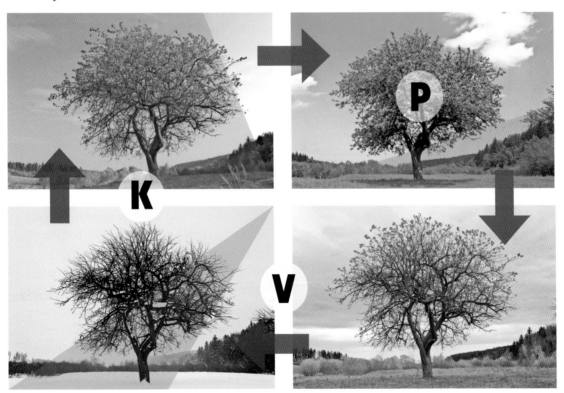

DOSHIC IMBALANCE

You have a unique balance of doshas – your constitution – which is determined at conception. When the current ratio of your doshas is different from your constitution your doshas are out of balance. Words used in the West to describe out of balance doshas include high, low, increased, decreased, excessive, disturbed, deranged, provoked, aggravated. The changes in doshic states are relative, and all the circumstances must be considered. Hot, spicy foods increase pitta and decrease vata and kapha, but it is when you have eaten an excessive amount for *you* that your pitta dosha is aggravated. The same food may help pacify your kapha dosha if it is excessive, or perhaps maintain your balance if you have a vata constitution.

All your experiences have qualities, each related to the qualities of vata, pitta, and/or kapha. A dosha is increased by those experiences that have similar qualities to the doshas and decreased by opposing qualities. Something with opposing qualities may "pacify" an increased dosha. So, how does one of your doshas become imbalanced? The answer is when you experience too many of a particular dosha's qualities without enough of their opposite qualities (see p. 32) to pacify or reduce the excessive doshic energy.

A key to understanding Ayurveda is to realize that you are most susceptible to increases in the dosha that predominates in your constitution. Remember, like attracts like. For example, if you have a pitta constitution, pitta qualities predominate in you. You will have a natural inclination toward those things that also have pitta qualities, thus increasing your current pitta energies. This attraction to

similar qualities may make it psychologically difficult to add opposite qualities to your lifestyle when you wish to pacify a dosha.

Imagine, for instance, you have a number of vata-genic factors (those that increase vata) in your lifestyle. These may include living in a cold climate, having a job that involves much travelling, especially flying, eating at irregular times, or habitually eating vata-aggravating foods (see Food Charts, pp. 132–43). These will increase your vata energy until your vata dosha becomes excessive – unless there are opposite qualities in your life. Lifestyle factors that increase pitta include habitually eating salty or spicy foods, or other foods that aggravate pitta; living in a hot climate; or having a high-powered or competitive job. A kapha-genic lifestyle could include overeating, especially foods that aggravate kapha, not exercising, sleeping excessively, and having a sedentary job.

Further, if your illness is due to an excess of the same dosha as that predominating in your constitution, it is harder to treat. For example, a vata disorder (see p. 74 for examples) in someone with a vata constitution will be more difficult to control (as the constitution reinforces the disorder) than in someone with a kapha constitution.

Chilli Peppers

Chilli peppers increase the pitta dosha, but pacify vata and kapha. Your constitution, current doshic state, and the seasons should all be considered when deciding if hot, spicy foods should be part of your diet.

DOSHIC IMBALANCE ASSESSMENT

When you have understood your constitution you can then determine if your doshas are in balance. An imbalance is assessed by reading the signs and symptoms in your mind and body that are manifested by the doshic energy that is excessive for YOU. If you have a persistent or chronic condition, complete this assessment in conjunction with the Ailment Assessment on page 80.

Repeat the physiological and psychological sections of the constitutional assessment (see pp. 38–41), to assess how you are NOW and have been recently. Differences in this and your original assessment indicate which dosha is excessive if the assessments have been done accurately.

If you are experiencing any digestive discomforts, negative emotions, or sleeping problems, write down what you are experiencing and then relate their qualities to vata, pitta, and kapha, using the information on pages 30–1, 68–9, 75–7, 78, and 124.

This information will help you decide whether you are experiencing excess vata, pitta, or kapha. If you are, you should look at your lifestyle (see Chapter 5) and diet (see Chapter 6) to see what factors in your life are contributing to the imbalance. Then you can take steps to restore your balance and prevent illness developing.

The ideal situation is to be able to read the doshas in your body, and live a life that maintains your constitutional balance. If circumstances, either external or internal, arise that cause an imbalance, the sooner you restore the balance the better. Ways to pacify the doshas will be discussed in Part Three, based on the principle that "opposites decrease".

Generally, it is an "excess" of a particular food, substance, activity, or emotion that will disturb a dosha, and so may start the disease process. What is excessive will vary from individual to individual, and will also vary for each individual at different times of his or her life. Your individual tolerances at any particular time are related to your constitution, the current state of your doshic energies, your age, and the season.

Some Factors Affecting Wellbeing

All our experiences and circumstances have qualities and these can be related to the qualities of vata, pitta, and kapha. Those that have similar qualities to a dosha will increase it; those with dissimilar qualities will decrease it.

Place & climate
Traumas

Age
Constitution
Season

Suppression of
natural urges
Lifestyle
Occupation
Misuse of the mind,
inappropriate actions
and speech
Diet
Digestion & metabolism

Immunity
Misuse, or over- or
underuse of the senses
Mind & emotions

Increasing VPK

The table (opposite) lists frequent causes of disturbance to each dosha. Under the tenet of "like increases like" you may see why some aspects of your life increase your doshas. Generally, it is habitual excesses that aggravate the doshas. But if one of your doshas is already increased, then you may be intolerant even to small amounts of something with qualities similar to your increased dosha.

FACTORS THAT INCREASE VPK

VATA

Exposure to cold

No routine in your life

Eating too much dry, frozen or left-over food, or foods with bitter, pungent or astringent tastes

Fasting

Too much travelling

Too much or inappropriate exercise

Misuse/overuse of senses

Too much sex

Alcohol

Suppressing natural urges

Abdominal surgery

Stimulants and other drugs

Too little sleep, staying up late, working nights

Not oiling the skin

Frequent colonics/enemas

Worry, fear, anxiety, grief — and repressing these

Autumn and early winter

PITTA

Exposure to heat

Eating too much red meat, salt, spicy or sour foods

Indigestion and irregularity of meals

Exercising at midday

Drugs, especially antibiotics

Too much intellectual work/thinking

Alcohol

Fatigue

Anger, hate, fear of failure, and repression of these emotions

Summer

KAPHA

Exposure to cold

Eating too much sweet food, meat, fats, cheese, milk, ice cream, yogurt, fried foods

Excessive use of salt

Excessive intake of water

Eating after satisfaction

Taking naps after meals

Not exercising

Underuse of the senses

Too much sleep

Doing nothing

Sedatives and tranquillizers

Doubts, greed and possessiveness, lack of compassion and staying attached to these emotions

Late winter and spring

INTESTINAL GASES

Gases indicate poor digestion and the formation of ama (p. 77); they prevent proper absorption of water, minerals, and prana in the colon. Associated mainly with excess vata, they may result from poor digestion due to disturbance of any dosha. Their causes are mainly dietary, but they may also be due to inadequate sleep, nervousness, shock, worry, stress, or anger.

ADVICE FOR PREVENTING AND RELIEVING GASES

- Follow a diet suitable for your doshic needs and the rules of eating (see Chapter 6).
- Do not eat foods that are difficult to digest or that create gases in their digestion.
- Do not eat between meals, or too much at any meal, or too late at night.
- Leave at least three hours between meals to allow the stomach time to do its work.
- Avoid the sweet taste or only take small amounts on its own. Desserts after meals contribute to fermentation and gases.
- Use carminative (gas-dispelling) herbs in moderation when preparing foods (see pp. 158–9).
- For relieving gases, do knee-to-chest exercises (p. 127) and abdominal massage (p. 120).

HABITUAL SUPPRESSION OF NATURAL URGES

Charaka Samhita lists 13 natural urges and the symptoms that can occur if they are habitually suppressed (see text under each urge). Vata is the dosha that causes these urges and suppressing them disturbs vata. The symptoms are all therefore examples of disturbed vata. The symptoms, which may arise from habitual suppression of the natural urges, could be relieved by taking steps to pacify vata and by allowing expression of these urges in a manner that does not cause offence to other people.

URGE: Urination
POSSIBLE SYMPTOMS
Pain in the bladder and urethra, dysuria (painful or difficult urination), headache, stiffness in groin.

URGE: Hunger
POSSIBLE SYMPTOMS
Emaciation, weakness, body ache, anorexia, giddiness, poor complexion

URGE: Burping
POSSIBLE SYMPTOMS
Hiccups, shortness of breath, anorexia, tremors

URGE: Thirst
POSSIBLE SYMPTOMS
Dryness of throat and mouth, deafness, fatigue, depression, cardiac pain

URGE: Passing gasses
POSSIBLE SYMPTOMS
Retention of faeces, urine, and gases, flatulence, pain, exhaustion, and other disorders in abdomen due to vata imbalance

URGE: Defecation
POSSIBLE SYMPTOMS
Colic pain, headache, retention of gases and faeces, cramps in calf muscles, and flatulence

URGE: Ejaculation of semen
POSSIBLE SYMPTOMS
Pain in penis and scrotum, body ache, pain in cardiac region, and obstruction in urine

URGE: Yawning
POSSIBLE SYMPTOMS
Convulsion, numbness, tremors

URGE: Vomiting
POSSIBLE SYMPTOMS
Itcing, urticarial rashes, anorexia, blackish spots on the face, swelling, anaemia, skin diseases, nausea, and erysipelas

URGE: Sneezing
POSSIBLE SYMPTOMS
Stiffness of back of neck, headache, facial paralysis, migraine, and weakness of sense organs

URGE: Tears
POSSIBLE SYMPTOMS
Coryza (catarrhal inflammation of nasal mucous membrane), eye diseases, heart diseases, anorexia, giddiness

URGE: Sleep
POSSIBLE SYMPTOMS
Yawning, body ache, drowsiness, head disorders, and heaviness in eyes

URGE: Strong breathing or panting due to exercise
POSSIBLE SYMPTOMS
Heart diseases and fainting

Caution:
The above lists indicate the possible outcome of habitually suppressing your natural urges. However, the symptoms may arise for other reasons. Do not assume, for example, that all heart disease is caused by not breathing properly after exercise.

EARLY STAGES OF THE DISEASE PROCESS

According to Ayurveda an imbalance of the doshas lies behind all illness. An imbalance occurs when the current state of your doshas differs from your constitution. There are many ways in which the doshas can be disturbed (see pp. 64–5). A change or accumulation of a dosha may result from one primary cause, or from the cumulative effects of many causes. The cause may be strong and sudden (for example, receiving news of a sudden death), and have an immediate impact on the doshas.

Stage One: Accumulation

The first stage is an increase in a dosha. The dosha accumulates in its seat, but at a rate faster than the body expels the excess. You may not notice the first signs of the disease process, since they are initially discomforts (see examples on chart opposite), and are not the sort of thing for which you are likely to seek therapeutic help. Many of us accept a modicum of discomfort as part of life or "my age".

Stage Two: Provocation

If the accumulation is not stopped at Stage One, the excess dosha is provoked to leave its seat in the gastro-intestinal tract (see p. 46). The signs of an aggravated dosha become more noticeable (see p. 69).

Stage Three: Spread

In this stage, the aggravated dosha spreads into the tissues. If there is a weakness in a particular tissue it will deposit itself there (see p. 70). At this stage, you may notice a change in the symptoms, but you may still find it difficult to pin-point what exactly is wrong.

If you pacify the excess dosha before the fourth stage of the disease process is reached (see p. 70), no lasting damage is done to the body. It is easier to regain your constitutional balance before the excess dosha settles into the tissues.

One, two, or all three of the doshas can be upset at any one time. Even where the initial difficulties arose from an excess of a single dosha, if left unchecked, the other two doshas are also likely to become disturbed in time. By then, a complicated illness will have developed.

More usually, the cause is weak and builds up slowly over time. It may come from an external source: eating an inappropriate diet over a number of years would, for example, cause a gradual change in the balance of the doshas. Or the cause of the disturbance of the doshas may come from within the body: for example, an accumulation of toxins due to poor metabolism would impede the movement of vata and disturb the doshas (see also pp. 76–7). To maintain wellness, observe and analyze your lifestyle to see if you are accumulating too many qualities of a particular dosha, and make any changes needed to balance your doshas (see Chapter 8).

Ayurveda describes the disease process in six stages. The first three are described on these pages, the final three on pages 70 and 72.

Chart of Signs and Symptoms

The first signs of the first three stages of the disease process are grouped according to which dosha is in excess of its constitution balance. You may only have one of the symptoms on this list; everyone has a different balance of doshas at work in the body, and this means that symptoms are different for everybody. Remember – do not read one symptom in isolation. Signs of increased doshas are sometimes felt, with the experience of negative emotions (see p. 78).

AGGRAVATED DOSHA	ACCUMULATION STAGE	PROVOCATION STAGE	SPREAD STAGE
EXCESS VATA	Constipation Intestinal gases Dry mouth Craves warmth Fear/anxiety	Increased gases & constipation Cold hands & feet Dryness in body	Distension relieved Fatigue Restless mind Worries/fear/anxious
EXCESS PITTA	Stomach acidity Burning sensations Anger/criticism	Heartburn Acid indigestion Burning pain in navel area Hypercritical	Burning sensation on passing urine/stools Yellowish stools Painful digestion
EXCESS KAPHA	Lethargic Low appetite Heaviness	Nausea Bloating Desire to sleep Increased salivation	Heaviness Swelling, Edema Increased mucus Vomiting

WEAK SPOTS

The fourth stage of the diseases process starts when the spreading excess dosha finds a weak spot in one of the tissue types (see pp. 56–7), and settles there. The first warning signals of illness will be felt and, in the West, this is the point at which we begin to feel that all is not well and take note of our lack of health. Through pulse diagnosis and a deep knowledge of the human body, an experienced Ayurvedic physician can read these warning signals and the earlier signs, and have a good indication of the disease that will follow if the excess dosha is left unchecked.

Inherited Weak Spots

Asymptomatic weakness in the tissues arising from cellular memory of parents' and grandparents' illnesses.

Physical and Psychological Traumas

Tissues that have been physically damaged may retain a cellular memory of the trauma. Psychological trauma may weaken tissues. Certain negative emotions have an affinity to certain organs (see p. 172).

Previous Infections and Illnesses

A tissue is weakened when it is affected by disease, making it more vulnerable in the future.

Unresolved Emotions

Weakness in organs from unresolved or repressed emotions (see pp. 172–3).

Addictions

Tissues are damaged by addictions. Alcohol, for example, weakens the liver, smoking attacks the lungs, mind-altering drugs affect the brain, and an addiction to sex damages the genitals.

Past Life Actions

In cultures that accept reincarnation, a weakness can be brought from previous lives. "Past life" also includes previous actions and attitudes in this life, and also a poor lifestyle.

Weakness in Tissues

Weakness or defects in tissues arise from many causes, but can be classified as one of six types (above). Weak spots can be present in any part of the body, but symptoms from them only arise when an excess dosha has settled in the affected tissue.

LATER STAGES OF THE DISEASE PROCESS

The fourth stage will only be reached if there is a weakness in one of the tissue types. If there is no such weakness, the excess dosha remains in circulation in the body, but causes no additional signs. Once Stage Five is reached, the disease needs rooting out and treatment is required. At Stage Six, the excess dosha will leave a weakness in the body and, unless pacified, will spread to other tissues.

Stage Four: Deposition

The excess dosha settles in the first tissue type that has a weakness. The dosha combines with the tissue, causing it, together with the by-products and "raw" materials, to become inferior. It may also produce toxins. If the tissue agni is strong, it will protect the tissue from the effects of an excess dosha.

Stage Five: Manifestation

At first, the effect of an excess dosha during deposition may be minor. But like a weed the disease grows and needs eradicating by elimination the excess levels of the imbalanced dosha. Ayurvedic physicians may recommend panchakarma and/or herbs (see pp. 186–7) to restore the doshic balance. You should complement any treatment with changes to your diet or lifestyle to pacify the excess dosha and prevent recurrence of the illness.

Stage Six: Differentiation

The excess dosha has disrupted the integrity of the system and the disease and its complications can be named. The disease, like the perennial weed, may broadcast the seeds of future illness, or it may lie dormant only to grow again when conditions permit. Even if the excess dosha is pacified, a weakness remains in the body. If the dosha is not pacified, and only the symptoms ameliorated, the excess dosha may move and settle into other tissues, where further ramifications will ensue.

SIGNS WHEN DOSHAS ENTER TISSUES

When considering your ailments from the Ayurvedic point of view, try to think about the qualities of the signs and symptoms and relate these to vata, pitta, and kapha, and to the tissue types affected.

For instance, symptoms that have qualities of a mainly dry or degenerative nature are a result of imbalanced vata, as are those relating to underweight and loss of, or interference with, movement. Heat or inflammation qualities are connected with pitta, as is bleeding. Excess kapha is connected with being overweight, or other increases in body mass or excess fluids, such as tumours and swellings.

However, the story is not that simple, since the doshas also interact with each other. When this happens the experience of an Ayurvedic practitioner is required. A build-up of excessive kapha can, for example, block the free movement of the vata energy. Although impaired movement is the obvious symptom, kapha is at the root of it.

Dryness may be due to the heat of pitta drying the body. In this case, pitta, rather than vata, should be pacified. In making an assessment of doshic disturbances, Ayurvedic practitioners may trace the sequential pattern of disturbance from the order in which the symptoms arose.

Abnormal movements may arise because of problems with muscle or nerve tissue types. An Ayurvedic practitioner is trained to observe the interactions and know which tissues are disturbed by the excess doshas and how the doshas are interacting.

The table on page 74 is not comprehensive, yet it gives examples of how excess doshas may manifest in the seven tissue types. Symptoms should not be read in isolation but as part of an overall picture. In the West, words used to describe illness often involve one or more doshas or tissues, and do not class qualities separately. Eczema, for example, may be either dry or weeping, and Ayurveda says the root cause is different in each case.

SOME SIGNS OF DOSHA ENTRY INTO TISSUES

Tissue Type	Excessive dosha	Symptoms
Lymph	V	Cold hands and feet – Dehydration, dry skin – Sunken eyes – Tingling, numbness in the skin – Looks undernourished – Feels fear – Insecurity, anxiety, lack of confidence
	P	Fever – Acne, pimples – Hot flushes – Eyes sensitive to bright light – Critical, short tempered
	K	Retention of water – Indigestion – Loss of appetite – Lethargic – Colds – Bronchial congestion
Blood	V	Anaemia – Dizziness – Abnormal pulsations – Contraction of blood vessels – Dry eczema
	P	Inflammatory conditions – Rashes – Fevers – Bruises easily – Nose bleeds – Bleeding under the skin – Psoriasis – Dermatitis – Multiple moles
	K	Weeping eczema – High cholesterol – Enlarged liver/spleen (dealing with excess fat)
Muscle	V	Muscle atrophy – Increased tone – Spasticity – Loss of movement – Tremors
	P	Repeated attacks of tonsillitis – Muscle abscess
	K	Muscle hypertrophy – Decreased tone, flabby muscles – Cysts on muscle tendons
Fat	V	Dry skin – Low backache – Cracking of joints
	P	Profuse sweating – Cellulitis – Burning hands and feet – Burning sensation at tip of penis
	K	Excessive thirst – High cholesterol – Obesity – Thick white vaginal discharge
Bones	V	Hair loss – Brittle nails – Deformities of nails – Pain in the bones – Degenerative arthritis – Receding gums – Dental caries – Pain due to unresolved emotions
	P	Inflammatory arthritis – Bone abscesses
	K	Bone tumours
Nerve	V	Dizziness, fainting – Lack of co-ordination – Paralysis – Confusion – Loss of memory
	P	Paralysis – Multiple sclerosis – Aplastic anaemia – Misunderstandings
	K	Tumours – Misconceptions
Reproductive tissue	V	Sexual disability – Low fertility – Premature ejaculation
	P	Inflammation of genitals
	K	Enlarged prostate – Tumours of testicles or ovaries/uterus

PAIN

Vata is involved in all pain. If the vata flow of energy in the body is unobstructed there is no pain. Pain arises when the vata dosha is disturbed, or the flow of vata (the mobile dosha) is blocked by improper functions of pitta or kapha. Blockages may also be caused by accumulations of ama (see p. 77) or by the repression of emotions. Repressed emotions can disturb the doshas and be the root cause of pain. Understanding such emotions can bring release (see p. 168).

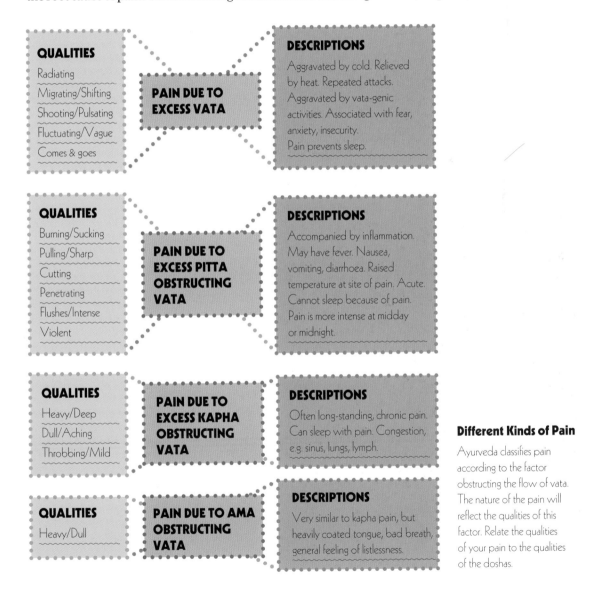

QUALITIES
Radiating
Migrating/Shifting
Shooting/Pulsating
Fluctuating/Vague
Comes & goes

PAIN DUE TO EXCESS VATA

DESCRIPTIONS
Aggravated by cold. Relieved by heat. Repeated attacks. Aggravated by vata-genic activities. Associated with fear, anxiety, insecurity. Pain prevents sleep.

QUALITIES
Burning/Sucking
Pulling/Sharp
Cutting
Penetrating
Flushes/Intense
Violent

PAIN DUE TO EXCESS PITTA OBSTRUCTING VATA

DESCRIPTIONS
Accompanied by inflammation. May have fever. Nausea, vomiting, diarrhoea. Raised temperature at site of pain. Acute. Cannot sleep because of pain. Pain is more intense at midday or midnight.

QUALITIES
Heavy/Deep
Dull/Aching
Throbbing/Mild

PAIN DUE TO EXCESS KAPHA OBSTRUCTING VATA

DESCRIPTIONS
Often long-standing, chronic pain. Can sleep with pain. Congestion, e.g. sinus, lungs, lymph.

QUALITIES
Heavy/Dull

PAIN DUE TO AMA OBSTRUCTING VATA

DESCRIPTIONS
Very similar to kapha pain, but heavily coated tongue, bad breath, general feeling of listlessness.

Different Kinds of Pain

Ayurveda classifies pain according to the factor obstructing the flow of vata. The nature of the pain will reflect the qualities of this factor. Relate the qualities of your pain to the qualities of the doshas.

DISTURBED METABOLISM

An imbalance of doshas can disturb agni and metabolism (see p. 48) and will impair your ability to digest food. If agni is low, toxic substances called *ama* (see p. 77) are produced. The body is not always able to expel ama, in which case it is deposited in various parts of the body, blocking or interfering with the free flow of dense and subtle matter through the body's channels.

Disturbed Digestive Agni

Ayurveda describes indigestion according to which excess dosha is affecting agni. The symptoms of poor digestion reflect the qualities of the imbalanced dosha. All three types of poor digestion produce ama.

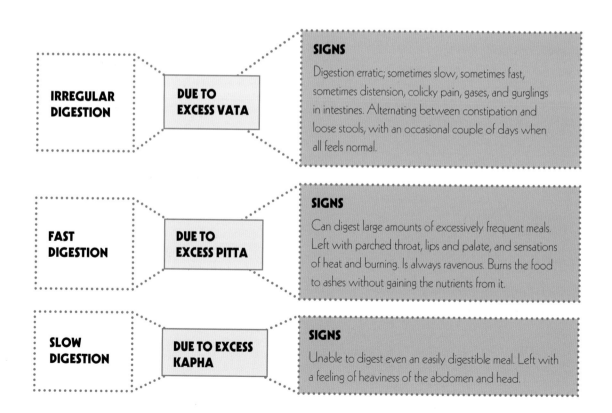

IRREGULAR DIGESTION

DUE TO EXCESS VATA

SIGNS
Digestion erratic; sometimes slow, sometimes fast, sometimes distension, colicky pain, gases, and gurglings in intestines. Alternating between constipation and loose stools, with an occasional couple of days when all feels normal.

FAST DIGESTION

DUE TO EXCESS PITTA

SIGNS
Can digest large amounts of excessively frequent meals. Left with parched throat, lips and palate, and sensations of heat and burning. Is always ravenous. Burns the food to ashes without gaining the nutrients from it.

SLOW DIGESTION

DUE TO EXCESS KAPHA

SIGNS
Unable to digest even an easily digestible meal. Left with a feeling of heaviness of the abdomen and head.

This is especially so in the case of the digestion agni. For example, chyle – the form food becomes as it is absorbed through the intestine walls – may contain partially digested food. Although this may be absorbed, partially digested food fails to provide, or inhibits the use of, nutrients needed by the body.

Derangements of agni and the production of ama are internal causes of disease. Deranged agni disturbs the doshas and also increases the production of ama. This will disturb agni still further, setting up vicious circles of cause and effect. The main causes of disturbed agni are:

- doshic imbalance
- excessive eating or drinking
- prolonged fasting
- eating between meals
- repressed emotions (see pp. 170–3)
- ignoring the rules of eating (see p. 154), but especially
  - wrong food combinations
  - foods inappropriate for your constitution
  - eating at unsuitable times
  - eating heavy, frozen, cold, or spoilt food
- improper use of purgatives or laxatives

If the tissue agnis (see pp. 56–7) are defective, inferior tissues and their by-products will result. Other effects of defective tissue agni are to lessen the body's ability to produce ojas (see p. 57) and to protect the tissues from the effects of excess doshas (see p. 72)

AMA

Ayurveda considers ama to be a major cause of illness. The Sanskrit word encompasses toxins in the body, whether these were originally external poisons introduced into the body or ones created internally due to low agni, poor food combinations, inadequate elimination of wastes, or disturbed doshas. Some of the literal meanings of ama include raw, uncooked, immature, and undigested.

A defective tissue agni will also result in ama during the production of the seven tissues (pp. 56–7).

A subtle ama is produced if our mental processes are impaired, or if we harbour unresolved emotions (see Chapter 7).

A whitish coating over the whole tongue indicates ama throughout the body. If the back third of the tongue is coated there is ama in the colon. If the coating is brownish, vata is disturbed as well. Bad breath and body odour are other signs of ama in the body. Ayurvedic physicians often recommend herbs to eliminate ama and balance agni.

NEGATIVE EMOTIONS

A doshic imbalance may have a negative effect on your mind and emotions. If a dosha is in excess you are more likely to display negative energy of a quality associated with it. The predominant dosha of your constitution becomes excessive more easily than the others. Thus, you will tend to experience its negative aspects more than others.

Negative emotions aggravate the dosha associated with them. For example, high kapha may mean you are more possessive but possessiveness increases kapha. The way to break this vicious circle is to pacify the aggravated dosha. Thinking in qualities and using Ayurveda in your daily life will help you to become more conscious of the qualities of your moods and to rate these as V, P, and/or K. This is a useful way to monitor small increases in a dosha, and to take steps to restore the balance sooner rather than later.

Relate the qualities of your moods to the qualities in other aspects of your life. Remember "like increases like". If you are impatient or critical (pitta), check if you have eaten pitta-genic foods or been exposed to pitta-provoking experiences.

Negative States

The lists below classify negative emotional and mental states according to excess doshas. By referring to the lists on pp. 30–1 and the positive states (see Chapter 7), you can compare how excess doshic energy may affect your mind and feelings.

EXCESS VATA

Nervousness — Anxiety —Fear — Confusion — Grief — Sadness — Insecurity — Lack of integrity — Loss of creativity — Lack of communication — Moodiness

EXCESS KAPHA

Boredom — Carelessness — Lack of compassion — Greed — Feeling lack of support or love — Obsessive behavior — Unkindness — Lack of interest

EXCESS PITTA

Ambition — Anger —Envy — Fear of Failure — Frustration — Hate — Jealousy — Judgmental or critical tendencies — Snappy speech and actions — Lack of discernment — Pride — Scepticism

AILMENTS

The Ayurvedic concept of the disease process is difficult to grasp initially, since it challenges how we have been taught in the West. As we have seen, symptoms of ill health can be classified into vata, pitta, and kapha, and this will indicate which dosha is likely to need pacifying (see table on page 74). Sometimes, the idea may seem too simple to be credible, and at other too complex to master. This is a natural reaction of the mind to new ideas. As you observe your life and body in terms of doshas you will see these concepts working in practice.

The first stages of the disease process deal with minor ailments that can be ameliorated by knowing yourself, and making appropriate adjustments to your lifestyle. The ability to read the initial signs of imbalances is the key to regaining wellness.

In the latter stages of the disease process the balance between your doshas, tissues, and agni has been seriously disturbed, and often complicated further by the presence of ama. You should seek qualified help in these stages, but lifestyle and diet are still important to support any treatments undertaken.

Symptoms of PMS

When you are assessing any ailment from the Ayurvedic perspective, it is important to look at the qualities of each symptom and classify them according to VPK. The name given to your ailment is not the key factor as the illness may be due to a disturbance of any one of the doshas. The symptoms of PMS are well known, and are related to VPK in the lists below.

VATA	PITTA	KAPHA
Bloated belly	Hot flushes	Retention of water
Low backache	Red, sensitive eyes	Breasts enlarged and full and tender
Painful joints	Nipples sensitive to touch	Gains weight
Stiffness and tightness in muscles	Burning sensation in urethra	Tiredness, excess sleep, lethargy
Insecurity, anxiety, fear	Burning sensation in hands and feet	Craves/eats sweet taste,
Irregular menstrual periods, with light flow	Migraine headache	especially chocolate
	Anger, criticism	Very possessive
	Argumentative	Heavy flow

AILMENT
ASSESSMENT

The interactions of the doshas in the body are complex. Give yourself time first to learn the qualities each dosha may manifest (see pp. 30–1) and also to understand your constitution (see pp. 38–41). Then you can start to appreciate if any excess doshic energy is affecting you. Remember, skilful reading of the doshas in the body comes with practice. As your knowledge of Ayurveda increases you will make more accurate assessments of your doshic state. But initially focus on your most intense, persistent, or chronic symptom or ailment. First, assess your doshic imbalance (p. 63). Then describe the ailment you are experiencing and answer these questions to help you grasp the qualities in your ailment and to relate them to VPK:

- What predominant qualities are you experiencing?
- Describe the quality of the pain, if any (see p. 75)
- When did the symptoms begin? In which age (see p. 10), season (see p. 150), and climate?
- Do your symptoms change with the seasons, climates, or at different times of the day or night (see p. 151)?
- Did you experience any major life events before the symptoms began (see p. 170)?
- What steps have you taken to alleviate the symptoms? What qualities did these measures have? What effects did the alleviating steps have?

See pages 30–1 and this chapter to help you decide if an excess of VPK is causing your symptoms. Remember to seek the advice of your medical adviser if you have an ailment or illness.

Maintaining good health is an ongoing process. The more you practise thinking in qualities and about Ayurveda, the more you will refine your perspective about your condition and learn how much emphasis to give to the variety of factors. At the same time, you will improve the way you adjust your diet and lifestyle to maintain your doshas in balance. If this balance is restored, you will have no excess dosha to cause symptoms of ill health.

AYURVEDIC PROFILE
GILES

Age: 30

Height: 1.93m (6ft 4ins)

Weight: 95kg (210 lbs)

Constitution: Kapha, with pitta as secondary dosha

After finishing school, Giles took a desk job, ate a diet of junk food, did his fair share of drinking, smoked, and indulged in recreational drugs. At 22, he married and became a student for three years. He reduced his alcohol intake and only smoked and took drugs under stress. He continued eating a diet rich in dairy, sweet, and fried foods. On completing his studies, he joined a personnel department where he still works. Five years ago, his grandfather – with whom he had been close – died. His wife left him a year ago and he still feels the pain of desertion.

As a child, Giles caught mumps, measles, and whooping cough but has had no major illnesses since. For some years, he has suffered congestion of the nasal sinuses, which is worse in winter and spring. He often has cold hands and recently has been drinking more fluids and urinating more often.

A year ago, Giles started coughing, expelling thick mucus from his lungs. The expectoration is worse in the evenings. He likes plenty of sleep and he sleeps deeply. He often feels very heavy after eating. His bowel movements are regular but slow, and his stools are soft and sticky with some mucus.

INTERPRETATION: The ailments that Giles is experiencing have kapha characteristic – obstruction, coldness, heaviness, excess mucus, and a desire for more fluids. The drinking, smoking, and drugs may have caused weak spots in his liver, lungs, and brain respectively.

Find out more about Giles on pages 156–7

PART THREE

MAINTAINING
WELLNESS

5. DAILY
ACTIVITIES

तस्याशिताद्यादाहाराद्बलं वर्णश्च वर्धते ।
यस्यर्तुसात्म्यं विदितं चेष्टाहारव्यपाश्रयम् ॥

He, who indulges daily in healthy foods and activities, who discriminates (the good and bad of everything and then acts wisely), who is not attached (too much), to the objects of the senses, who develops the habit of charity, of considering all as equal (requiring kindness), of truthfulness, of pardoning and keeping company of good persons only, becomes free from all diseases.

(*Astanga Hrdayam* Chapter 4: 36)

Everything we do has particular doshic characteristics. The way we eat, sleep, work, and enjoy ourselves – all have qualities of VPK. It is important to realize that everyone can adjust their personal daily routine to redress a doshic imbalance and maximize wellbeing. If, however, you continue to behave in ways that increase any imbalance in your doshas, you will not experience the satisfaction of a high level of wellbeing. A sustained imbalance in your doshas will lead to illness.

Achieving a doshic balance does not happen overnight – you have to work at it. The best way to start is to ask yourself questions about how you lead your life. Truthful answers will begin the process of raising your awareness, which will guide any adjustments you then decide to make. Remember that change has to come from you. Other people's suggestions can only help you if you have truly accepted the changes that you are trying to bring about.

Some of your daily activities are more fixed than others. The nature of your work, for example, may be difficult to change, whereas you can design leisure activities to counteract the excessive influence of a particular dosha. Use your exercise and leisure activities as opportunities to counter any imbalances that arise from your working patterns (see pp. 88–91), and allow yourself time to nurture your mental, emotional, and inner aspects.

Some of the guidelines in the pages that follow apply to everyone. Others are intended to adjust specific doshic imbalances. This chapter provides basic routines that can help you balance your doshas. It may require great effort to change established habits, but once you notice the small benefits of initial changes you can move from a downward spiral of ill health to an upward path of wellness.

The way of Ayurveda is to look at changing the balance of all activities, not to try to tackle symptoms in isolation. If you make general changes in your life that are right for you, your doshic balance will improve so that, when you no longer have excess doshic energy, many symptoms you might have will disappear of their own accord.

TELEVISION

Watching too much television increases vata due to overstimulation of the eyes and ears. It also increases kapha due to the passive nature of watching. The subject matter watched may also affect the doshas. In Ayurveda, the principle of "like increases like" is important; for example, if the overall quality of a program has negative pitta emotions (see p. 78), these may be impressed on a subtle level on the mind, and may then increase pitta. If and how these subtle impressions manifest themselves in an individual depends on many factors, but it is unlikely that a direct correlation is possible. Habitually listening to fearful news bulletins may increase your vata levels. Be selective in your viewing and listening so you can take in only those subtle qualities you would like to have.

DAILY ROUTINE

Give a little thought to your daily routine and arrange the events of your life for your optimum wellbeing. Ask yourself whether your commitment, habits, and preferences are benefitting or disturbing your doshic balance. Modern pressures can make you feel that you have little choice over many aspects of your life. Yet, the accumulated benefits of small changes can make a noticeable difference to you. Your constitution will influence the way you arrange your life. Read the following guidelines to see whether your approach to daily routine is helping you keep your doshas balanced, or whether you need to make adjustments to help prevent increases of your predominant dosha.

VATA

Vata types need to introduce regularity to their lives and keep it — one of the hardest things for a vata person to achieve. But in succeeding you will experience less erratic levels of energy and a decrease in the discomforts caused by excess vata, such as insomnia and weariness.

Eat regularly and establish a routine for going to bed and getting up. Keep your routine even when your energy is good. Note when you are running on overdrive — unable to pay enough attention to your current task, frantically doing three things at once, or talking fast and frequently, skipping from subject to subject. Slow down and give yourself time to think; you will still achieve all you need to, but will be less tired.

PITTA

Pitta types may have already organized themselves efficiently — and often those around them, too. You tend to be precise about following your plans, as this helps you achieve your objectives. Avoid becoming too goal oriented. Take time to do things just for the sake of doing them — take a relaxing walk instead of playing a competitive game. Sitting outside on a clear summer's night staring at the moon is very soothing for pitta.

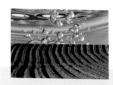

KAPHA

If you already have a fixed schedule and don't like change, you are probably a kapha type. Review your routine often, making deliberate changes to prevent yourself from getting stuck in a rut. Overcome your kapha dislike of change by making a pact with yourself to do something in a slightly different way each day — for example, vary your route to work.

YOUR ROUTINE

A routine that is balanced for your constitutional type will allow you to enjoy freshness and vitality every day.

VPK AT WORK

You may spend as much as a third of your day working, so the many qualities associated with your work and working environment will affect your doshas. If your assessments (see pp. 104–5) show that the accumulated effects of your work result in a steady increase of one or more doshas, then you may have to adjust your diet, daily routine, and leisure pursuits to balance it.

The qualities of different occupations can be related to the qualities of vata, pitta, and kapha (see right). Bear these qualities in mind when recruiting others and look for someone with a good balance of the necessary qualities in their constitution. However, if in excess these doshic qualities will manifest themselves as negative characteristics. For example, a reliable administrator (kapha) may be unwilling to accept change if her kapha increases excessively. Similarly, the efficient manager (pitta) may concentrate on his or her personal objectives rather than company ones, and the creative designer (vata) may have unworkable ideas.

Much tension arises when you have to work with someone who evokes strong emotions in you. These will also affect your doshas (see p. 78). Reflect on these difficulties in your quiet times to tease out the different levels in the problem and why you react as you do. Look deeply, but without being hard on yourself. Try to understand the situation, without attributing fault. You may find ways of resolving the problem. It may not be easy to change the outer circumstances but you can limit the detrimental effects on your wellbeing by becoming an "observer" (see Chapter 7).

When considering the effect of work on your doshas, you need to take into account the qualities of your working environment. There may be subtle psychological influences. For example, the threat of redundancy brings with it a fear of unemployment and change, which increase vata; or competitiveness, instead of co-operation with your colleagues, increases pitta.

OCCUPATIONAL VPK

VATA	PITTA	KAPHA
Dancing	Management	Nursing
Acting	Politics	Administration
Designing	Surgery	Cooking
Teaching	Law	Building
Writing	Finance	Counselling
Photography		Manual labour

Constitutional Suitability

The chart on the left shows examples of occupations related to the qualities of vata, pitta, and kapha (VPK). The airy qualities of vata are good for communication skills; the ether element adds creativity. A strong intellect is associated with pitta; so too is the precision exhibited, for example, by competent engineers. The steadiness and compassion of kapha is appreciated in the caring professions, and the earth element in kapha finds good expression in horticulture and catering. Inevitably, many occupations call on qualities from all doshas.

The Working Environment

Using the examples in the chart below, try to relate the qualities of your working environment to vata, pitta, and kapha.

EFFECT OF WORKING ENVIRONMENT ON DOSHAS

ENVIRONMENT	CONDITIONS	INCREASED DOSHA
Air-conditioned office or department store	Lack of prana in atmosphere	Vata
	Lack of natural light	Kapha or Vata
	Flickering artificial light	Vata
Airplane	Movement, lack of prana, dehydration	Vata
Car/truck	Movement	Vata
Kitchen	Heat	Pitta
Furnace, foundry	Heat	Pitta
Cold store	Cold	Vata and Kapha
Check-out near exit door	Noise and draughts	Vata

Excess experience	Increases
Boredom	Kapha or vata
Challenges	Pitta; also vata, if they evoke fear
Competition	Pitta
Concentration	Pitta
Decision making	Pitta
Frustrations	Pitta
Interruptions	Vata
Repetitive tasks	Kapha
Small repetitive task involving the same muscle action	Vata
Responsibility	Pitta; also vata, if you worry about it
Sitting/standing	Kapha
Talking	Vata
Telephoning	Vata

Qualities at Work

Arrange the qualities of your work environment to help you keep your doshas balanced. Try to have natural light and ventilation, freedom from intrusive noise, the right space and a pleasing décor.

The Nature of your Work

When you assess any detrimental effects your work has on your doshas, consider those qualities that become excessive. Study the table (left) and the effects that an excessive experience can have on the doshas.

COMPUTERS

Computers have become part of modern life, in both the work place and at home. Some of their adverse effects are now known, and guidelines have been laid down for working practices to limit adverse influences on health.

If you spend too much time working or playing with a computer it will increase all three doshas, but especially vata. The speed at which the information on the screen changes, the flickering of the screen (often subliminal), and the repetitive sensory and motor stimulation all disturb vata. The precision needed, and the many frustrations that arise in obtaining the required results, increase pitta. Eye strain can disturb both vata and pitta. The sedentary nature and repetitive routine of computer work increase kapha.

Take steps to pacify vata by massaging your face, hands, and forearms with oil. Take frequent breaks away from your computer, preferably in fresh air; and move and stretch your body frequently, in particular the fingers, hands, arms, and shoulders. Spend a few minutes, two or three times a day, resting your eyes. One way to do this is to rest your elbows on your desk or your knees, close your eyes, and cover them with your palms.

LEISURE PURSUITS

By understanding the qualities associated with your leisure activities you will, in the short term, be able to add opposite qualities to reduce some of the adverse effects caused, for example, by your working life. Choose activities for relaxation and leisure to suit your constitution and so lead to balance and harmony in your life. For example, gentle, soft music will soothe vata, but kaphas may need the stimulation of louder, livelier music.

Consider the long-term consequences of your leisure pursuits on your doshas – you may be having fun now, but are you building up trouble for the future? For instance, you may enjoy being very active in your twenties and thirties, but could overstep the fine line between a healthy level of activity, which varies for each individual, and being slightly hyperactive. Hyperactivity increases vata energy. If the increase is gradual, you may not notice the effects until you are in your forties or fifties, by which time the excess dosha has moved into the deep tissues (see pp. 68–74).

VATA

Vata is easily increased by misuse or overuse of the senses, since vata predominates in the nervous system. Very loud music, fast flashing lights, and computer games all overuse the senses. If you have a vata constitution you are naturally drawn to fast action and new experiences, but you should spend time doing calm, gentle, creative pursuits, such as painting and spinning wool. You will also benefit from saunas, because of their warm and moist qualities.

PITTA

Pittas are attracted to competitive, mentally challenging situations. You should be challenged enough to avoid the risk of boredom, but not in ways that make you aggressive or increase your determination to win. You should avoid competitive one-to-one contests.

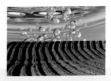

KAPHA

If allowed to, kaphas enjoy sitting doing nothing, whereas you would be better taking part in activities that are both physically and mentally stimulating. Make a concerted effort to take on new activities, but do not let these degenerate into unconscious habits. Keep adding variations to your leisure pursuits — for example, devise new aerobic sequences regularly.

Sports and Pastimes

If you frequently engage in sports, select those with qualities that help you balance the doshic qualities of your other activities, particularly your work. The table (see right) is given as a guide to help you relate sports and their various qualities to vata, pitta, and kapha. Remember that "like increases like". For example, engaging in vata-genic sport will increase your vata dosha. The way in which you play a sport may also alter the qualities. For example, if you are aggressive, this will increase your pitta, as will competitiveness. Movement, speed, and action are vata qualities, and will therefore increase vata.

KAPHA

Angling – Bowls
Weightlifting
Wrestling – Shot put

PITTA

Archery – Chess
Fencing – Shooting

VATA/KAPHA

Sailing – Windsurfing

VATA/PITTA

Football – Motor racing
Squash – Table tennis
Tennis – Track sports
Horse racing

PITTA/KAPHA

Billiards – Snooker
Golf
Javelin throwing
Boxing

VATA

Bobsledding
Bungee jumping
Cycling – Gymnastics
Horse riding
Ice skating
Parachuting
Roller skating
Skiing

Leisure Choice

Look at the doshic guidelines opposite to help you choose leisure activities appropriate to your constitution.

GARDENING

Gardening benefits all the doshas. It helps bring vatas down to earth, unless they are overly enthusiastic and exhaust themselves. Planning and the challenge of growing new varieties of plants or old ones more productively will keep pittas stimulated. Kaphas have an affinity with the land, and benefit from the physical work of gardening. The fresh air will also give extra prana which balances all the doshas.

ON VACATION

Vacations give you a chance to have a change of scene, a break from your commitments, and time to relax once you arrive at your destination. All types of travel, especially flying, increase vata. Anxiety about flying also increases vata, making you even more anxious. Take steps to pacify vata on your journey. Avoid alcohol, since it aggravates dehydration, drink dilute sweet fruit juices instead; drink ginger tea or take ginger tablets; massage your face and hands with a light oil, perhaps with one drop of lavender essential oil per 5 ml (1 teaspoon) of base oil; and eat small, easily digestible meals.

VATA

If you have a vata constitution you will be most affected by change and new experiences. Sight-seeing and touring are vata-genic. You would benefit most by having a vacation in a single destination with plenty of sun and warmth, though not in an arid climate. You will find locations at sea level less vata-aggravating than those at altitude. Resist packing your days and nights full of activities that leave you feeling tired. Find a beautiful place and enjoy being idle.

PITTA

If you have a pitta constitution avoid hot climates. Be sufficiently active to keep your mind satisfied by challenging yourself, rather than others. Try activities such as backpacking, canoeing, or skiing. Aim to let your holiday unfold and do not organize it to such an extent that you become frustrated if things do not go as planned.

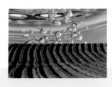

KAPHA

If kapha predominates in your constitution, you may be most contented lying in the sun doing as little as possible. However, a touring or activity vacation, which brings new interests each day, would be more beneficial.

Choosing a Vacation

The type of vacation you take will affect your doshas. Select a vacation that has the right qualities to help balance your lifestyle.

A Change of Scene

Backpacking in snow-covered mountains is strenuous and challenging. It makes a suitable vacation if you have a pitta constitution, but is not so good for vata types.

TAKING EXERCISE

Regular exercise helps improve the digestion: it raises agni, keeps the channels unobstructed, expels the wastes of cell metabolism, and keeps the muscles supple. Almost everyone will benefit from exercise, but the exercise must be suitable for your constitution. Too much exercise increases vata.

Exercise and VPK

Read the following guidelines to help you determine the best exercise for your constitution.

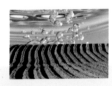

VATA

If you have a vata constitution, you are attracted to vigorous exercise, such as aerobics or jogging, and you often exercise to the point of exhaustion. However, exercising to this level increases vata, and in the long run will have a damaging effect on your joints, which are particularly vulnerable in people with a vata constitution. Have a regular amount of gentle exercise every day.

PITTA

If you have a pitta constitution, you should resist competitive sports, such as tennis or squash. Your determination to win may cause you to take the sport too seriously. Water and winter sports will cool the heat of your pitta constitution.

KAPHA

If you have a kapha constitution, you may dislike exercising. You would benefit from vigorous exercise, though you may need a lot of encouragement to do so, until it is established as part of your routine. You will have the stamina to exercise for longer than those with a vata constitution.

The ideal amount of exercise varies with each individual. Ayurveda says you should exercise to half your capacity. For instance, if you know that after running for thirty minutes you are exhausted, then you should not run for more than fifteen minutes. Another way to tell when you have had the optimum amount of exercise is when sweat comes to your forehead, armpits, and along your spine.

Yoga, walking, and swimming are good exercise for all constitutional types, balancing for all three doshas, and can be done alone or with others. If you are a vata type use your enthusiasm to start a new exercise programme to encourage one of your kapha friends to join you. A weekly arrangement for you and your kapha friend to meet together at the swimming pool or yoga class will help you sustain the habit when your initial excitement wears off. Your pitta friend might join you once he sees how he will benefit.

Receiving a massage is a passive form of exercise, giving the physiological benefits of exercise. It also helps counteract the stresses of modern life, particularly if you can lie down for an hour in a pleasant and relaxing atmosphere and let someone give you their full and caring attention. Incorporate a regular weekly, fortnightly, or monthly massage into your lifestyle in order to experience the accumulating benefits.

Exercise need not be limited to times when you have an hour to spare. Small amounts of exercise throughout the day are beneficial. A short walk after eating will aid digestion. Get into the habit of stretching and relaxing different muscle groups occasionally, especially if you have to sit for long periods of time. Stretching or warm-up exercises first thing in the morning balance the somnolence of the night. Such exercises can also be done at any other time of the day, but not after eating.

Caution:

Do not take strenuous exercise if you have acute indigestion, chest complaints, infections or inflammatory complaints, or if you are very old or very young.

SIMPLE EXERCISE SEQUENCE

Before you begin the exercises, sit still in the kneeling position (see right). Attune to your breathing, taking several deep, rhythmic abdominal breaths – let your abdominal muscles expand as you inhale and gently contract as you exhale. As you perform the sequence of exercises remain aware of your breathing and try to co-ordinate your movements with your breath.

When you first try these exercises do them slowly, taking one or two inhalations and exhalations in each position before moving to the next. Be aware of the stretching and contraction of your muscles. Do not strain in any way. Then sit in the kneeling position and, still maintaining the deep rhythmic abdominal breathing, picture your body performing the sequence of exercises. You can do this by visualizing the movements or imagining the feelings in your body, particularly your muscles, as you do them. Then repeat the exercises.

When you are familiar with the exercises, practise them daily to help keep your body flexible. Start with three rounds of the sequence and slowly increase to ten. It is important to remember that, before starting each sequence, to attune to your breathing since this will affect the speed at which you do the exercises.

When you are familiar with the exercises and are able to perform them with ease, you can

do the sequence as a more dynamic exercise, especially if you have a kapha constitution, but remember to keep the co-ordination of breath and movement. When you have finished the sequence, remain for a few moments in the kneeling position – physically relaxed and mentally calm – and observe your breath.

The Kneeling Position
Kneel down, with your knees and heels slightly apart, but with your big toes touching. Then sit back so that your buttocks sit comfortably on your heels, hands resting on your thighs just above the knees. Check that your spine is straight but relaxed and your chin level so your neck and head feel aligned with your spine.

1.The Upward Stretch
Inhaling, remain kneeling, and simultaneously raise your buttocks and stretch your arms up in line with your ears, palms forward and fingers pointing to the ceiling.

2.The Resting Position
Exhaling, bend forward, bringing your forehead, hands (slightly apart), and elbows (bent) to rest on the floor, with your buttocks resting on your heels.

3 All-fours Position

Inhaling, without moving the position of the hands and knees, raise yourself to kneeling on all fours, with chin and buttocks up. Drop your abdomen and small of the back toward the floor to create a smooth curve in the lumbar area.

4a Preparation

Prepare to move into the inverted-V position by tucking your toes under, but remaining on all fours.

4b Inverted-V Position

Exhaling, push into the floor with your hands, straighten your legs so your buttocks go high into the air making your body into an inverted-V shape; put your head between your arms aiming the crown of your head at the floor, and feel that your back and shoulders are flat. Place your heels flat on the floor but do not force them.

Note

If your heels do not easily go flat in the inverted-V position, practise walking on the spot by alternately bending one knee forward as the opposite heel goes down on the floor. Keep your toes on the floor as you do this.

5 Return to All-fours

Inhaling, return to the all-fours position.

Return to Resting

Exhaling, return to the resting position.

7 Back Stretch

Inhaling, slide your arms straight out in front, come on to your knees, move forward with your body, dropping your hips and buttocks toward the floor. Keep your arms straight so your body weight is held on the heels of your palms of the hands. Keep your chin up and look up.

8 Return to Resting

Exhaling, return to the resting position.

9 Upward Stretch

Inhaling, move into the upward stretch.

10 Return to Kneeling

Exhaling, return to the kneeling position, with spine erect and hands on thighs.

WORK, LEISURE AND EXERCISE ASSESSMENT

As you assess the doshic qualities of your work or your main daily activities you have to consider the strength of their influence, which may change from time to time. The overriding qualities of your office job may increase kapha, but if a new boss tries to undermine you or give you new responsibilities, that is likely to increase vata and pitta, too.

Use the list of questions below to start your work and leisure assessment. Write qualitative descriptions of all aspects of your work. Then, using the lists of qualities (see pp. 28–31 and 88–91), assess the effect your work has on your doshas. Ask which aspects need to be balanced, either by changing your working habits (if this is possible) or by altering other areas of your life, to bring overall doshic harmony. Consider also how much exercise you do and what you do in your leisure time. Look at the qualities to see the relationship between what you do and the doshas. Is this the right way for you to spend your time?

Work Assessment Questions

● What skills do you use in your job?

● What intellectual, physical, and emotional demands are made on you while you are working?

● What is your working environment like?

● Does your job require you to sit or stand in a particular posture, or to hold or use part of your body in a particular way over long periods of time?

● What are the small experiences that you encounter day in and day out in your job?

● How much time do you spend working at a computer?

● How do you feel about your work?

● Are there any difficult relationships connected with your work?

Leisure and Exercise Assessment Questions

● How much leisure time do you have in a day/week?

● What exercise do you take? Is it too much or not enough?

● What sports do you play? How do your mind and body feel during and after sport?

● What are your hobbies and pastimes? What intellectual, physical, and emotional experiences are involved? What are their qualities?

● Do you experience any discomforts before, during, or after your leisure time, such as headaches or weariness?

● Do you watch television, listen to music? What other sensory experiences do you have?

● Do you regularly spend time, however short, with your partner, children, or friends?

AYURVEDIC PROFILE
MARTIN

Age: 45

Height: 1.79m (5ft 10in)

Weight: 70.5kg (155 lbs)

Constitution: Pitta

An ambitious lawyer described by his friends as a workaholic, Martin expects unrealistic standards from his employees. He makes fast decisions, hates failure, and has a quick temper. He can skip meals when engrossed in work, but this makes him very critical and when he stops work he is ravenous. He enjoys Italian and very hot Mexican foods. He plays squash and likes fast cars. He experiences acid indigestion and frequently has red spots and blotches on his face and neck. Once or twice a year, he gets a mild lung infection. Over the last year, he has had occasional but intense headaches.

INTERPRETATION: Martin is experiencing pitta ailments. His pitta constitution makes him intellectually capable and ambitious, but excess pitta drives him too hard. He fears failing so does not allow himself to ease up or to listen to advice until his body can no longer take the strain. His work and leisure activities are pitta-increasing

Find out more about Martin on pages 156–7 and 182–3.

MORNING ROUTINE

Your body readily adapts itself to your habits, so it is important that you establish a routine that contributes to improving your overall health and vitality. Good habits often seem the most difficult to acquire. Your mind may resist change or may tell you that you are missing out on some of life's pleasures. But following a few simple guidelines (see pp. 108–9) for a short time each day – this may only involve thinking about something in a different way – is preferable to times of discomfort and illness that may affect you for longer periods.

Your current morning routine will probably have evolved to take into account the needs of getting to work on time and/or getting children up and off to school. You may feel that there is no time in the morning to do anything new or different. Introducing change may mean doing things in a slightly different way or getting up earlier (see pp. 112–13). If you decide to introduce changes to your morning habits, choose one or two alterations at first and gradually build up to a healthier routine.

Early morning is the main vata time (see p. 151). Vata energy in the pelvic cavity is responsible for expelling urine and faeces. Ayurveda teaches that the natural urge for defecation should arise in the early morning soon after naturally waking up from sleep. As well as proper elimination, other important parts of the daily routine include stretching, or exercise (see pp. 96–103), and a few moments watching the breath. Together, these prepare the body and mind for a fresh intake of nutrients and experiences.

Morning Exercise

Regular stretching and gentle exercise as part of your morning routine help to regulate your body's metabolism.

SUGGESTIONS FOR A MORNING ROUTINE

The following suggestions for a morning routine are suitable for all constitutional types. Use the suggestions to decide how you wish to alter your morning routine.

1. On waking, lie in bed for a few moments and become aware of how your body is feeling, and of your attitude toward the new day. Think about all levels of your being, and your part in universal creation. Whatever the difficulties or challenges you may face during the day, start it with kind and loving thoughts about yourself. Adopt an attitude of thanks; this will keep your heart open to the wonder of the universe and its blessings. Try and carry this attitude of awareness into all your daily activities.

2. Rub your palms together and hold or gently rub them over your face before getting out of bed. Feel energy and vitality flowing into your being.

3. Greet yourself in the mirror, a reminder that you love and respect yourself.

4. Visit the bathroom and attend to the natural urges of elimination, which should arise in the morning (see pp. 126–7).

5. Gently scrape your tongue with a tongue scraper or teaspoon. This stimulates the digestive system through subtle channels (similar to meridians) that connect with the tongue. If you have ama (see p. 77) in your body you may have a coated tongue and scraping it will help remove some of this.

6. Clean your teeth. If you have receding gums, massage them with your forefinger after dipping it in sesame oil. Repeat this in the evening.

7. Clean your nasal passages. Hold one nostril as you clear the other using deep abdominal breaths. Do not use short, shallow, or forceful breaths. Using your little finger, carefully massage each nostril with sesame oil, this will help prevent the mucus membranes drying. Your fingernail must be kept short if you do this.

8. Oil your skin (see p. 117).

9. Take a hot or warm shower or bath. Use only warm water on your head.

10. Do some stretching exercises (see pp. 98–103) or yoga. And follow this with meditation or a quiet time.

11. Dress in fresh, clean, comfortable clothes. Select colours according to their effects on your doshas (see pp. 110–11).

12. Eat breakfast, if it is appropriate for your constitution (see p. 151).

THE EFFECTS OF COLOUR

Different qualities are associated with different colours. You can relate the colours to vata, pitta, and kapha and use colour to affect your wellbeing, particularly through the colours you choose for your clothes and the décor of your home and work place. The range of hues reflects the different facets of a colour. For example, red is associated with heat, violence, aggression, passion, power, domination, but it can also be stimulating, warming, and comforting.

CONSTITUTIONAL TIPS

Each constitutional type should ideally decorate their home in colours that pacify their predominant dosha. Vata's homes should be in warm pastel colours; pitta's in cool blues and greens; kapha's with bright designs and colours.

Kapha

Avoid using white if you are a kapha. All colours pacify kapha, except greens and dark blues. Choose bright, strong, bold colours and designs that will excite you.

Vata

If you are vata type, blue and other dark shades probably predominate in your wardrobe. Ideally, you should avoid dark colours, especially black, browns and blues. You should also avoid vivid colours which may disturb the sensitivity of the nervous vata. Choose pastel shades instead.

Pitta

Eliminate red and black from your wardrobe if you are a pitta type. Use cool, soft, pale colours and blues as much as possible.

YELLOW AND ORANGE

Yellow and orange are warm, simulating colours that increase pitta. Their strong, dark shades are not advised if you have a pitta constitution or high pitta dosha, but sunny yellows will cheer vatas who are prone to depression.

RED

Red will over-stimulate pitta, but can be warming for vata, and provide necessary stimulation for kapha. Pink is gentler, embracing, loving, and calming, but if you have a kapha constitution it may make you more lethargic. Red cars are not to be recommended, as they could add a touch too much aggression to your driving, especially if you have a pitta constitution.

GREEN

Green with a yellow hue will increase pitta and decrease vata. Blue-greens will cool and calm pitta, and increase kapha.

BLUE AND PURPLE

Blue and purple are cooling colours that can be worn to good effect by those with pitta constitutions.

GOLD

Gold, the colour of the sun, is warming, and can be used if you have a vata or kapha constitution. Silver is connected with the moon and is cooling. If you have a pitta constitution you could perhaps wear silver jewellery rather than gold.

MORNING ASSESSMENT

Few of us look in detail at our experiences between waking and starting the day's main activities. List the things you do in the morning and in what order you do them (see below). Add how you feel when you awake and your attitude to starting the day. Compare your list to the suggested routine on pages 108–9 to see if you need to make adjustments. What changes would you like to make (for example, get up 20 minutes earlier to do stretching exercises or sit down to eat breakfast) and what do you need to make them happen?

If part of your schedule involves getting your child up and off to school, include in your assessment what you do for your child, and any feelings and frustrations you have. Do you wish to adapt some of these habits and attitudes as your child's ability to care for him or herself increases?

The following questions can help you become aware of your morning habits – are they right for your doshas?

- What time do you wake up? Does it allow you enough time to prepare for the day without rushing?
- How long do you lie in bed before you get up? What do you think about? Are you looking forward to a new day?
- Do you get the urge to eliminate your bowel and bladder first thing in the morning? Do you attend to them? Are two or three bowel movements necessary? Do you need to drink tea or coffee to stimulate a bowel movement?
- How many cups of tea, coffee, or other drinks do you have in the morning?
- Is your skin dry? Do you oil it regularly or apply drying products, such as talc or alcohol-based perfumes?
- Do you stretch or exercise your body?
- Do you meditate or take time to compose your thoughts?
- Is the television or radio on? Is it background noise or are you paying attention to it?
- Do you eat breakfast, and if so at what time? Do you sit down or eat as you go?
- How do you feel by the time you are ready to start your day's pursuits?

AYURVEDIC PROFILE
VICKY

Age: 60

Height: 1.61m (5ft 3in)

Weight: 48kg (105lbs)

Constitution: Vata

Vicky retired 6 months ago. Although she has had no serious illness, for most of her life she has suffered frequent indigestion, variable appetite, gases, and alternating bouts of constipation and loose stools. She has dry skin, a dry cough, and often feels cold, especially her feet. She sleeps fitfully, and most of the time feels weary. Recently, she noticed tics in her hands and fingers.

Vicky has a general anxiety that does not allow her to relax. She has a coated tongue and often has bad breath. She has little routine in her life, going to bed at any time between 8 pm and midnight depending on how she feels. Occasionally, she takes a walk. She says she takes no other exercise as she is always running around. Her mind jumps from idea to idea and she starts more projects than she will ever finish.

INTERPRETATION: Vicky is experiencing ailments due to an excess of vata energy, enhanced by the changes brought on by retirement. The bad breath and coating on the tongue indicate toxins, perhaps due to poor digestion resulting from increased vata and poor food combinations. Vicky will find it hard to get into and stick with a daily routine, yet this is the best way for her to pacify her vata. Vicky is establishing a new morning routine. She rises at 6.30 am and attends to elimination, which is becoming regular since she started taking triphala (see pp. 128–9) each evening. She applies sesame oil before showering, and cleans her mouth and nasal passages. Since joining a weekly yoga class Vicky practises for half an hour with a 10-minute breathing and quiet time at the end. At 7.45 am, she eats breakfast.

Since retiring, Vicky has looked at the colours of her clothes. When shopping, she is still drawn to blue, her favourite colour, but has decided to add pink and beige. She could also try warm reds, especially in winter.

Find out more about Vicky on page 156.

HOMECOMING

Late afternoon and early evening are vata times. For many people, this is the time to leave work, to travel home, and to change their activities. It is easy to take this diurnal increase in vata energy into your evening. As soon as you get home, shower, change into fresh clothes, and have 10 minutes' quiet time. Use this time to detach yourself from the day's events and remind yourself "who you really are" (see Chapter 7).

Try not to take your concerns about work home with you. If you do, make a mental effort to put them to one side, until it is the appropriate time to deal with them again. At the same time, ask yourself to be receptive to the guidance of your intuition in your decisions and actions regarding your concerns. It may take practice before this works well for you, but sincerity and persistence will be rewarded.

You can also use the quiet time to connect with your inner wisdom regarding conflicts and difficulties in your domestic life. If your household arrangements, or the need to prepare the evening meal, make it difficult to take a few quiet moments, remember that it is your conscious attitude that really makes the difference and that you are never separated from your inner wisdom.

Eat your evening meal early to allow time for the food to digest before engaging in other activities. You should leave at least two hours between eating and going to bed.

Spend some time with your children, your partner, your friends, or with yourself each evening, without modern distractions, such as the telephone or television. Give your attention to the moment, unfettered by your regrets from the past or your concerns about the future. Tiredness can make you irritable and snappy in company, but by really listening to each other, and by allowing time and space for acceptance, you will be able to foster spontaneity and understanding.

Inner Tranquillity

Take a few moments at the end of your working day to close your eyes and contact your inner beauty and peace.

INTIMACY

The natural time for intimacy is during kapha time in the evening, as the sexual act increases vata due to the amount of energy expended throughout the mind and body.

Satisfying sexual union between two people brings increased health, vitality, ojas (see p. 57), and thus immunity. It has to be developed over time, with each partner being concerned most with their partner's satisfaction on physical, mental, emotional, and deep inner levels. Thus, they build up a trust that allows the surrender of the defences of their innermost being, allowing each to open completely to the other and the unity of orgasm.

Reciprocal satisfaction cannot be hurried and needs a certain propriety. Though touch and smell are the primary senses of intimacy, every sense should be satisfied. Intimacy needs pleasant surroundings – flowers, soft music, sweet foods. Bathe in warm water perfumed with oils. Healthy sex also needs the clarity of total awareness (see pp. 176–7).

Gratification of lust and unsatisfying sex will bring ill health due to increased doshas, loss of ojas, and thus reduced immunity. Excessive loss of reproductive tissue weakens other tissue types and this is aggravated by dryness in the cells from increased vata. Unsatisfying sex also disturbs the emotions, and thus the doshas, principally pitta from anger and frustration, but also vata if fear or vulnerability is experienced, or kapha if you are possessive.

Desire to gratify lust may lead to an addiction to sex and frequent changing of partners in vain attempts to reach the deep satisfaction that can be found in sexual union. Vatas may change their partners because they seek satisfaction through new experiences; pittas in search of an intensity they cannot, or feel unable to, achieve; and kaphas because, once interested in sex, they have big appetites.

The frequency of sex depends on your constitution and also the seasons – it is more depleting in hot weather than cold. Kaphas have greater stamina and are able to partake more frequently and for longer than vatas and pittas.

REPRODUCTIVE TISSUES

Milk, honey, ghee, and onions are nourishing foods for the reproductive tissues. But onions arouse the body, which could cause further sexual desire. Warm milk with honey and almonds is advised after sex to help replenish the tissues.

OILING

Regularly oiling the skin keeps it smooth and supple. It is a very useful way to pacify vata, counteract dryness, and reduce anxiety. If you have a vata constitution or are in the vata age (see p. 10), try to oil yourself at least three times a week. A weekly oiling of the whole body is recommended for everyone (unless there are contra-indications).

Sesame oil is favoured in Ayurveda. It is warming and heavy and very pacifying for vata. Kapha is naturally oily and those with increased kapha should use oils very sparingly. Sesame oil may be too heating for pittas; sunflower or coconut would be more suitable. Use organic, cold-pressed oils; these are available from wholefood shops.

Contra-indications

Do not use oil:

• If you have a medical condition or are pregnant, unless with the knowledge of your medical adviser.

• Over any areas that are painful, unless you have guidance from your medical adviser or a massage therapist.

• Over any areas of broken, damaged, or infected skin.

• Within an hour of eating.

• If you have a thick coat on your tongue, an indication of ama.

Tips about Using Oil

• Oil, especially sesame oil, is very penetrating and difficult to remove from fabrics, particularly man-made ones. Do not use your best towels, keep one specifically for use when oiling up. Put on cotton socks after oiling your feet to protect carpets and bedding.

• Do not put oil on the soles of your feet if you are going to bathe or shower afterward since they will be slippery. Take care in the shower or bath since any excess oil on your body may leave a film on the bath. Clean the bath immediately.

• Warm oil is comforting and penetrates the skin better than cold.

• If you have long hair and find it difficult to get the oil on to your scalp, use a small dropper filled with oil and run the tip along your scalp slowly releasing the oil. Then massage.

• Keep oil in a small bottle with a nozzle to help control the amount used.

• Warm the oil by putting the bottle in a bowl of warm water.

• Keep paper towels to hand for wiping your hands and any spills immediately.

Instructions for Oiling

- Have an attitude of nurturing and love toward yourself and your body. Keep your attention on the part of your body you are oiling.
- Sit or stand on a large towel spread on the floor in a warm place.
- Use small amounts of oil, adding more as it is absorbed. Using both hands and adapting to the contours of your body, work in generous circular movements and long strokes from the extremities toward the body. Vatas should be gentle with themselves but kaphas can be more vigorous.

Oiling Head and Feet

A shorter method of applying oil, which can be used at night to bring calmness and aid sleep, is to apply oil to your head and feet. Apply oil to the crown of your head and massage for a few moments with your fingertips. If you do not like getting oil on your hair, apply it to the forehead and temples instead. (A towel over your pillow will help protect it from the oil.) Sitting on the floor, apply oil to the soles of your feet and massage them for a minute or so. Put on cotton socks. Never oil your feet on tiled or other slippery surfaces. Use common sense regarding the risk of falling: broken limbs aggravate all doshas and are painful and inconvenient.

Massaging the Scalp

A sense of calmness and tranquillity comes from massaging your scalp with oil. Such a massage pacifies vata and can reduce feelings of general anxiety.

Sequence for Oiling

- Work oil into your fingers, thumbs, and hands.
- Work up both arms to your shoulders and into your armpits.
- Apply oil to your toes, especially around the nails, and then work over the tops of your feet and up your legs.
- A very comfortable way to oil your abdomen is to lie on your back on the floor with your knees bent and your feet flat on the floor. However, you can do it sitting or standing. Place one hand flat on your abdomen and put the other over it. Work in the direction of flow in the colon: come up your right side to your rib cage, across your middle, down to your left hip, and across to your right hip.
- Starting at hip level and working up to your armpits (working around the breasts) make alternating horizontal strokes, first with one hand and then the other, from each side to the middle of your body.
- Work along your collarbones and all around your shoulders.
- Using your fingers work up and down the back of the neck, and more gently at the front.
- Using your fingertips work gently, but firmly, over your face (avoiding your eyes). Also, oil your scalp if you wish.
- Only oil those parts of your back that you can reach easily.
- Shower or bathe after you have finished.

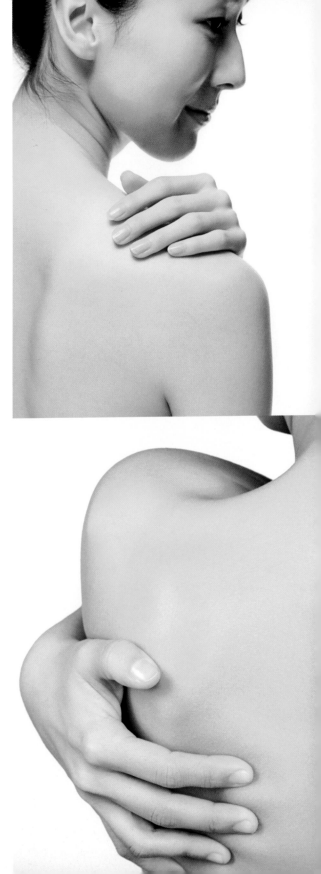

OILING WITH A FRIEND

It can be very relaxing to have someone apply the oil for you. This person can be a partner or a friend whom you can trust. They do not need to oil your whole body, just your back, or head and feet, or your face.

Sit or lie in a comfortable position – this will depend on which parts of your body are to be oiled. As you relax, your body temperature naturally drops a little so it is important that only the part being massaged is uncovered. Feeling chilled will prevent you from relaxing. And make sure your "oiling friend" has warm hands. Give your friend feedback about the pressure they are applying – whether it is too light or too heavy, or if it is just right.

Getting Ready

Make sure your "oiling friend" is comfortable, to avoid a stressed back through bad posture. If you lie down, use a massage table or the floor. Avoid using a bed, if possible, as it offers you little support and the height will almost certainly be wrong for your partner. Remember, your partner's clothes need to be protected from the oil by using a towel either as an apron or placed on their lap if massaging your hand.

Your "oiling friend" should use circular strokes to work the oil into your skin with their fingers or hands, depending on the area being oiled.

For the Vata Age

Oiling is very beneficial to counteract the dryness experienced in the vata age (over 55). Many who are well into the vata age will enjoy having oil rubbed gently into their hands. One drop of lavender oil per 5 ml (one teaspoon) of base oil will give added comfort.

SLEEP AND DREAMS

Evening is kapha time, which brings a natural heaviness to your mind and body. The main requirement for a good night's sleep is the complete digestion of all the day's mental and emotional experiences, and also of food.

Too much sleep increases kapha. Kaphas and those with excess kapha should avoid sleeping during the day or having a lie-in. Vatas need plenty of rest to replenish their nervous system and should avoid late nights and night shifts. Pittas sleep soundly, generally require less sleep than other doshic types, and usually wake with an alert mind.

Sleep problems can be related to the doshas. Going to sleep easily but having difficulty waking can indicate excess kapha. Waking around midnight relates to increased pitta. Difficulty going to sleep, waking frequently – especially between 2 and 4 am – indicates that your vata is too high.

If you find it hard to go to sleep, train your mind and body to accept that going to bed means going to sleep. Set a time for going to bed, preferably between 10 and 11 pm. Massage your head and feet with sesame oil (see p. 118). Drink a cup of milk (see pp. 160–1). If you are taking triphala (see pp. 128–9) in the evening, you need to alter your routine: take the triphala at least an hour and a half after eating and a milk drink at least an hour and a half after the triphala.

Dreams

During sleep, the mind withdraws the senses from the outer world. It has the opportunity to finish digesting the day's experiences and completing unfulfilled desires. When you remember your dreams you may be recalling fragments of these processes.

Dreams can be related to the doshas. Vata dreams are either active with movement, such as flying, chases, jumping or falling from heights, or are frightening. Pitta dreams can be violent or angry, or have sharp instruments or fighting in them. Kapha dreams are gentle, often featuring calm water, lakes, or oceans.

Your dreams will tend to relate to your predominant dosha (see pp. 38–41). A change in the type of dreams you have may indicate a doshic imbalance (see p. 62). For example, if you start experiencing dreams with vata qualities, they may indicate an increase in your vata dosha.

Occasionally, you may have a dream that seems significant to you. Trust yourself to interpret it. Ask yourself questions, about the people, objects, situations, and relationships in the dream. Be guided by your inner wisdom as you enquire, remaining open in order to gain the insights that will be useful to you.

Sequence to Combat Insomnia

- Sit on your bed and watch your breath for a few moments, give thanks for the day's experiences, joys and tribulations.

- Get into bed, put the light out.

- Still watching your breath get into a position that is comfortable for sleeping. If you are restless, just know that it is your excess vata energy wanting to fidget.

- Stay watching your breathing. Imagine what your body feels like when it is asleep. Let your breath slowly deepen. Repeat this exercise if you wake in the night. Often insomnia makes us feel that we will be tired the next day, but by doing this exercise you can ensure that your body at least will be rested.

A Pleasant Bedroom

Use fresh bed linen, soft lighting, and gentle music. Do not have a television or reading matter by the bed, other than perhaps a book of inspirational quotes.

CONSTIPATION

The colon is the seat of vata (see p. 46), and an important organ for the overall wellbeing of the body. It is part of the food and prana channels: an unhealthy colon means that elimination and digestion may be impaired and absorption of prana from food reduced. In addition, toxins may be assimilated into the body, and vata could increase, possibly leading to excess vata spreading to other parts of the body.

Chronic constipation tends to be connected with increased vata, but may be due to an increase in the other doshas. The excess heat of pitta may cause dry stools. The downward movement of the vata energy, which is responsible for defecation, may be blocked by too much mucus in the intestines (increased kapha) or by an accumulation of undigested foods or ama.

An inappropriate diet with poor food combinations is a major cause of chronic constipation and gases. Lack of sleep, anxiety, and other factors that increase vata (see p. 65) may also contribute to constipation and gases. Habitually suppressing the natural urge for defecation, or excessive use of laxatives or colonics may also result in constipation, since they all upset the body's natural intelligence to regulate itself.

Early morning is the vata time of day and the best time for elimination. Waking around 6 am to attend to the natural urges of defecation with complete and satisfying elimination helps to maintain the health of your colon.

The Squatting Position

Stand with your feet hip-width apart and toes turned outward. Bend the knees and slowly ease yourself down as far as you can comfortably go. Practise moving up and down until you can squat comfortably. Eventually, you will be able to wrap your arms around your knees and hug them. This position may take many weeks of practice. Do not force this position, and if it becomes uncomfortable, release it.

Knee-to-chest Exercises

1 Lie on the floor and bend your right knee. Hold your leg just below the knee and pull it toward your abdomen. Release your leg and return it to the floor. Repeat with the other leg.

2 Lie on the floor and bring both knees up simultaneously. Wrap your arms around your legs, just below your knees, and hug them. Pull them in toward your abdomen. Hold for a few moments. Relax and return your legs to the floor. Try to do this exercise twice a day.

Some Ways to Help Relieve Chronic Constipation

• Check your diet, especially for inappropriate food combinations and excess of vata-genic foods (see the NO column of food charts – pp. 133–43). Check other factors that may be disturbing your doshas and slowly make changes in your diet and lifestyle.

• Condition your colon to regular elimination. On rising, go to the bathroom, even if you do not have the urge to defecate. Sit or squat (see left), pull in your anal muscles firmly, and relax. Repeat three times. Don't push or strain as you try to pass stools.

• Drink a glass of warm water to help stimulate the gastro-intestinal reflex.

• Take triphala before going to bed (see pp. 128–9).

• Practise squatting twice a day (see left), and if possible use this position instead of sitting when passing stools as it aids complete elimination.

• Do the knee-to-chest exercise twice a day.

• Massage the abdomen (see p. 120) with or without oil. If you cannot easily fit this into your daily routine, do it in bed before rising.

• Attend to the natural urges of your colon when they arise.

TRIPHALA

Triphala is an Ayurvedic herbal compound made up of three fruits or herbs – amalaki (*Embelica officinalis*), bibhitaki (*Terminalia belerica*), and haritaki (*Terminalia chebula*). The combination of the three herbs makes it a regulator of all three doshas. Triphala generally comes in powdered form, but many people prefer tablets or capsules because they do not like the taste.

Triphala has a laxative effect, but does not create dependency, nor disturb healthy intestinal flora. It regulates and rejuvenates the colon. It normalizes digestion and metabolism, and helps expel gases from the intestines. It aids weight reduction by assisting in the removal of toxins and fat from the cells. It is a source of vitamin C.

Triphala can be taken daily as a general tonic and bowel regulator. If you take it over a long period, then stop taking it for two to three weeks at approximately ten-week intervals. Although it is not addictive, the body will adapt to its regular long-term use, thereby making it less effective. It is best to take triphala in the evening, at least one and a half to two hours after food, and about half an hour before going to bed. In any case, do not eat for one and a half hours afterward.

You will need to find out how much triphala is right for you. Do not exceed 5 ml (one teaspoon) per day. When you start taking it, use a smaller amount, such as 1.25–2.5 ml (quarter or half of a teaspoon), increasing the amount gradually. When you first take it you may experience an increase in passing wind.

The triphala is not creating these gases but helping expel old gases trapped in pockets in the intestines. If you experience loose stools when you start taking triphala, reduce the amount of triphala.

AMALAKI
A regulator for pitta energy

HARITAKI
A regulator for vata energy

BIBHITAKI
A regulator for kapha energy

Caution:

Do not take triphala in cases of diarrhoea or dysentery, or during pregnancy.

Preparing Triphala

Triphala can be prepared in a number of ways. Try each of them to discover which suits you and your routine best.
The strongest action will be obtained by simmering the triphala, and the weakest by soaking it and leaving the dregs.

• Soak it in a cup of water at room temperature for eight hours. Drink the water, leaving the dregs.

• Mix it in a cup of tepid water and drink the water and the dregs.

• Put it in a cup and fill with boiling water. Leave to "brew" for 5 minutes before drinking. You can drink it either with or
without the dregs.

• Simmer with about one and a half cups of water in a pan for 20 minutes — or longer if you want it stronger. Strain and drink.

6. FOOD AND DIET

मात्रावद्द्यशनमशितमनुपहत्य प्रकृतिं
बलवर्णसुरवायुषा यीजयत्युपयीक्तारमवश्यमिति ॥

Taken in appropriate quantity, food certainly helps the individual in bringing about strength, complexion, happiness, and longevity without disturbing the equilibrium of dhatus (tissues) and doshas of the body.

(*Charaka Samhita* Chapter 5: 8)

For thousands of years, Ayurveda has taught that what we eat plays a big part in determining health. All matter consists of the five elements (see p. 22), which are a manifestation of consciousness. As you eat you take into yourself the subtle influences attached to the food and prana as well as the physical form of the food. Even the stages of production to which food is subjected affect its qualities. Food is part of the dynamic dance of life and its qualities, both obvious and subtle, affect your wellbeing.

The immediate connection between the qualities of food and their impact on your health is not always obvious, due in part to the complexities of Western diets and the effects the digestive process has on food. *Charaka Samhita* lists eight specific factors

that you should take into account when determining a diet appropriate for you. Consider your diet in relation to these factors, since each will, to some degree, help you determine if your diet is right for you in your current circumstances, or indicate where you could make beneficial changes. The eight factors listed by *Charaka Samhita* are:

1. The natural qualities in foods
2. How the natural qualities in foods can be altered
3. The effects of combining foods
4. The quantity of food eaten
5. The place(s) and climate where the food was grown, prepared, and eaten
6. The effects of the seasons and time of day
7. General guidance on eating habits
8. Individual differences in the consumer of the food

Food Charts

Before looking at each of these factors, the following pages provide an overall classification of foods according to whether they tend to increase or pacify each dosha. Prepared by Dr. Vasant Lad, Director of the Ayurvedic Institute, Albuquerque, New Mexico, these charts take into account the combined effects of the tastes, energetics, and post-digestive effects of the foods (see Chapter 3) and their qualities (see p. 144). The charts are general and are designed to help everyone, so let your individual circumstances and tolerances guide you. Remember, too, that different methods of preparation and combination may modify the effects of the foods on your doshas.

You may find that, on first looking at these charts, your favourite foods are in the column that increase your predominant dosha (see Constitutional Assessment on pp. 38–41). This is understandable, since you are attracted to things that have similar qualities to yourself, as the principle "like attracts like" suggests.

One way to become familiar with this classification of foods is to copy the list, display it prominently (e.g. on the refrigerator door), and refer to it while you prepare meals. As you cook, look on the list to see the doshic classification of the foods you are using. If your meals are prepared for you, then daily review what you have eaten against the list.

When you have started using Ayurvedic principles to adjust your diet, have a copy of the list with you when shopping. If you refer to it when selecting food, you will develop new shopping habits and be less likely to arrive home with items that are unsuitable for your doshic needs.

Assessing your Current Diet

Learning to classify your food – and hence your overall diet – as increasing or pacifying vata, pitta, or kapha, gives you the starting point for making changes. To do this, keep a record of everything you eat and drink for at least seven days.

Remember to record all snacks and nibbles as well as meals, and the times when you ate them. For each day, use headings of breakfast, lunch, evening meal, and snacks. Leave space to note later whether the foods tend to increase or pacify vata, pitta, or kapha; and make notes, too, about how your food combinations affect your overall doshic picture and digestion (see Chapter 3).

You may find recording your diet a hard exercise. Not only do you have to remember to write it down, but if you snack frequently or eat foods judged as "bad", then seeing it written down may make you feel guilty. If you have a problem making your dietary record, regard it as an exercise in observation, and accept yourself as you are. Be kind and gentle with yourself. Guilt or shame may make you want to eat more, leading to more guilt and self-recrimination. Knowing what you are eating means that you are in a better position to make permanent changes, if that is what you choose.

With the qualities of the doshas (see Chapter 2) and the food charts to guide you, analyse your dietary record to see if foods that increase one dosha predominate in your diet. Use a different coloured pen for each dosha and mark the food items for each meal according to which dosha they increase.

FOOD CHARTS

Food Charts

The following pages give lists of foods that influence vata, pitta and kapha. Each dosha contains two lists:

NO means that the foods aggravate/increase the dosha. Avoid eating these foods if you are following a diet that pacifies the dosha.

YES means that the foods pacify/decrease the dosha. Select foods from this column if you are following a diet that pacifies the dosha.

The Ayurvedic Institute
Food Guidelines for Basic Constitutional Types

NOTE: Guidelines provided in this table are general. Specific adjustments for individual requirements may need to be made, e.g. food allergies, strength of agni, season of the year, and degree of dosha predominance or aggravation.

* OK in moderation ‡ OK occasionally

A Word of Caution

These are guidelines only, and not meant to substitute in any way for the advice of a qualified physician or nutritionist. Ayurveda always recommends a slow and steady approach to changes in your diet. Do not try to do everything at once!

After you have discovered which diet is for you (see pp. 154–5), remember to listen closely to your body as you try different foods. If for instance you get gas, or heartburn, it may not be the food for you. Everyone is completely individual, and even though the food is on your list, it might not agree with you. So be gentle and loving with yourself. Slowly with this list and your own listening will come a way of eating that will bring great balance and health into your life. Also Ayurveda says that it is not what you eat occasionally that creates a serious imbalance, but what you consume on a day-by-day basis.

VATA		PITTA		KAPHA	
NO	**YES**	**NO**	**YES**	**NO**	**YES**

FRUITS

Generally most dried fruit	Generally most sweet fruit	Generally most sour fruit	Generally most sweet fruit	Generally most sweet & sour fruit	Generally most astringent fruit
Apples (raw)	Apples (cooked)	Apples (sour)	Apples (sweet)	Avocado	Apples
Cranberries	Apple sauce	Apricots (sour)	Apple sauce	Bananas	Apple sauce
Dates (dry)	Apricots	Bananas	Apricots (sweet)	Coconut	Apricots
Figs (dry)	Avocado	Berries (sour)	Avocado	Dates	Berries
Pears	Bananas	Cherries (sour)	Berries (sweet)	Figs (fresh)	Cherries
Persimmons	Berries	Cranberries	Cherries (sweet)	Grapefruit	Cranberries
Pomegranates	Cherries	Grapefruit	Coconut	Grapes*	Figs (dry)*
Raisins (dry)	Coconut	Grapes (green)	Dates	Kiwi	Peaches
Prunes (dry)	Dates (fresh)	Kiwi‡	Lemons*	Lemons*	Pears
Watermelon	Figs (fresh)	Lemons	Grapes (red &	Limes*	Persimmons
	Grapefruit	Mangoes (green)	purple)	Mangoes‡	Pomegranates
	Grapes	Oranges (sour)	Limes*	Melons	Prunes
	Kiwi	Papaya*	Mangoes (ripe)	Oranges	Raisins
	Lemons	Peaches	Melons	Papaya	Strawberries*
	Limes	Persimmons	Oranges (sweet)	Pineapple	
	Mangoes	Pineapple (sour)	Pears	Plums	
	Melons	Plums (sour)	Pineapple (sweet)	Rhubarb	
	Oranges	Rhubarb	Plums (sweet)	Tamarind	
	Papaya	Strawberries	Pomegranates	Watermelon	
	Peaches	Tamarind	Prunes		
	Pineapple		Raisins		
	Plums		Watermelon		
	Prunes (soaked)				
	Raisins (soaked)				
	Rhubarb				
	Strawberries				
	Tamarind				

VATA		PITTA		KAPHA	
NO	**YES**	**NO**	**YES**	**NO**	**YES**

DAIRY

VATA NO	VATA YES	PITTA NO	PITTA YES	KAPHA NO	KAPHA YES
Cheese (hard)*	Most dairy is good!	Butter (salted)	Butter (unsalted)	Butter (salted)	Butter (unsalted) ‡
Cow's milk (powdered)		Buttermilk	Cheese (soft, not aged, unsalted)	Buttermilk*	Cottage cheese (from skimmed goat's milk)
Goat's milk (powdered)	Butter	Cheese (hard)	Cottage cheese	Cheese (soft & hard)	Ghee*
Yogurt (plain, frozen or with fruit)	Buttermilk	Sour cream	Cow's milk	Cow's milk	Goats' cheese (unsalted & not aged) *
	Cheese (soft)	Yogurt (plain, frozen or with fruit)	Ghee	Ice cream	Ghee*
	Cottage cheese		Goat's milk	Sour cream	Goat's milk (skimmed only)
	Cow's milk		Goat's cheese (soft, unsalted)	Yogurt (plain, frozen or with fruit)	Yogurt (diluted)
	Ghee		Ice cream		
	Goats' cheese		Yogurt (freshly made & diluted)		
	Goat's milk				
	Ice cream*				
	Sour cream*				
	Yogurt (diluted & spiced)				

SWEETENERS

VATA NO	VATA YES	PITTA NO	PITTA YES	KAPHA NO	KAPHA YES
White sugar	Barley malt	Honey*	Barley malt	Barley malt	Fruit juice concentrates
	Fructose	Jaggary	Fructose	Fructose	Honey (raw & not processed)
	Fruit juice concentrates	Molasses	Fruit juice concentrates	Jaggary	
	Honey		Maple syrup	Maple syrup	
	Jaggary		Rice syrup	Molasses	
	Maple syrup‡		Sucanat	Rice syrup	
	Molasses		Turbinado	Sucanat	
	Rice syrup		White sugar‡	Turbinado	
	Sucanat			White sugar	
	Turbinado				

VEGETABLES

Generally frozen, raw, or dried vegetables	In general vegetables should be cooked	In general pungent vegetables	In general sweet & bitter vegetables	In general sweet & juicy vegetables	In general most pungent & bitter vegetables
Artichoke	Asparagus	Aubergine	Artichoke	Courgette	Aubergine
Aubergine	Beets	Beet greens	Asparagus	Cucumber	Artichoke
Beet greens‡	Cabbage*	Beets (raw)	Beets (cooked)	Olives, black or	Asparagus
Bitter melon	Carrots	Burdock root	Bitter melon	green	Beet greens
Broccoli	Cauliflower*	Carrots (raw) *	Broccoli	Parsnips‡	Beets
Brussels sprouts	Courgette	Corn (fresh) ‡	Brussels sprouts	Potatoes, sweet	Bitter melon
Burdock root	Coriander	Daikon radish	Cabbage	Pumpkin	Broccoli
Cabbage (raw)	Cucumber	Garlic	Carrots (cooked)	Spaghetti squash*	Brussels sprouts
Cauliflower (raw)	Daikon radish*	Green chillies	Cauliflower	Squash, winter	Burdock root
Celery	Fennel (Anise)	Horseradish	Celery	Taro root	Cabbage
Corn (fresh) ‡	Garlic	Kohlrabi‡	Coriander	Tomatoes	Carrots
Dandelion greens	Green beans	Leeks (raw)	Courgette		Cauliflower
Jerusalem artichoke*	Green chillies	Mustard greens	Cucumber		Celery
Kale	Horseradish‡	Olives, green	Dandelion greens		Coriander
Kohlrabi	Leeks	Onions (raw)	Fennel (Anise)		Corn
Leafy greens*	Mustard greens*	Peppers (hot)	Green beans		Daikon radish
Lettuce*	Okra	Prickly pear (fruit)	Jerusalem artichoke		Dandelion greens
Mushrooms	Olives, black	Radishes (raw)	Kale		Fennel (Anise)
Olives, green	Onions (cooked) *	Spinach (raw)	Leafy greens		Garlic
Onions (raw)	Parsnip	Tomatoes	Leeks (cooked)		Green beans
Parsley*	Peas (cooked)	Turnip greens	Lettuce		Green chillies
Peas (raw)	Potatoes, sweet	Turnips	Mushrooms		Horseradish
Peppers, sweet &	Pumpkin		Okra		Jerusalem artichoke
hot	Radishes (cooked) *		Olives, black		Kale
Potatoes, white	Spinach (cooked)		Onions (cooked)		Kohlrabi
Prickly pear (fruit &	Squash, summer &		Parsley		Leafy greens
leaves)	winter		Parsnips		Leeks
Radish (raw)	Swede		Peas		Lettuce
Spaghetti squash*	Tomatoes (cooked) ‡		Peppers, sweet		Mushrooms
Spinach (raw) *	Taro root		Potatoes, sweet &		Mustard greens
Sprouts*	Watercress		white		Okra
Tomatoes (raw)			Prickly pear (leaves)		Onions
Turnip greens*			Pumpkin		Parsley
Turnips			Radishes (cooked)		Peas
Wheat grass sprouts			Swede		Peppers, sweet &
			Spaghetti squash		hot
			Spinach (cooked) ‡		

VATA		PITTA		KAPHA	
NO	**YES**	**NO**	**YES**	**NO**	**YES**

VEGETABLES (continued)

VATA NO	VATA YES	PITTA NO	PITTA YES	KAPHA NO	KAPHA YES
Radish (raw)			Sprouts (not spicy)		Potatoes, white
Spaghetti squash*			Squash, winter &		Prickly pear (fruit &
Spinach (raw) *			summer		leaves)
Sprouts*			Taro root		Radishes
Tomatoes (raw)			Watercress*		Spinach
Turnip greens*			Wheat grass		Sprouts
Turnips			sprouts		Squash (summer)
Wheat grass					Swede
sprouts					Tomatoes
					(cooked)
					Turnip greens
					Turnips
					Watercress
					Wheat grass
					sprouts

LEGUMES

VATA NO	VATA YES	PITTA NO	PITTA YES	KAPHA NO	KAPHA YES
Aduki beans	Lentils (red) *	Miso	Aduki beans	Kidney beans	Aduki beans
Black beans	Miso‡	Soy sauce	Black beans	Mung beans*	Black beans
Black-eyed peas	Mung beans	Soy sausages	Black-eyed peas	Mung dal*	Black-eyed peas
Butter beans	Mung dal	Tur dal	Butter beans	Soy beans	Butter beans
Chickpeas	Soy cheese*	Urad dal	Chickpeas	Soy cheese	Chickpeas
Haricot beans	Soy milk*		Haricot beans	Soy flour	Haricot beans
Kidney beans	Soy sauce*		Kidney beans	Soy powder	Lentils (red &
Lentils (brown)	Soy sausages*		Lentils (brown	Soy sauce	brown)
Peas (dried)	Tur dal		& red)	Tofu (cold)	Miso
Pinto beans	Urad dal		Mung beans	Urad dal	Peas (dried)
Soy beans			Mung dal		Pinto beans
Soy flour			Peas (dried)		Soy milk
Soy powder			Pinto beans		Soy sausages
Split peas			Soy beans		Split peas
Tempeh			Soy cheese		Tempeh
Tofu*			Soy flour*		Tofu (hot) *
White beans			Soy milk		Tur dal
			Soy powder*		White beans
			Split peas		
			Tempeh		
			Tofu		
			White beans		

	VATA			PITTA			KAPHA	
NO	**YES**		**NO**	**YES**		**NO**	**YES**	

CONDIMENTS

VATA NO	VATA YES	PITTA NO	PITTA YES	KAPHA NO	KAPHA YES
Chilli peppers*	Black pepper*	Chocolate	Black pepper*	Chocolate	Black pepper
Chocolate	Chilli peppers	Chutney, mango	Chutney, mango	Chutney, mango	Chilli peppers
Horseradish	Chutney, mango	(spicy)	(sweet)	(sweet)	Chutney, mango
Sprouts*	(sweet or spicy)	Dulse*	Coriander leaves	Dulse*	(spicy)
	Coriander leaves*	Gomasio	Hijiki*	Gomasio	Coriander leaves
	Dulse	Horseradish	Kombu*	Hijiki*	Horseradish
	Gomasio	Kelp	Lime*	Kelp	Mustard (without
	Hijiki	Ketchup	Sprouts	Ketchup‡	vinegar)
	Kelp	Lemon		Lemon*	Spring onions
	Ketchup	Lime pickle		Lime	Sprouts
	Kombu	Mango pickle		Lime pickle	
	Lemon	Mayonnaise		Mango pickle	
	Lime	Mustard		Mayonnaise	
	Lime pickle	Pickles		Pickles	
	Mango pickle	Salt (in excess)		Salt	
	Mayonnaise	Seaweed		Seaweed*	
	Mustard	Soy sauce		Soy sauce	
	Pickles	Spring onions		Tamari	
	Salt	Tamari*		Vinegar	
	Seaweed	Vinegar			
	Soy sauce				
	Spring onions				
	Tamari				
	Vinegar				

ANIMAL FOODS

VATA NO	VATA YES	PITTA NO	PITTA YES	KAPHA NO	KAPHA YES
Chicken (white)*	Beef	Beef	Buffalo	Beef	Chicken (white)
Lamb	Buffalo	Chicken (dark)	Chicken (white)	Buffalo	Eggs
Pork	Chicken (dark)	Duck	Eggs (albumen or	Chicken (dark)	Fish (freshwater)
Rabbit	Duck	Eggs (yolk)	white only)	Duck	Rabbit
Venison	Eggs	Fish (sea)	Fish (freshwater)	Fish (sea)	Shrimp
Turkey (white)	Fish (freshwater	Lamb	Rabbit	Lamb	Turkey (white)
	or sea)	Pork	Shrimp*	Pork	Venison
	Salmon	Salmon	Turkey (white)	Salmon	
	Sardines	Sardines	Venison	Sardines	
	Seafood	Seafood		Seafood	
	Shrimp	Tuna fish		Tuna fish	
	Tuna fish	Turkey (dark)		Turkey (dark)	
	Turkey (dark)				

VATA		PITTA		KAPHA	
NO	**YES**	**NO**	**YES**	**NO**	**YES**

NUTS

VATA NO	VATA YES	PITTA NO	PITTA YES	KAPHA NO	KAPHA YES
None	In moderation:	Almonds (with skin)	Almonds (soaked and peeled)	Almonds (soaked and peeled) ‡	Charoli
	Almonds	Black walnuts	Charoli	Black walnuts	
	Black walnuts	Brazil nuts	Coconut	Brazil nuts	
	Brazil nuts	Cashews		Cashews	
	Cashews	Hazelnuts		Coconut	
	Charoli	Macadamia nuts		Hazelnuts	
	Coconut	Peanuts		Macadamia nuts	
	Hazelnuts	Pecans		Peanuts	
	Macadamia nuts	Pine nuts		Pecans	
	Peanuts‡	Pistachios		Pine nuts	
	Pecans	Walnuts		Pistachios	
	Pine nuts			Walnuts	
	Pistachios				
	Walnuts				

BEVERAGES

VATA NO	VATA YES	PITTA NO	PITTA YES	KAPHA NO	KAPHA YES
Apple juice	Alcohol (beer or wine) *	Alcohol (spirits or wine)	Alcohol (beer) *	Alcohol (beer, spirits, sweet wine)	Alcohol (dry wine, red or white)
Black tea	Almond milk	Apple cider	Almond milk	Almond milk	Aloe vera juice
Caffeinated drinks	Aloe vera juice	Berry juice (sour)	Aloe vera juice	Caffeinated drinks‡	Apple cider
Carbonated drinks	Apple cider	Caffeinated drinks	Apple juice	Carbonated drinks	Apple juice*
Carob*	Apricot juice	Carbonated drinks	Apricot juice	Chai (hot, spiced milk)*	Apricot juice
Chocolate milk	Berry juice (except cranberry)	Carrot juice	Berry juice (sweet)	Cherry juice (sour)	Berry juice
Coffee	Carrot juice	Cherry juice (sour)	Black tea	Chocolate milk	Black tea (spiced)
Cold dairy drinks	Chai (hot, spiced milk)	Chocolate milk	Carob	Coffee	Carob
Cranberry juice	Cherry juice	Coffee	Chai (hot, spiced milk)	Cold dairy drinks	Carrot juice
Iced tea	Grain "coffee"	Cranberry juice	Cherry juice	Grapefruit juice	Cherry juice (sweet)
Icy cold drinks	Grape juice	Grapefruit juice	Cool dairy drinks	Iced tea	Cranberry juice
Mixed veg. juice	Grapefruit juice	Iced tea	Grain "coffee"	Icy cold drinks	Grain "coffee"
Pear juice	Lemonade	Icy cold drinks	Grape juice	Lemonade	Grape juice
Pomegranate juice	Mango juice	Lemonade	Mango juice	Miso broth	Mango juice
Prune juice‡	Miso broth	Orange juice*	Mixed veg. juice		Mixed veg. juice
Soy milk (cold)		Miso broth*	Peach nectar		Peach nectar
Tomato juice‡		Papaya juice	Pear juice		
Vegetable bouillon					

VATA		PITTA		KAPHA	
NO	**YES**	**NO**	**YES**	**NO**	**YES**

BEVERAGES (continued)

VATA NO	VATA YES	PITTA NO	PITTA YES	KAPHA NO	KAPHA YES
Herb teas:	Orange juice	Pineapple juice	Pomegranate juice	Orange juice	Pear juice
Alfalfa‡	Papaya juice	Tomato juice	Prune juice	Papaya juice	Pomegranate juice
Barley‡	Peach nectar	Sour juices	Rice milk	Pineapple juice*	Prune juice
Blackberry	Pineapple juice		Soy milk	Rice milk	Soy milk (hot &
Borage‡	Rice milk	**Herb teas:**	Vegetable bouillon	Sour juices	well spiced)
Burdock	Sour juices			Soy milk (cold)	Vegetable bouillon
Catnip*	Soy milk (hot &	Ajwan		Tomato juice	
Chicory*	well-spiced) *	Basil‡	**Herb teas:**		**Herb teas:**
Chrysanthemum*		Cinnamon‡		**Herb teas:**	
Corn silk	**Herb teas:**	Clove	Alfalfa		Ajwan
Dandelion		Eucalyptus	Bancha	Comfrey*	Alfalfa
Ginseng	Ajwan	Fenugreek	Barley	Marshmallow	Barley
Hibiscus	Bancha	Ginger (dry)	Blackberry	Red zinger	Basil
Hyssop‡	Basil‡	Ginseng	Borage	Rosehip‡	Blackberry
Jasmine‡	Camomile	Hawthorn	Burdock		Borage
Lemon balm‡	Cinnamon‡	Hyssop	Catnip		Burdock
Nettle‡	Clove	Juniper berry	Camomile		Catnip
Passion flower‡	Comfrey	Pennyroyal	Chicory		Camomile
Red clover‡	Elderflower	Red zinger	Chrysanthemum		Chicory
Red zinger‡	Eucalyptus	Rosehip‡	Comfrey		Chrysanthemum
Sage	Fennel	Sage	Corn silk		Cinnamon
Strawberry*	Fenugreek	Sassafras	Dandelion		Clove
Violet	Ginger (fresh)	Yerba mate	Elderflower		Corn silk
Wintergreen*	Hawthorn		Fennel		Dandelion
Yarrow	Juniper berry		Ginger (fresh)		Elderflower
Yerba mate‡	Kukicha*		Hibiscus		Eucalyptus
	Lavender		Hops		Fennel*
	Lemon grass		Jasmine		Fenugreek
	Licorice		Kukicha		Ginger
	Marshmallow		Lavender		Ginseng*
	Oat straw		Lemon balm		Hibiscus
	Orange peel		Lemon grass		Hops
	Pennyroyal		Licorice		Hyssop
	Peppermint		Marshmallow		Jasmine
	Raspberry*		Nettle		Juniper berry
	Rosehip		Oat straw		Kukicha
	Saffron		Orange peel*		Lavender
			Passion flower		

VATA		PITTA		KAPHA	
NO	YES	NO	YES	NO	YES

BEVERAGES (continued)

VATA		PITTA		KAPHA	
NO	YES	NO	YES	NO	YES
	Sarsaparilla		Peppermint		Lemon balm
	Sassafras		Raspberry		Lemon grass
	Spearmint		Red clover		Licorice*
			Saffron		Nettle
			Sarsaparilla		Oat straw
			Spearmint		Orange peel
			Strawberry		Passion flower
			Violet		Pennyroyal
			Wintergreen		Peppermint
			Yarrow		Raspberry
					Red clover
					Saffron
					Sage
					Sarsaparilla*
					Sassafras
					Spearmint
					Strawberry
					Violet
					Wintergreen
					Yarrow
					Yerba mate

SEEDS

VATA		PITTA		KAPHA	
NO	YES	NO	YES	NO	YES
Popcorn	Chia	Chia	Flax	Halva	Chia
	Flax	Sesame	Halva	Sesame	Flax*
	Halva	Tahini	Popcorn (no salt, buttered)	Tahini	Popcorn (no salt, no butter)
	Psyllium‡		Psyllium		Psyllium‡
	Pumpkin		Pumpkin*		Pumpkin*
	Sesame		Sunflower		Sunflower*
	Sunflower				
	Tahini				

VATA		PITTA		KAPHA	
NO	**YES**	**NO**	**YES**	**NO**	**YES**

SPICES

VATA NO	VATA YES	PITTA NO	PITTA YES	KAPHA NO	KAPHA YES
Caraway	**All spices are good!**	Ajwan	Basil (fresh)	Salt	**All spices are good!**
		Allspice	Black pepper*		
	Ajwan	Almond extract	Cardamom*		Ajwan
	Allspice	Anise	Cinnamon		Allspice
	Almond extract	Asafoetida (hing)	Coriander		Almond extract
	Anise	Basil (dry)	Cumin		Anise
	Asafoetida (hing)	Bay leaf	Dill		Asafoetida (hing)
	Basil	Caraway*	Fennel		Basil
	Bay leaf	Cayenne	Ginger (fresh)		Bay leaf
	Black pepper	Cloves	Mint		Black pepper
	Cardamom	Fenugreek	Neem leaves*		Caraway
	Cayenne*	Garlic	Orange peel*		Cardamom
	Cinnamon	Ginger (dry)	Parsley*		Cayenne
	Cloves	Mace	Peppermint		Cinnamon
	Coriander	Marjoram	Saffron		Cloves
	Cumin	Mustard seeds	Spearmint		Coriander
	Dill	Nutmeg	Turmeric		Cumin
	Fennel	Oregano	Vanilla*		Dill
	Fenugreek*	Paprika	Wintergreen		Fennel*
	Garlic	Pippali			Fenugreek
	Ginger	Poppy seeds			Garlic
	Mace	Rosemary			Ginger
	Marjoram	Sage			Mace
	Mint	Salt			Marjoram
	Mustard seeds	Savory			Mint
	Neem leaves	Star anise			Mustard seeds
	Nutmeg	Tarragon*			Neem leaves
	Orange peel	Thyme			Nutmeg
	Oregano				Orange peel
	Paprika				Oregano
	Parsley				Paprika
	Peppermint				Parsley
	Pippali				Peppermint
	Poppy seeds				Pippali
	Rosemary				Poppy seeds
	Saffron				Rosemary
	Sage				Saffron
	Salt				Sage
	Savory				Savory

VATA		PITTA		KAPHA	
NO	**YES**	**NO**	**YES**	**NO**	**YES**

SPICES

VATA		PITTA		KAPHA	
NO	YES	NO	YES	NO	YES
	Spearmint				Spearmint
	Star anise				Star anise
	Tarragon				Tarragon
	Thyme				Thyme
	Turmeric				Turmeric
	Vanilla				Vanilla*
	Wintergreen				Wintergreen

GRAINS[§]

VATA NO	VATA YES	PITTA NO	PITTA YES	KAPHA NO	KAPHA YES
Barley	Amaranth*	Bread (with yeast)	Amaranth	Bread (with yeast)	Amaranth*
Bread (with yeast)	Durham flour	Buckwheat	Barley	Oats (cooked)	Barley
Buckwheat	Oats (cooked)	Corn	Cereal, dry	Pancakes	Buckwheat
Cereals (cold, dry, or puffed)	Pancakes	Millet	Couscous	Pasta‡	Cereal (cold, dry, or puffed)
Corn	Quinoa	Muesli‡	Crackers	Quinoa	Corn
Couscous	Rice (all kinds)	Oats (dry)	Durham flour	Rice (brown, white)	Couscous
Crackers	Seitan (wheat meat)	Polenta‡	Granola	Rice cakes‡	Crackers
Granola	Sprouted wheat bread (Essene)	Quinoa	Oat bran	Spelt*	Durham flour*
Millet	Wheat	Rice (brown) ‡	Oats (cooked)	Wheat	Granola
Muesli		Rye	Pancakes		Millet
Oat bran			Pasta		Muesli
Oats (dry)			Rice (basmati, white, wild)		Oat bran
Pasta‡			Rice cakes		Oats (dry)
Polenta‡			Sago		Polenta
Rice cakes‡			Seitan (wheat meat)		Rice (basmati, wild)*
Rye			Spelt		Rye
Sago			Sprouted wheat bread (Essene)		Sago
Spelt			Tapioca		Seitan (wheat meat)
Tapioca			Wheat		Sprouted wheat bread (Essene)
Wheat bran			Wheat bran		Tapioca
					Wheat bran

[§]Always use suitable grains when 'generic' things are listed

VATA		PITTA		KAPHA	
NO	**YES**	**NO**	**YES**	**NO**	**YES**

OILS

VATA NO	VATA YES	PITTA NO	PITTA YES	KAPHA NO	KAPHA YES
Flax seed	**For internal & external use (most suitable at top of list):** Sesame Ghee Olive Most other oils **External use only:** Coconut Avocado	Almond Apricot Corn Safflower Sesame	**For internal & external use (most suitable at top of list):** Sunflower Ghee Canola Olive Soy Flax seed Primrose Walnut **External use only:** Avocado Coconut	Avocado Apricot Coconut Olive Primrose Safflower Sesame Soy Walnut	**For internal & external use in small amounts (most suitable at top of list):** Corn Canola Sunflower Ghee Almond Flax seed

FOOD SUPPLEMENTS

VATA NO	VATA YES	PITTA NO	PITTA YES	KAPHA NO	KAPHA YES
Barley green Brewer's yeast **Vitamins:** K	Aloe vera juice* Bee pollen Amino acids **Minerals:** Calcium, Copper, Iron, Magnesium, Zinc Royal jelly Spirolina Blue-green algae **Vitamins:** A, B1, B2., B6, B12, C, D, E, P (bioflavonoids) and Folic Acid	Amino acids Bee pollen‡ Royal jelly‡' **Minerals:** Copper, Iron **Vitamins:** B2, B6, C, E, P (bioflavonoids) and Folic Acid	Aloe vera juice Barley green Brewer's yeast **Minerals:** Calcium, Magnesium, Zinc Spirolina Blue-green algae **Vitamins:** A, B1, B12, D and K	**Minerals:** Potassium **Vitamins:** A, B1, B2, B12, D and E	Aloe vera juice Amino acids Barley green Bee pollen Brewer's yeast **Minerals:** Calcium, Copper, Iron, Magnesium, Zinc Royal jelly Spirolina Blue-green algae **Vitamins:** B6, C, P (bioflavonoids) and Folic acid

THE NATURAL QUALITIES OF FOOD

All foods have obvious and subtle qualities which affect your physical body and influence your doshas. Three contrasting pairs of natural qualities (see p. 32) which are most useful when first considering the effects of these qualities are: light–heavy; liquid/oily–drying; heating/hot–cooling/cold (the latter refers to both temperature and energetics – see pp. 52–3).

Select foods that have the natural qualities to give the results you desire. For instance, if your body is dry (signs include dry skin or hard dry stools), avoid drying foods and tastes (see pp. 54–5). You can change the qualities of food – for example, by steaming vegetables rather than eating them raw, or by adding an oil dressing. If there is too much heat in your body (one indication might be an itchy rash), cut down on "hot" foods, i.e. those that increase pitta.

Raw foods are often advocated to add roughage to the diet and if you suffer from constipation you may notice an initial improvement. But, in the long term, the roughness of too much raw food may increase vata and so contribute to the constipation.

Natural qualities

Heavy	Milk – Wheat – Brown rice – Fish – Red meat – Sesame oil
Light	Mung beans – Basmati rice – Leafy vegetables – Chicken – Apple – Sunflower oil
Cooling/Cold	Milk – Sunflower oil – Wheat – Apple – Ice cream – Coconut
Heating/Hot	Fish – Sesame oil – Onions – Eggs – Meat – Chilli
Oily	Most nuts – Fish – Eggs
Drying	Many vegetables – Pears – Millet

Foods and their Qualities

The table gives examples of qualities of some of the foods we eat. We may only become aware of the effects of qualities in foods, after we have been eating them regularly for some time. Even then we may not always relate the changes in our bodies to those foods.

ALTERING FOOD'S
NATURAL QUALITIES

The natural qualities of foods can be changed in obvious ways, such as cooking, but also in subtle ways – for example, through the attitudes of those involved in growing, preparing and marketing food.

Cooking alters the qualities of food. Cold foods can be made hot; dry foods made moist or oily. For instance, the qualities of muesli with cold milk are dry, cold, and heavy – qualities which increase vata and kapha. Oats made into porridge are a more suitable breakfast if you are following a vata-pacifying diet, because you have imparted moisture and warmth to the oats.

Although foods do not have a prana rating, lack of prana in your food will lead to low vitality and eventually fatigue (see pp. 50). Modern methods of production, processing, packaging, and distribution reduce the prana in food and microwave cooking may destroy it. Some processed foods contain substances to please the senses. Such substances, rather than adding nutrients that the body can use for healthy tissue building, may distort the body's natural intelligence and lead to ama. They may even make the mind crave inappropriate foods.

Aurveda teaches that subtle influences can affect us, and so the attitudes and emotions of those who prepare food will be imparted to it, so it is best to eat food cooked with love. Food cooked in anger may subtly upset the digestion. The subtle qualities of many processed foods are not known, nor are all the long-term effects of their habitual use. Any food taken in inappropriate circumstances or in excess will be "bad". What is inappropriate or excessive will vary for each person and their current doshic balance. Even "healthy" foods can be misused and create ama: raw honey in small quantities is beneficial, but cooked honey cannot always be assimilated and will create ama. We cannot always escape these influences, but we should be aware of them so that we can select, as far as possible, fresh foods that have been subjected to a minimum of commercial processing.

BAD INFLUENCES

It is likely that some manufactured products, which are designed to replace foods currently considered "bad" for you (such as sugar and butter), may not be made into healthy tissues; and if they are not expelled from the body they will result in ama and blocked channels.

COMBINING FOODS

According to the teachings in Ayurveda, particular foods should not be combined because they put a strain on the digestive process. All substances have their own tastes, energetics, and post-digestive effects (see pp. 52–3), which influence how the food is digested and utilized. The different digestive demands of foods eaten at the same meal may strain the digestive system and deplete agni. Such foods, when eaten at separate meals, may, however, be properly digested and so add to your wellbeing.

The antagonistic qualities of foods that are not ideally combined may be reduced by one-pot cooking (see below right).

Unfortunately, the rules about food combining cannot be simply set out as a comprehensive table that says, "Do not eat this with that". As with all things in Ayurveda, everything is relative and general rules have to be applied individually. If your digestion is poor you need to take more care about combining foods than if you have a strong digestive capacity.

It is essential that you learn to understand not only what your body is telling you but also the state of your agni or digestive capabilities, which will vary from time to time. You may already know that some foods do not agree with you, or that sometimes they do and on other occasions they do not. Your own observation is a good teacher.

Some General Rules about Food Combining

- Do not mix foods that have different energetic characteristics (see pp. 52–3) at the same meal. For example, do not mix milk, which is cooling, with fish or meat, which are both heating.
- Do not eat cooked and raw foods at the same meal. Raw foods are harder to digest.
- Do not eat fruit with other foods.
- Do not mix milk and yogurt.
- Do not mix milk and yogurt with sour or citrus fruits, fish, meat, eggs, nightshades (potatoes, tomatoes, or aubergine), or starches.
- Do not mix different types of protein, such as eggs and cheese.

One-pot Cooking

If you cook together foods of different tastes, energetics, or post-digestive effects (see pp. 52–3) in one pot, such as a casserole, you can substantially reduce the adverse effects of incompatible food combinations. The foods are formed into one "juice" that acts upon the digestive system. One-pot cooking is a good way to help settle the irregularities of excess vata on digestion (see p. 162 for the recipe for kitcheri).

QUANTITY OF FOOD

How much food you eat should primarily be related to your ability to digest it. You should neither eat too much or too little. Think of the digestion process as a fire. A fire reduced to embers will go out if you add a large amount of fuel. But a few, light kindling sticks will ignite, increasing the fire and allowing further fuel to be burnt. Likewise a fire that receives too little fuel will go out. Always aim to eat the amount that will restore or maintain a steady digestion.

Your digestive capacity is related to your constitution. Vata types tend to undereat or eat erratically, which makes digestion irregular; kaphas tend to overeat, which slows down digestion. Pitta types are more likely to have good digestive strength, though too much hot spicy food will make their digestive fire burn too fiercely (see pp. 76-7).

Other factors that determine the right quantity to eat include age, level of activity, occupation, the season, and time of day. If you are under-eating or over-eating, do not suddenly change the quantity of food you eat, but regularly eat a little more or less over a period of weeks.

The advice in Aurvedic texts about the optimum amount to eat at one meal varies between one third to one half of the stomach's capacity of solids, one quarter to one third for fluids, leaving one quarter to one third empty. Discover what suits you. In general, vata types should drink more fluids than kaphas. Fluids help in the digestion and absorption of food;

space is needed for the proper mixing with the digestive juices. Generally, when you are ill, you should eat a little less than you are hungry for.

It is vital to eat the right amount of individual foods. According to Ayurveda, a suitable diet is 40-60 per cent grains, 10-20 per cent protein, and 30-50 per cent vegetables and fruit. Adjust this according to your constitution. Kaphas could benefit by eating at least 40 per cent of their diet as vegetables, because they are generally light, whereas vatas should have more grains than vegetables. About 10 per cent of the diet for all doshas should be fruit, but not eaten with other foods.

Eating meat

Ayurveda does not recommend meat as a regular part of the diet because it is heavy to digest. However, it can be eaten when necessary to strengthen the body, prepared in a way that assists its digestion, such as in soups or casseroles.

THE IMPORTANCE OF PLACE

The quality of, and the qualities in, food are influenced by the place where the food is grown and produced. Try to obtain food that has come from a wholesome environment – for example, from a non-polluted place with fertile soil, and grown by people who enjoy producing food.

When *Charaka Samhita* was written about 3000 years ago, most food would have been grown and prepared within the community that ate it. Nowadays, we need to consider the effects of foods brought in from other parts of the world as well as the effects on the subtle energies in food caused by modern methods of food production. The conditions in which animals live and die have a subtle influence on the products we consume from their carcasses. We may also ingest with our food residues of chemicals used in current agricultural methods. The subtle qualities of food grown in a naturally rich soil will differ from the qualities of food grown in a depleted soil with the aid of chemicals. The subtle energies of such chemicals may impair the normal functions of the doshas as well as creating ama.

The climate of your local environment should guide your decision when selecting foods. For example, if you live in an arid climate, foods with rough or sharp qualities will be antagonistic to your body. So, too, would cold, heavy foods eaten in a cold, damp place.

Climate and geographical locations are interlinked and have doshic qualities. Places at sea level and places with cold, wet climates have strong kapha qualities. Places at altitude and places with a low rainfall or a lot of wind have strong vata qualities. Sunshine brings pitta qualities. The ideal climate is a place such as Hawaii, where no doshic quality is excessive. If you move to a different environment your body will need time to adapt, and you may need to take extra measures to compensate. For example, moving to the altitude and dryness of New Mexico after a life by the ocean in California may increase your vata. If so, you should adapt your diet and oil your skin more often.

The Ideal Climate

The tropical islands of Hawaii are blessed with a balanced climate in which neither vata, pitta, nor kapha are excessive.

THE SEASONS OF THE YEAR

The natural progress through the stages of life (see p. 10), the changes in the seasons, and time of day are external factors over which you have no control. They all have qualities that can affect your health. If you understand these qualities then you are in a position to reduce possible adverse effects by incorporating the opposite qualities into your lifestyle. To some extent you already do this when you wear a warm coat in winter, or a sun hat in summer. By understanding the cycles of these external factors in relation to the qualities of VPK, you are in a better position to plan your lifestyle and diet to match your doshic needs (see also p. 61).

Adjust your diet to your stage of life, especially in the vata-age (55 and over)

when you should eat raw and dry foods only occasionally. Also adjust your diet according to the seasons because of their effect on the doshas. In winter, you eat warmer and heavier foods than in summer, unless a constitutional or doshic imbalance indicates the contrary. In general, salads are more appropriate in the summer to cool pitta; ginger tea in winter to warm vata and kapha.

VPK and the Seasons

A dosha is naturally increased during the season that has similar qualities. You should take these into account in your eating habits and especially during the season which aggravates your predominant dosha.

VATA

The vata season is autumn and early winter. The sap withdraws from the leaves, which dry and blow away in the wind.

PITTA

Pitta energy increases in late spring with the increase in temperature and throughout the summer, the hottest part of the year and the longer sunny days.

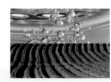

KAPHA

The coldest part of winter when nature is frozen and solid is the season when kapha is naturally disturbed. The liquid quality of kapha is experienced during early spring with the melting of winter's ice, and the rising of the sap.

TIME OF DAY

The time you eat your meals also affects the doshic qualities of the meals. It is advisable not to eat late at night, and to leave at least two hours before going to bed to allow for digestion. If you have a kapha constitution or are following a kapha-pacifying diet, remember that eating at kapha times of the day will increase the heaviness of eating. Breakfast is not generally recommended for those with a kapha constitution for the same reason, but always take your individual circumstances into account. If you are following a kapha-pacifying diet, eat breakfast before 7 am and do not have your evening meal after 7 pm.

People with pitta constitutions should aim to have their main meal around midday when the sun, pitta, and agni are at their highest. If you have excess pitta you may be more critical until you eat.

The main vata time is early morning. Late afternoon and early evening are also vata times, the "autumn" of the day. If you are dealing with excess vata or managing a vata constitution then the most important thing is to eat at regular times. Breakfast around 8 am, lunch at 12.30 pm, and an evening meal around 6 pm is probably the best for you. Sometimes, however, you may need to eat a smaller meals four or even five times a day.

Daily Rhythms

The rhythms of the day have their own qualities of VPK. The beginning of the day, when movement and activity begin, is the main vata time. The middle part of the day is the main pitta time. Slowing down and sleep come at the end of the day, the principal kapha time. Each of the three doshas' energies peak to a lesser extent at other times. For example, the other pitta time is midnight. An ailment whose symptoms are worse at midday or midnight is likely to be the result of excess pitta.

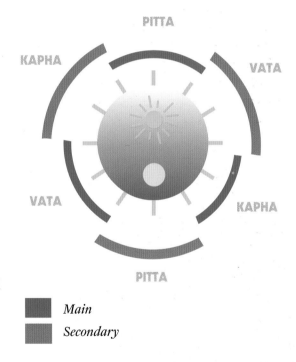

Main

Secondary

GENERAL RULES
ABOUT DIET

The principles outlined on the preceding pages of this chapter will help guide you toward eating the appropriate amount, at appropriate times, of the right kinds of foods that do not disturb your doshas or agni. You are aiming to eat foods that: are compatible and easily digested, absorbed, and assimilated; provide your body's requirements for building tissues; and satisfy your senses and mind.

All the guidelines for choosing foods need adjustment to suit individual doshic requirements. However, some rules for good eating apply to almost everyone – and most of them are common sense.

THE CONSUMER

The individual factors to consider in order to assess the right diet for you are:

- Your constitution (see pp. 38–41)
- Any current doshic imbalances (see pp. 62–3)
- Age (see p. 10)
- The strength of your digestion (see pp. 49–50)
- Your lifestyle

Iced Water

Iced water inhibits digestion, which leads to the production of ama and disturbances of the doshas. As Dr. Vasant Lad says, "Ice is not nice".

- Is your desire to eat coming from your mind or body? Eat only when your body is naturally hungry.
- Do not eat until your stomach has finished working on the previous meal.
- Do not eat when you are very emotional, angry, worried, or upset, as this disturbs agni.
- Avoid incompatible food combinations.
- Do not over-eat or under-eat.
- Eat wholesome foods that are pleasing to the senses.
- Avoid foods you don't like, as they won't satisfy the mind.
- Avoid under-cooked, over-cooked, or burnt foods.
- Do not eat unripe or over-ripe fruits.
- Avoid eating leftovers, or habitually eating reheated foods, as they will have little prana.
- Do not drink iced water before, during, or immediately after a meal. Coldness shocks the body; it also inhibits agni and causes ama. If you wish to drink with your meals, have drinks that are warm, or a small amount of wine, which can aid digestion.
- Eat in congenial company or pleasant silence.
- When eating, do not talk too much, watch TV, listen to the radio, or read. These activities distract your senses from the food you are eating and from observing and responding to the promptings of your body.
- Stop eating when your body is satiated.

CONSIDERING CHANGES TO YOUR DIET

Deciding on a diet that is right for you is often the hardest part about using Ayurvedic principles. There is no easy answer, but it is important not to make quick or dramatic changes. This gives you time to learn about the doshic classification of foods (see pp. 133–43) and to become more aware of the effects your current diet may have. Then, if you make one small change at a time, you will experience for yourself how foods affect your wellbeing.

The changes may involve eating different foods, different combinations of foods, or preparing foods by different methods. If you propose using different food items then you need to consider ways that these can be incorporated into your diet. Generally, it is not easy to give up foods you eat habitually, and you will find it hard initially to think of suitable alternatives. Your digestive system will have adapted to the foods you eat, and sudden or big changes will act as a shock to the system and may lead to digestive or other problems. Make gradual changes over weeks and months.

Pacifying the Doshas

The lists below summarize the main rules for each dosha-pacifying diet. In addition, you should choose foods from the YES column of the food charts to pacify that dosha (see pp. 133–43) and avoid those in the NO column. Occasional lapses will not hurt, it is what you do habitually that matters.

PACIFYING PITTA

YES	NO
Eat salads	Avoid sour, salty,
Use only cooling	spicy foods
herbs and spices	Avoid alcohol
	Avoid meat
	Avoid fried foods

PACIFYING VATA

YES	NO
Use spices	Avoid raw foods
Eat heavy, warm,	Avoid dry foods
oily, moist foods	Avoid leafy
Have regular meal	vegetables
times	Avoid cold foods
	Avoid frozen
	foods

PACIFYING KAPHA

YES	NO
Eat plenty of	Avoid sweet and
vegetables	salty foods
Eat salads	Avoid dairy
Eat dry, light foods	products
Use spices	Avoid fried foods
	Avoid frozen
	foods

WHICH PACIFYING DIET?

Once you know your constitution (see pp. 38–41), then you can select foods that tend to pacify your predominant dosha, since this is the dosha that tends to increase most easily. Pacifying your predominant dosha allows you to gain increased vitality by producing a better balance of doshic energy than exists in your constitutional balance. Before you follow a pacifying diet for your predominant dosha, check your other doshas are in balance (see p. 63).

If you have a duo-type constitution, you need a diet that does not increase either of your predominant doshas. For example, if you have a pitta–kapha constitution you should select foods that will not excessively increase pitta or kapha. In addition, you will have to make seasonal adjustments, so that a pitta-pacifying diet will be appropriate in the pitta season (summer) and a kapha-pacifying diet in winter.

However, if one of your non-predominant doshas is excessive (see p. 63), then follow a diet that pacifies the excessive dosha until that

Selection of Diet

Look at the lists below to identify your doshic state and then follow the appropriate diet indicated at the top of the column. For instance, if you have a vata constitution with increased pitta, follow a pitta-pacifying diet. To discover which foods suit which diets, see the food charts on pages 133–43.

Vata-pacifying Diet for:
- Vata constitution with no increased dosha
- Vata constitution with increased vata
- Pitta constitution with increased vata (but do not increase pitta)
- Kapha constitution with increased vata (but do not increase kapha)

Kapha-pacifying Diet for:
- Kapha constitution with no increased dosha
- Kapha constitution with increased kapha
- Vata constitution with increased kapha (but do not increase vata)
- Pitta constitution with increased kapha (but do not increase pitta)

Pitta-pacifying Diet for:
- Pitta constitution with no increased dosha
- Pitta constitution with increased pitta
- Vata constitution with increased pitta (but do not increase vata)
- Kapha constitution with increased pitta (but do not increase kapha)

dosha has returned to your constitutional norm. At the same time, try to avoid increasing your predominant dosha. Follow the advice given for people with duo-type constitutions above. For example, if you have a pitta constitution but your vata is excessive, follow a vata-pacifying diet, but avoid eating too many foods that increase pitta. Monitor the signs of excess doshas in your mind and body (see p. 63) and when the excess vata has been eliminated, follow a pitta-pacifying diet.

As your understanding of Ayurveda grows, so too will your confidence in preparing balanced meals. Remember, food is to be enjoyed so do not let anxieties about getting it right spoil your meals. Strong digestion, clear perceptions, good company, and fresh food cooked with love allow you to experience the natural deliciousness of food and satisfaction in body and mind.

Preparing Food for a Family

If everyone in your household follows the same dosha-pacifying diet then whoever organizes the meals can plan menus around the appropriate ingredients and principles. But if you all have differing doshic requirements, planning an appropriate menu can be complicated. Do not try to change the meals until you feel familiar with the general principles – providing a diet suitable for everyone will seem impossible to start with unless you cook separate meals!

Before you make any changes, classify the foods you buy into vata, pitta, and kapha. If you intend to pacify two doshas, look for items in the food charts (see pp. 133–43) that apply to both, and substitute these where possible. There is no easy solution, but moderation and individual use of condiments and garnishes will help. The selection of suitable side dishes in Indian cooking is a very useful way to make a tri-doshically balanced meal. Another way is to use one-pot cooking as often as possible (see p. 146).

Garnishes

You can add garnishes individually according to dosha: for example, pittas can add coriander leaves, mint, raita (yogurt-based condiment), or shredded coconut; vatas and kaphas can add fresh ground pepper or ginger pickle.

FOOD PROFILES

Vicky's Diet (p. 112)

Vicky is a vegetarian with a vata constitution and a vata imbalance. She also has toxins due to her incapacity to digest fully improper food combinations. She should eat regularly and simply, and in particular avoid raw and dry foods. She should select foods from the vata-pacifying (YES) column of the food charts (see pp. 133–43).

Giles's Diet (p. 81)

Giles has a kapha constitution and his favourite foods tend to increase kapha. He should avoid fried, dairy, and sugary foods, and select foods from the kapha-pacifying (YES) column of the food charts (see pp. 133–43).

Martin's Diet (pp. 105, 182–3)

Martin has a pitta constitution and excess pitta. His current pitta-increasing diet should be altered to reduce pitta. He should avoid fried foods, alcohol, and coffee, and cut down on meat, especially red meat. He should select foods from the pitta-pacifying (YES) column of the food charts (see pp. 133–43).

VICKY'S DIET

Meal	Summary of Diet from Weekly Diet Record	Suggestions to Adjust Diet to Help Pacify Vata
Breakfast	Oat-based muesli with dried fruit, cold milk, and yogurt. Boiled egg with toast. Coffee.	Cooked oats. Eat fruits separately, and soak dried fruit. Do not mix milk and yogurt. Scrambled eggs.
Lunch	Salads of lettuce, tomatoes, and cucumber, with quiche or cheese and baked potato.	Vegetables sautéed or steamed. Replace hard cheese with cottage cheese. Use freshly ground black pepper. Eat sweet potato or cook white potato with oil and spices. Whole wheat macaroni and sauce. Lassi.
Evening meal	Lentil, bean, or nut dishes with salad or vegetables. Rice pudding. Yogurt, cheesecake, or fruit.	Limit use of legumes to mung beans, some soya products, and red lentils. Use cumin, coriander, and fennel in bean dishes to help reduce gases and their tendency to cause constipation. Try kitcheri with bread or chapattis and pickle. Have lassi in place of yogurt. Eat fruit as snacks on its own.
Snacks	Rice cakes, chocolate. Occasional alcoholic drink, apple juice, carbonated water.	Sweet fruits. Wholewheat or oatmeal cookies with spices, e.g. cinnamon and ginger. Ginger tea, hot spiced milk. Small amount of alcohol to stimulate the appetite.

GILES'S DIET

Meal	Summary of Diet from Weekly Diet Record	Suggestions to Adjust Diet to Help Pacify Kapha
Breakfast	Sugar-coated cereals with cold milk. Toast with butter and jam. Coffee. At weekends, a cooked breakfast with fried bacon, eggs, tomatoes, and bread.	A light breakfast before 7.30 am of muesli (without wheat) and drink juice, such as apple, instead of cold milk.
Lunch	Cheese sandwiches or pizza or scampi and chips. Danish pastry or other dessert. Beer.	Soups or salads, but with very little oil-based dressing. Lassi.
Evening meal	Pies, e.g. steak and kidney, or roast beef or chicken, with boiled or roasted vegetables. Likes dessert most days, sometimes with cream.	Freshwater fish or chicken, steamed vegetables. Dishes with basmati rice or millet. Baked apples with clove and cinnamon.
Snacks	Chocolate biscuits, tea, squashes, and fizzy drinks.	Fruit. Apple juice, grape juice, herb teas.

MARTIN'S DIET

Meal	Summary of Diet from Weekly Diet Record	Suggestions to Adjust Diet to Help Pacify Pitta
Breakfast	If away from home, fried breakfast. Coffee. At home, coffee and skips breakfast. More coffee and whatever is to hand on arrival at the office.	Have breakfast. Oatmeal, shredded wheat, toast, or pancakes.
Lunch	Sandwich unless having business lunch often at Italian or Mexican restaurants. Wine.	Stick to the salad bars. Do not have alcohol.
Evening meal	A large variety of different foods, often steaks. Likes tasty sauces, especially those with tomatoes, garlic, onions, or chilli. Wine and liqueurs.	Rice dishes and pasta. Have herb sauces in place of spicy ones. Reduce the amount of alcohol.
Snacks	Salty snacks. Coffee. Spirits.	Sweet fruits. Cold drinks, dilute sweet fruit juices, mint tea.

In Western cookery, spices and herbs are used in small amounts, mainly for flavouring. Ayurveda has a wider approach. In addition to adding deliciousness to food, spices and herbs stimulate the appetite and aid digestion, by increasing secretion of digestive juices, by increasing absorption in the intestines, by reducing gases, and by influencing the doshas. There are some spices that should be in every home. If you have not tried cooking with spices before, the ten that follow will give you a good foundation.

The energetics (see pp. 52–3) of each herb and spice is shown – either heating or cooling. The spices also affect the doshas, either by increasing (I) or pacifying (P); the effect is given in the order on V, P, and then K.

P = pacifies I = increases
* = Pacifies unless used in excess

Nutmeg

Heating P I P
Helps with absorption. Is calming.
Use ground and sparingly.

Black Pepper

Heating P* I P
Increases appetite and agni. Aids the digestion of dairy products. Too much will cause irritation and dryness. Use freshly ground.

Cinnamon

Heating P P* P
Stimulates agni. Is less likely than ginger to affect pitta. Use powdered, sticks, or pieces.

Clove

Heating P I P
Stimulates agni and helps with absorption. Use whole or ground.

Cumin

Slightly heating P P* P

Pacifies vata and kapha without increasing pitta unless used in excess. Helps reduce ama and gases and tones the digestive system. Use the seeds whole or powdered.

Ginger

Heating P I P

Highly regarded in Ayurveda. Works on all tissues, especially digestive and respiratory. Stimulates agni, helps relieve gases and constipation, and vata or kapha indigestion. Do not use if there is high pitta, temperature, bleeding conditions, or ulcers. Use root, either fresh or dried. Fresh is best for vata and dried for kapha.

Fennel

Cooling P P P

Increases agni without increasing pitta. Helps prevent gases. Either chew the seeds after a meal or add to vegetables that end to produce gas when cooking. Use seeds, whole or powdered.

Coriander

Cooling P P P

Helps counteract the effects of pungent foods. Eases gases and generally tones the digestive system. Use whole seed or powdered. Use leaves as a garnish.

Cardamom

Heating P P* P

Kindles agni without increasing pitta, unless used in excess. Reduces the mucus-forming effects of dairy products. Use in coffee to counter some effects of caffeine. Use powdered or whole seeds.

Turmeric

Heating P* P* P

Strengthens digestion and generally improves metabolism. Aids the digestion of protein. The root is used ground. Widely used in Indian cooking, giving dishes a yellow color. It can stain clothes, work surfaces, and china.

DRINKS FROM HERBS AND SPICES

Be flexible in your use of herbs and spices; select them according to your needs and to the seasons. If you have a lot of heat in your body (for example, those with a pitta constitution, or excess pitta), then hot, pungent spices will not be good for you. However, you can use black pepper, cardamom, cinnamon, and turmeric in moderation (see pp. 158–9). Coriander and fennel are cooling and therefore beneficial for you. People with a naturally cold make-up (those with vata or kapha constitutons) can use all the spices. The heating ones, such as ginger, black pepper, and clove are especially useful in the winter months. Whatever your constitution, make sure your kitchen contains a selection of spices.

A good way for you to become familiar with the taste and effects of spices and herbs is to make drinks from them. Enjoy making your own teas according to your specific requirements, and drink them as alternatives to the usual tea or coffee. Here are some recipes for various drinks which you can try. The amounts given are a guide; adjust them to your own preferences.

Ginger Tea

This very warming drink can be made with fresh or dried ginger. For one mug, use EITHER about a teaspoon of grated or finely chopped fresh ginger OR a flat quarter teaspoon of dried ginger. Then add boiling water. Let it steep for five minutes. Strain before drinking. Add honey or brown sugar if desired.

Heating Drink

A mixture of five ground spices, this is easiest to prepare in small batches and then store in a jar. The proportions are one part black pepper and four parts each of cardamom, cinnamon, clove, and ginger. Experiment to see if these are your favoured proportions, but beware of overdoing the black pepper or it will dominate. Mix these together until they are well blended. You can make a simple tea using a flat quarter teaspoon of the mixture per mug and then adding hot water; let it brew for a few minutes. Add honey or brown sugar if desired when the drink has brewed. You could also add a couple of pinches of this mixture to a cup of ordinary tea – just for a change.

Cooling Drink

This tea is cooling in its energetic properties rather than its temperature and is good for all constitutional types. It is made with equal proportions of the seeds of cumin, coriander, and fennel. Allow one teaspoon of seeds per mug. Add hot water and allow to brew before straining and drinking. An easy way to make this tea is to mix a batch of the seeds, store them in a jar, and use a mesh tea ball for the seeds when you need a drink.

Spiced Milk

To a small mug, add generous pinches (such as a quarter teaspoon) of ground ginger, cardamom, and cinnamon, and a small pinch of nutmeg. Fill with hot milk. When it has cooled slightly, add honey to taste if desired. Stir well. This makes a good bedtime drink, soothing vata and encouraging sleep. You can try different proportions or spices, such as clove in place of the cinnamon.

Lassi

This drink changes the natural properties of yogurt and is recommended at the end of a meal to help digestion. Adjust the spices according to your constitution. Vata and kapha types could have cumin, ginger, cardamom, and/or black pepper. The black pepper will give it a kick, so use with care. Pitta types should use coriander or fennel. Blend equal parts of yogurt and water and add, in total, a half to one teaspoon of your chosen spices. Mix in a small amount of sweetener, such as honey or maple syrup, if you so desire.

KITCHERI

Kitcheri is a one-pot dish made with rice, beans, spices, and often with vegetables. You can adapt the spices and vegetables to your tastes and doshic needs. Nutritious and very easy to digest, kitcheri is recommended for irregular digestion (see pp. 76–7). If you use rice in the proportion of two to one with beans, the amount of protein available to the body will be more than if the rice and beans are eaten separately. If you have low digestive strength, kitcheri should be cooked to the consistency of mashed potatoes.

Ingredients:

Oil	Spices
Basmati rice	Split yellow mung beans
Water	Vegetables

You can vary your choice of spices and also the amounts you use. Initially, try half a teaspoon per person of cumin, coriander, and fennel seeds and half a teaspoon of turmeric powder. This will make a dish suitable for all constitutional types. For a warmer kitcheri, add ginger.

For each person, allow a handful of Basmati rice (about 1oz or 30g) and half as much split yellow mung beans. Mix rice and beans together and wash in cold water.

162

In a pan, melt one teaspoon of ghee or oil and add the seeds. Cook for a minute. Then add the ground spices and washed grains and beans, stirring them to coat with the oil. Add sufficient hot water to cover the grains and beans by about 2in (5cm), bring to the boil and simmer gently, stirring occasionally. Make sure the pan does not become dry and add more water as required.

Add diced vegetables if you like – root ones with the rice, and leaf or softer ones nearer the end of the cooking time. Select vegetables that are appropriate for your doshas (see food charts on pp. 133–43). The dish is cooked when the rice is soft and a grain easily squashes between thumb and forefinger. Most of the liquid should have been absorbed or evaporated. Kitcheri can be served with chapattis. Pitta types could use coriander leaves as a garnish. Vata and kapha types can have some pickle.

A One-pot Dish

Kitcheri, a rice and bean dish, is nutritious and easy both to prepare and to digest. As a note of caution, kitcheri may cause constipation if eaten regularly. Adding diced vegetables will prevent this (see main text).

EATING VEGETABLES

Vegetables should form 20 to 40 per cent of your diet. If you have a kapha constitution eat plenty of vegetables because generally they are light.

Ayurveda does not recommend eating raw vegetables because they are rough and hard to digest. However, they are fine on occasions if your digestion is good. Salads are better in summer than winter as they pacify pitta but increase vata. If you are in the vata age (over 55) eat salads only occasionally, and with an oil dressing. Raw tomatoes disturb all the doshas, so avoid eating them regularly. Raw vegetables take longer to digest than cooked ones so try not to mix them in the same meal.

As far as possible, buy organic vegetables that are in season and locally grown or, even better, eat ones you or your friends have grown with love.

When deciding how to cook your vegetables, think of the qualities the cooking will add. If you stir fry or sauté vegetables, the oil will increase kapha and pitta but not vata. If the vegetables are crunchy, they will still tend to increase vata and be harder to digest. Steaming vegetables preserves their flavour as well as making them easier to digest. Potatoes are vata-genic and baking dries them further. The "jacket" adds another vata quality – roughness – and is hard to digest. So enjoy baked potatoes when your vata is not aggravated. You can

reduce the vata-genic qualities of potatoes by cooking them in the way suggested below.

Cooking diced vegetables with spices in a small amount of water is suitable for all doshic types. You can experiment with different combinations of spices and vegetables. Select one or more vegetables that are suitable for your doshic requirements (see food charts on pp. 133–43). Wash them and cut them into bite-size pieces. A little creative chopping adds to the visual appearance of the dish.

Use a large, heavy-bottomed, preferably stainless steel, shallow pan with a lid. Over a moderate heat, add 2–3 tablespoons of oil – do not overdo the oil if you have a kapha constitution. Then add your chosen spices. Select them to benefit your agni and doshas (see pp. 158–9) but also for their aromas and flavours. If spices are new to you, start with a half a teaspoon each of cumin seeds and mustard seeds – black mustard seeds are stronger than yellow ones.

If you use whole seeds, put them in the oil and cook them until they begin to pop. Then add your selection of ground spices (e.g. turmeric or fennel), and cook for a moment before adding the chopped vegetables.

Stir the vegetables for a minute to coat them in the spices and oil, and then add a small amount of water.

Bring to the boil, put the lid on, and turn down to a low to moderate heat until the vegetables are cooked. The amount of water needed depends on the type of vegetables you are cooking – root vegetables need more than softer vegetables such as courgettes – and the size you have cut them. Essentially, the aim is to leave no excess water when the vegetables are ready to eat (you can add more water if necessary during the cooking).

Kitcheri and vegetables cooked in this way, with garnishes suitable for your doshas (see p. 155) and chapattis or other flat bread followed by a glass of lassi (see p. 161) makes an easily digestible, nutritious, tasty, and inexpensive meal that is balanced for all doshas.

Fresh Vegetables

Enjoy the flavours and freshness of recently picked, locally grown vegetables. Select ones that are suitable for your doshas.

7. MIND AND
EMOTIONS

यद्गुणं चाभीक्ष्णं पुरुषमनुवर्तते सत्त्वं
तत्सत्त्वमेवीपदिशन्ति मुनयी बहुल्यानुशयात् ॥

According to the Acharyas the mind of a person is qualified on the basis of the type of his repeated
action; it is so because that quality must be predominating in him.
(Charaka Samhita *Chapter 8: 6*)

The perfect human being experiences no disturbances in energy flow, since all levels function in harmony. Body, senses, mind, consciousness, and those parts of us that are beyond description, together express the wonder and beauty of life. Disturbances at any level can affect health.

Your body, the most accessible part of your being, is a reflection of the less tangible parts of you; an expression of all your experiences and how you have assimilated them. Your body requires proper care, which may be lacking as the everyday mind continuously seeks fresh experiences.

Ayurveda teaches that the everyday mind has qualities and therefore must be physical, though more subtle than the body. Like the body, it has to be balanced to function properly. The mind is faster and more demanding than the body, and thus harder to bring under proper control. Ahamkara (see pp. 18–21) may identify with itself so strongly that the link with your inner wisdom appears lost, along with the unity of being part, with all other, of cosmic consciousness.

According to Ayurveda, all illnesses are psychosomatic. Both mind and body are involved and should be considered in restoring health and maintaining wellness, as benefits at one level of being will be reflected at other levels.

The Everyday Mind
Your everyday mind and ordinary intellect link your senses and actions. They regulate the interfaces between your external and internal environments, and the changes that happen internally. Your mind pervades your whole body.

Everything we experience on the physical level comes via one or more of our senses. All our perceptions have qualities related to VPK. This is most easily demonstrated with taste (see pp. 54–5), but it applies to other sense as well. A violent film, for example, has pitta-aggravating qualities. Tickling enhances vata.

You cannot be conscious of every sensation you receive, but remember that the qualities of sensations may increase your doshas according to the principle of "like increases like". So limit your exposure to those qualities you do not want, but enjoy those that will add to your wellbeing.

The clarity of your mind is affected by how you use it. Like a muscle, it needs the right kind of use and neither too little nor too much. Pitta types tend to have sharp, quick minds – they love reading and doing mental puzzles – which they easily overuse. Kaphas are slower thinkers who generally would benefit from more mental stimulation than they are used to. Vatas dream up projects, and have new schemes every time you meet them. They need to concentrate on one or two of their sound ideas, in order to move forward into the planning and execution stages.

Whatever your constitution, too much intellectual work aggravates pitta. Too much sensory stimulation, such as watching TV and VDUs disturbs vata. Boring, repetitive tasks dull the mind and increase kapha. What is "too much" depends on the individual and their current circumstances.

We usually eat sweet foods when we crave comfort. Comfort foods often have kapha qualities in both their taste and texture. As you heal your emotional hurts, use senses other than taste to give yourself comfort and nurturing, such as the company of friends, an aromatherapy massage, or relaxing music.

Sensory Experience

The smell of a rose is sweet, a quality associated with kapha.

UNDERSTANDING EMOTIONS

Those who express their emotions often feel that this is better than suppressing them. Ayurveda says it is better to understand emotions rather than suppressing or expressing them. In understanding them, they are transformed and released. If you are angry, look behind the events that triggered your anger. Then look behind the anger. Behind anger, or fear, and other negative emotions there is usually a hurt. A deep, deep hurt that you have tried to silence.

Deep unresolved emotions can disturb the mind. They suck your energy to parts seemingly beyond your control or manifest themselves as illness in the body. You may not be able to resolve all emotional pains as they occur, particularly if an event overwhelms you or if emotional traumas happen before you have the maturity to digest and assimilate them.

The body and mind have powerful survival instincts which can override conscious processes. Phobias, or less clearly labelled but equally inappropriate and habitual actions, may be behaviours set up as defence or denial mechanisms. The problem of the phobia diverts attention from the unresolved hurt. Energy is used to maintain the denial or avoidance rather than for creating wellness.

The resolution of pain releases the energy used in denial or avoidance, or that manifests as physical symptoms. Take time to resolve your emotional pains. It is a process of small steps forward, and some seemingly backward until at the right time you experience the change inside. The change comes through understanding, acceptance, and letting go.

Contacting your inner wisdom (see p. 174) helps when you are trying to resolve your deep emotional hurts. Observe your body and mind as you enquire about what you are experiencing. Ask yourself why you are experiencing this. Let your connection with your inner wisdom grow, and let it show you your unique way to understanding. Open yourself to the inner guidance that is always ready to reveal the opportunities you truly need. You have to have awareness to see them. Then it is vital to act upon them.

Start by seeing coincidences or synchronistic events in your life. Ask yourself simple questions as if a wise person were listening to you. Immediate or direct answers are not necessarily given. As you go about your daily life something may happen that seems coincidental. Someone may say something or give you a book that has something that strikes a chord in you, or you meet someone who opens new ideas about your internal questions. The circumstances of these coincidences are unique to each individual, and easily dismissed by the logical mind. However, use common sense and discrimination, but do not miss the quiet way in which the guidance comes. This gets easier with practice, and in time you will find yourself becoming more and more in flow with your life.

You may be guided to seek support from someone as you come to understand and acknowledge all you experienced, how you reacted at the time, and how you have been affected. When this inner acknowledgement comes, you will feel the force that held the pain dissolving. You are ready to assimilate the good squeezed from the pain.

COMING THROUGH PAIN

Emotional hurts can be very painful and you may feel unwilling to face that pain. Coming through emotional pain is one way to release it. It is generally acknowledged, for example, that the only way to resolve the pain of bereavement is to come through it. If the grieving process stops before the pain is resolved then different psychological and physical problems arise, which may not be seen as connected to the bereavement. Apply this principle of "coming through pain" to all types of pain you experience.

LOVE YOURSELF

The release is a process, a means by which we grow. Take it in small sips. Remember to love yourself through all this. Your mind and body always strive toward health, but their starting point is how they are now. They need time, nurturing, routine, and gentle discipline.

EXPLORING YOUR PAIN

When you experience pain, either emotional or physical, or you have an emotional problem, take time to stop and see how you think about the pain or problems well as taking practical steps to alleviate it.

Watch and experience the pain dispassionately with an enquiring mind. Relate the qualities of your experiences to the doshas (see pp. 30–1, 75, 78). Ask yourself questions about what you are experiencing. Be patient; it usually requires practice to obtain the insights. Learn to recognize your way of knowing that you have received a meaningful insight. Trust yourself to receive the counsel of your inner wisdom, which may be hidden by the chatter of the everyday mind.

You can do this enquiring, observation exercise with any problems in your life. Be with the problem and explore all its facets. Remember, you are the observer. Lovingly, patiently, diligently search for the keys to understanding and resolution.

LIFE EVENTS
AND CHANGE

Traumas and life events, even good ones, affect our health because change aggravates vata. Vata is the most volatile of the doshas; according to ancient texts, over 50 per cent of illness is due to vata disturbances. Many symptoms of stress in modern life are due to excess vata. Take extra care of yourself at times of change, to prevent vata imbalance. Try to understand how your doshas are affected by change and life's events, and how they affect your reactions to them. And try to see times of ill health or stress as indicators of the adjustments required in your lifestyle.

Major life events include changes in both family circumstances (e.g. divorce, marriage, pregnancy, childbirth, children leaving home) and working life (a new job/boss, redundancy, retirement, moving to a new location). The death of someone we love leaves us empty (vata), but other emotions may be bound up in the pain: for example, anger (pitta) at the circumstances of the death, or difficulty in letting go (kapha).

Assessing Life Events

Use these headings to assess the major events in your life:

• Description of the event

• Duration of the event

• Season when the event took place

• Effects of the event on your body

• Thoughts and emotions experienced

Think about the qualitative effects on your mind and body. Relate these to the qualities of VPK (see pp. 28–31, 37) and to emotions (see pp. 36, 78, 168–9), in order to assess the doshic effects of your experiences.

Compare the chronological order of your life events with previous ailments or illnesses, and use the ailment assessment (see p. 80) to understand which excess dosha mainfested the symptoms. This helps build the picture of the doshic patterns in your life and to show tendencies in the way you react. Ask an empathetic friend to help you.

A Newborn Baby

The arrival of a new human being signals many changes in
a family. All doshas can be affected by the physical and
emotional experiences. Vata, in particular, will be increased
by the birth process itself, by the change in routine, and by
the interruption to, and loss of, sleep.

REPRESSED EMOTIONS
AND THE BODY

We have seen that negative emotions and repressing emotions aggravate the doshas (see pp. 78, 168–9). Unresolved emotions can also cause weak spots (see p. 70), which show no symptoms unless the doshas are aggravated and spread into the tissue types. Massage can reach the seven tissue types, which according to Ayurveda are connected to the layers of the skin.

Massage is known to improve metabolism and to have other physiological effects; and, in the right conditions, massage can help release repressed emotions. This takes time, and the environment must be safe, physically and emotionally. Also, the masseur's touch and manner must be caring and sensitive. In these conditions you have the opportunity to be with and let go of repressed emotions, but only when you are ready to release them. Tears are a sign that the body is cleansing emotions. Always be gentle and loving toward yourself. Trust what you are experiencing. Never force anything. It has taken time to become as you are and time will be needed to change.

ORGANS AND NEGATIVE EMOTIONS

Organ	Emotion
Adrenals	Anxiety, sense of lack of support
Bladder	Insecurity
Colon	Nervousness
Heart	Sense of lack of love, feelings of deep hurt
Lungs	Sadness and grief
Kidney	Fear
Gall bladder	Hate
Liver	Anger
Small intestine	Sense of failure
Spleen	Greed, attachment, possessiveness
Stomach	Lack of fulfilment, lack of contentment

Negative Emotions

Dr. Vasant Lad teaches that certain negative emotions have an affinity with some organs (see table). All experiences are impressed on the memory of muscle tissues. Within Ayurveda's understanding of the body there are specific connections between certain emotions and muscles, and between those muscles and certain organs. The layers of skin are related to the seven levels of tissue; thus all the tissues can be affected by massage.

RELATIONSHIPS

Life is relationships. Your wellbeing affects and is affected by your relationships with yourself, your body, your pains, your thoughts, your emotions, your partner, your family, your friends, your colleagues, your work, your leisure activities, and your environment.

When your relationship with yourself is right the rest will move into balance. The key is to love yourself, which means accepting yourself just as you are. In loving yourself you are able to love the rest of creation. You reflect what you are. Awareness of who you really are and understanding of your uniqueness will allow you to love yourself. By loving yourself, you will give yourself the time needed for the welfare of your body and mind and spirit

Through learning to love yourself, you will also come to respect yourself. You will also find the resources within that allow you to make adjustments to your attitudes and your life, which will help to bring your other relationships into balance. If you find your place in the dance of creation, it helps those around you find their places, too.

Some situations in life do not seem to find proper resolution, and you may have to face hard decisions and painful acceptance. Not accepting a situation, having regrets over your actions, or not feeling able to act, all take energy and can affect your physical health.

The qualities of the emotions in your relationships affect your doshas. If there is much anger, pitta increases. Fear deranges vata. Possessiveness affects kapha. As you deal with difficult times, look after your physical health by taking practical steps through your diet and lifestyle to keep your doshas balanced.

Meditation and awareness (see pp. 176–7) will help you understand your relationships. Learn to be the observer. See what is happening, but do not judge. Many human communications are clouded by the filters of past hurts and judgmental attitudes.

SPACE TO GROW

When your doshas are balanced, positive aspects are naturally expressed in all your relationships. For example, communication (vata), attention (pitta), and support and compassion (kapha). This brings space, allowing all your relationships to grow and develop. The space gives room for unconditional love, the energy of the universe, and the source of healing.

INDIVIDUAL IDENTITY

Inappropriate opinions and judgments, or the harbouring of deep hurts, can bring a sense of isolation, separation, or division. We lose the awareness that we are a part of universal creation and cannot be separated from it. We take our hurts and pains personally, when we forget that we share in the pain, and also the joys, of humanity.

Modern pressures make it hard to remain connected with "who we really are", especially if we identify ourselves as only our emotions, thoughts, everyday mind, and physical body. When we acknowledge hidden levels of our being we touch our inner wisdom and come to know "who we really are" – the experiencer experiencing existence.

It is important to have a strong individual identity, or ahamkara (see pp. 18–21), so we are not open to unwelcome influences. In building our identity, the mind may want to gain power and perpetuate itself, rather than be a servant of "who we really are". This is subtle, but we can end up defining ourselves as our own strong attitudes and opinions. If this happens we forget "who we really are" and lose the awareness of how and why the attitudes were formed, and whether they are still relevant for our wellbeing.

This is a very difficult and often painful part of ourselves to look at. For most of us it strikes at what we regard as the core of our being. Courage is needed to examine and, perhaps, change these structures of our minds. Often, they are self-made filters that colour and weaken our connection with "who we really are" and cause us to act in ways that prevent us realizing our full potential.

Identity with deep attitudes does not change easily. Ask yourself why you think as you do about issues affecting your wellbeing. Do your opinions help you obtain the best outcome, or would a change in your approach open up greater possibilities? If you find yourself resisting change, ask yourself why, but without being critical. Change should only happen at the appropriate time. Gradual change is preferable and less distressing than sudden change.

WHO AM I?

This is a question that has no answer. But if asked in stillness or meditation it brings growing awareness of parts of your being that are beyond words — insights of "who you really are". It heals internal wounds and brings integration. Everyone experiences this in different ways. As you continue to ask "Who am I?" your inner wisdom will grow whatever your outer circumstances, and a light will shine through any pains you still have to bear.

Integration

Regular meditation, stilling the mind, allows the gradual integration of all aspects of your being.

AWARENESS AND MEDITATION

Meditation maintains mental and emotional health by allowing you to be aware of "who you really are". If you already meditate then continue as usual, otherwise the first step is to practise stilling the everyday mind (see below). When you first start, many questions arise: how should you meditate correctly, what are you trying to achieve, or how can you understand what you experience? Let the questions pass without worrying or trying to answer them. Give yourself a regular quiet time when you can become aware of your inner wisdom, which can guide all aspects of your life.

Life is Meditation

Meditation can be more than spending 10 minutes every morning and evening letting your mind be still, although this in itself is important. You can live your whole life as a meditation, as the observer witnessing your life. You are vital, aware of how your thoughts and actions affect your wellbeing and the wellbeing of those around you.

Living life in this state of awareness is a skill that needs practice until it becomes part of you. Start by taking a few moments (at different times during the day) consciously to observe how your body is feeling. Do this at any time – at the bus stop, at your desk, while driving, or preparing a meal. Are both sides of your body balanced or are you putting more weight on one side? Adjust your posture if necessary, but do not worry if a few moments later you are back in your habitual position. Do you have tension or aches in any part of your body – for example, in your shoulders or legs? If you do, do not make a judgment about that or yourself; just gently move the tense muscles or rub the aches and carry on with what you are doing.

Consciously note the state of your everyday mind. Is that little voice chattering away in your head, repeating judgments from the past and worries about the future? Is the chattering interfering with your mind's clarity, clouding your perceptions and actions now? That little voice is one of the hardest things to control. Become aware of the tone of its chatter. It can act like brainwashing. Often, these repetitive thoughts are unloving and critical of yourself. Even if you cannot turn it off you can change the record so that it has positive and loving messages. Every time you catch yourself thinking negative thoughts, cancel them mentally and create a positive thought. A regular 10 minutes' quiet time really helps quieten the mind.

As you learn more about Ayurveda and the doshas, you will find you put your awareness increasingly into your daily activities. You use the qualitative way of thinking to see what is happening around and within you, and then make conscious instead of habitual choices.

STILLING THE EVERYDAY MIND

If meditation is new to you, here is a simple way to learn to still the mind. Make yourself comfortable, preferably sitting on the floor or a chair. Sit with your spine upright but relaxed. Focus your attention on your breath. Observe it going in and coming out. Do not change how you are breathing, just watch. On the inhalation silently say "SO", and on the exhalation "HUM". When you notice that the mind has wandered away from the breath, gently bring it back and continue with "SO-HUM".

" Meditation is one of the most serious things. You can do it all day, in the office, with the family, when you say to someone, "I love you", when you are considering your children … And when you so meditate you will find in it an extraordinary beauty; you will act rightly at every moment; and if you do not act rightly at a given moment it does not matter, you will pick it up again — you will not waste time in regret. Meditation is part of life, not something different from life. "

Krishnamurti, *Meditation*

8. MAKING
CHANGES

ॐ☙

क्रमेणापचिता दीषाः क्रमेणीपचिता गुणाः ।
सन्ती यान्त्यपुनर्भावमप्रकम्प्या भवन्ति च ॥

The bad effects diminished gradually and the good effects increased gradually, attain (the state of)
non-recurrence and become stable.
(*Astanga Hrdayam* Chapter 7: 50)

You need to apply Ayurveda in your life to experience its benefits. Before this can happen, you need to take many factors into account. And as you examine the qualities in your life more closely, you find that the doshic influences are not always clear cut, making it confusing which dosha you need to pacify. You end up thinking you need to pacify them all! So where do you begin?

First have confidence and trust in yourself. You already feel and think in qualities; now you can begin to use qualitative information in logical and intuitive ways. You know your mind and body very well, though often your inner wisdom may seem obscured by habits detrimental to your health. The very first step to maintaining good health is to make sure you have good digestion (see p. 179). This prevents ama (see p. 77) and builds healthy tissues,

which results in sufficient ojas (see p. 56). Ojas, if not depleted through poor lifestyle, will make you more resilient to the doshic influences you encounter day by day.

You should also observe the variety of experiences that arise in your mind and body. Note whether they relate to positive or negative aspects of vata, pitta, or kapha. As you do this, you will see how you respond to different qualities in your daily activities. Then you start making choices about the qualities you want to incorporate into your life. You learn to distinguish where your cravings come from: your inner wisdom to balance a dosha or supply a genuine need of your mind or body; or an excess dosha, seeking to increase itself under the principle of "like increases like". Develop your awareness, as your everyday mind will try many tricks to confuse you.

Reviewing your Assessments

Understanding your doshas is an ongoing process, which you will follow automatically as you learn to read the doshas in and around you. Therefore you need to review your assessments to see the doshic patterns in your life.

Try if you can to become aware of any deep feelings that may be subtly influencing your life. These will be very personal and private, but if left unaddressed they may gradually affect your health adversely. Be the observer, and be gentle with yourself as your awareness of these feelings grows.

Use the information from the summary of your assessments (see p. 181) to help you decide which areas of your life you wish to change. Make sure that you are following the correct doshic-pacifying diet (see pp. 154–5).

If you have any current ailments or any doshic imbalance (see p. 63), then you should remove or reduce factors that are increasing the excess dosha(s), or practise acceptance of factors you feel you cannot change (see Chapter 7). You should follow a lifestyle that will pacify the increased dosha(s). As you deal with your current imbalance, try not to disturb your predominant dosha, if it is different from the increased dosha.

When you have no doshic imbalances, follow a diet and lifestyle that will pacify your predominant dosha(s). This will help you work toward a "better" doshic balance, thereby preventing ailments and illnesses, increasing your vitality, and slowing down the ageing process.

Review possible changes to your lifestyle under these headings: digestion, diet, work, leisure pursuits, exercise, quiet times, morning routine, and responsibility to relationships. Write down your proposals in a positive way rather than a negative way. Let the mind

IMPROVING DIGESTION

- Correct factors that are disturbing your agni (see p. 76).
- Choose a diet suitable for your doshas (see Chapter 6).
- Take appropriate exercise (see pp. 96–7).
- Eat at regular times and observe the rules of eating (see Chapter 6).
- Use herbs and spices that stimulate agni and aid digestion when preparing food and drinks (see pp. 158–65).
- Improve your elimination (see pp. 126–7).

concentrate on the new actions so the old ones will wither through lack of attention. Change should be gradual to be beneficial. Remember that as you change those close to you will have to adjust to the new you.

Make broad statements of intent if you wish to make big changes and then note down the first few small practical steps toward the bigger goal. From your overall list, select two or three small steps to start the process of change. Keep taking further appropriate steps, until you have learned to live and respond to your current experiences, but not with habitual reactions, but through aware choices that maintain the natural balance of your doshas.

SEASONAL VARIATIONS

Whatever your circumstances, you should adjust your lifestyle to allow for seasonal variations (see p. 150).

DIETING

Your body has adapted to your eating patterns. A sudden change in diet can make you body or mind feel deprived. But if the changes are made slowly, both your mind and body have time to adapt. Permanent changes in weight need to be achieved slowly. Generally, a kapha-pacifying diet will result in weight loss, while a vata-pacifying diet will help you gain weight (see pp. 154–5).

Excess weight may be due to a number of causes, e.g. ama, poor digestion, wrong food combinations, low agni, or overeating (either to satisfy the mind's desire for comfort or the body's need for prana).

Assessment Summary

Use Martin's assessments (see pp. 182–3) to help you summarize your own data. Mark in the related doshas (use the following questions as a guide):-

- What is your constitution or predominant dosha(s)? (See pp. 38–41)
- Are your doshas balanced? (See p. 63)
- Are your predominant dosha(s) or any imbalances increased or pacified by:
 - Your diet
 - Aspects of your work
 - Unresolved emotions
 - Your relationships
 - Your leisure activities
 - Your attitudes
 - Your life events?

VPK and Daily Living

The VPK guidelines below remind you of key points, in addition to the correct diet, for day-to-day living for each constitutional type.

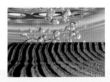

VATA

- Have a regular routine
- Oil your skin regularly
- Take gentle exercise daily
- Have plenty of sleep and rest
- Keep warm
- Nurture your senses

PITTA

- Achieve your ambitions without pressurizing yourself
- Use constructive criticism rather than confrontation
- Take non-competitive exercise daily
- Keep cool
- Enjoy outdoor activities that challenge you

KAPHA

- Vary your routine
- Have plenty of mental stimulation
- Take vigorous exercise daily
- Get up early, go to bed late
- Keep warm

Caution:

If you have any medical condition, dietary or lifestyle changes should be made in consultation with your medical adviser. However, following the correct diet and lifestyle for you will assist any treatments you have.

MARTIN'S ASSESSMENTS

Martin's Ayurvedic profile was described on page 105 and his diet assessed on page 157. Here his life is related to VPK, and changes and first steps recommended.

Aged 45	Pitta age
Constitution	Pitta

Ailments

Acid indigestion	Pitta
Red spots/blotches	Pitta
Lung infections	Pitta
Headaches	Pitta/Vata

Life Events/Relationships

Aged 18 University	34 Daughter born
28 Partner in law practice	37 Son born
31 Married	38 Father died

These all involved changes and increase in vata, but did not have any noticeable effect on his health. At 28, he achieved an ambition, but no definite goals since.

Morning Routine

Erratic, rushing	Vata

Work

Responsibilities	Pitta
Sedentary	Kapha
Travel	Vata
Challenging	Pitta
Many demands	Pitta/Vata
Frustrations	Pitta
Interruptions	Vata

Leisure

Squash	Pitta
Social drinking and eating	In excess, will increase pitta, kapha

Digestion

Strong, fast	Pitta
Diet	Pitta

Attitudes and Emotions

Frustrations	Pitta
Deep fear of failure	Pitta
Deep fear of emptiness in life	Vata

The Summary of Martin's Assessments

Martin's profile reveals a pitta imbalance and a number of pitta influences, though there are also factors which may increase vata. In the past, his health has not been affected by increased vata. But if the vata-increasing factors are not addressed they will be more likely to lead to ailments when he approaches the vata age. Then his body will have less resilience to tolerate further imbalance of doshas due to the prolonged increase of his pitta dosha.

Martin looked closely at his deep inner feeling. In his late teens and twenties, he used his natural pitta energy and the mental abilities manifested from it to gain his legal qualification and successful professional reputation. He developed the habit of achieving, for in addition to his intellectual gifts he had to be very goal-oriented to accomplish his ambition. This habitual way of working (which increases pitta), combined with a deep and private fear of failure, locks him into a pitta-genic lifestyle. Unless he makes changes, such a lifestyle will take him from the early to the later stages of the disease process.

If Martin could reduce his excess pitta energy he would more easily move into the mature stage of his career, reaping broad benefits established by his earlier hard work. He now knows that he should put his positive or natural pitta energy to good use, not only for himself but also for his family and colleagues.

Suggested Changes for Martin to Reduce Pitta

Diet — Pitta-pacifying (see pp. 133–43)

Work — Reduce the demands, frustrations, and interruptions by leading a team to whom he can delegate with confidence, and whose respect he will gain by sharing his experience, by acknowledging their strengths, and by constructively criticizing their weaknesses.

Lesiure Pursuits/Exercise — More outdoor activities with his family, e.g. cycling. Some individual sessions with a yoga therapist to establish suitable exercises that he can do each day whether he is home or away.

Morning Routine — Get up early enough to spend half an hour doing yoga or having a quiet time. Eat breakfast with his children.

Responsibility to Relationships — Give uninterrupted time to children/wife without expecting responses or results (since they are unused to this, expectations will limit what could develop). Achieve a better balance between energy and time given to work and family.

Martin's First Steps

Martin accepts that he needs to make changes and apart from the morning routine, the changes he lists are general aims. His first steps are: eating breakfast at the same time as his children; choosing foods more carefully when eating out; becoming aware of when he is impatient or critical with his personal assistant; reflecting on more appropriate ways of responding; and making an appointment with a yoga therapist.

SEEKING ADVICE

If you feel unsure about taking steps to change your lifestyle and would like Ayurvedic advice, then you can seek either an Ayurvedic physician or practitioner. The former has had extensive and rigorous training: a degree in Ayurvedic Medicine and Surgery, which takes five years to complete, is followed by a period of supervised practical experience – similar to the internship of newly graduated Western doctors.

In 1980, Dr. Robert Svoboda (who wrote the foreword to this book) became the first Westerner to graduate from a recognized university or college with such a degree. He is one of a very few fully trained Ayurvedic physicians practising in the West. This situation may slowly change. In India, more Ayurveda students than ever are receiving training and more Ayurvedic clinics are catering for Westerners.

Currently, in the West, Ayurveda is used primarily for prevention and alleviation of digestive disorders. Increasing numbers of Westerners are seeking training in its principles and practice. They may become Aurvedic practitioners, not physicians. Those sufficiently trained already can offer guidance on panchakarma (see p. 186), herbs, diet, and lifestyle. Some Western health-care practitioners and alternative therapists are receiving instruction in Ayurveda to complement their professional expertise. This will enable them to make individual assessments, be more effective in selecting treatments, and offer dietary and lifestyle advice using Ayurvedic principles.

Finding an Ayurvedic physician or practitioner can be difficult. Not only are they few and far between at present, but also standards may vary. However, this will change, too. Standards of training for different levels of practitioners and registers of practitioners are yet to be established. Consequently, when you try to find a competent Ayurvedic physician or practitioner, use your common sense and be guided by your inner wisdom – do not let your good judgment be clouded by a desperate desire to find help.

Assessing Ill Health

Good powers of observation and a deep understanding of the body enable Ayurvedic physicians to read information about health and illness from small signs. They then build a complete picture of a patient's doshic balance or imbalance.

In making an assessment, the physician needs to ascertain which doshas, tissues, channels, and organs are affected, and will need to discover your constitution, the strength of your agni and your strength to undertake treatment. Physicians ask questions to confirm assessments they make by reading the pulse or observing the tongue, iris, face, skin, urine, and stools.

Ayurvedic Treatments

The object of treatment in Ayurveda is to restore the patient's natural balance of the doshas by pacification, thus removing the cause of the illness as well as the symptoms. When the doshic balance is restored, the tissues weakened by the illness need to be rejuvenated. The effectiveness of the treatment will depend on many factors including your physical and mental strength to overcome the illness, the length of time you have suffered from it, your age, your diligence in following the advice, and the accuracy of the advice. The longer you have had an illness, the longer and harder it is to restore your doshic balance. It is also harder to restore the doshic balance and rejuvenate the tissues completely when you are in the vata age since your metabolism is naturally slowing down.

Herbs, panchakarma (see p. 186) and shirodhara (see above) are the principal treatments used in Ayurveda in the West, but many other treatments now available in the West as complementary therapies have been used within Ayurveda for thousands of years. These include massage, marma point manipulation (similar to acupressure), colour and gem therapy, essences and potencised remedies, music and chanting, meditation, yoga, and balancing nadi energy (on which polarity therapy is based).

The Use of Herbs

In Ayurveda, herbs are often used for pacification (and the rejuvenation that follows) and the general maintenance of health. A vast range of herbs is available and their effectiveness is due to detailed knowledge of their special actions, or prabhav (see p. 53) and correctly matching these to the doshas, tissues, and agni.

Ayurveda understands herbs in terms of their qualities and their effects in the body and on the doshas. Thus it is concerned with the overall strengthening or diminishing action in the body not the "active" ingredient of each herb. In Ayurveda, a medicine should do its job in the body and leave without side effects. Although many Ayurvedic herbal formulae are available as general tonics, individual treatments are finely tuned to the patient's constitution and specific circumstances as well as the doshas and tissues involved.

PACIFICATION

This involves "burning" ama, enkindling agni, and removing excess doshas, using herbs, fasting under supervision, exercise, and pranayama.

Panchakarma

If you have the physical strength, the physician may suggest purification in the form of panchakarma. This deep cleansing process, which is unique to Ayurveda, enables the body to release excess doshas and toxins from its cells, gather them in the gastrointestinal tract, and expel them. Panchakarma means five actions. These are therapeutic vomiting to remove excess kapha, therapeutic purgation to remove excess pitta, therapeutic enema to remove excess vata, nasal administration in cases of diseases of the head and neck, and blood-letting in cases of blood disorders.

The body has to be properly prepared for a number of days. This involves deep, generous oil massage followed by steam treatment. The steam helps the oil penetrate the skin as well as releasing surface toxins. Herbs may be used with the oil or steam. When the oil has penetrated deeply and the body is fully prepared, the appropriate "action" is taken. Each panchakarma programme is individually tailored to the patient.

Caution:

Panchakarma is very powerful and should be carried out by an experienced practitioner.

Pulse Diagnosis

Some Ayurvedic physicians rely solely on pulse diagnosis to determine health. Usually taken at the radial arteries in the wrist, it is a skill that requires great sensitivity, clarity, and dedication to acquire. In the hands of an expert, it is very accurate, though you may find it disconcerting to have such a short consultation.

INDEX

RESOURCES

Further Reading

Charaka Samhita Vols 1 to 3
Editor/Translator Prof. Priya Vrat
Sharma (Chaukhambha Orientalia,
9th edition, 2005)

Astanga Hrdayam Vol 1
Translated by Prof. K. R. Sri Kantha
Murthy (Krishnadas Academy, 1991)

Ayurveda: Life Health and Longevity
Dr. Robert Svoboda (Arkana, 1992)

The Yoga of Herbs
Dr. David Frawley and Dr. Vasant Lad
(Lotus Press, 2nd edition, 2001)

Ayurvedic Cooking for Self Healing
Usha Lad and Dr. Vasant Lad (The
Ayurvedic Press, 2nd edition, 2006)

The Ayurvedic Cookbook
Amadea Morningstar (Lotus Press,
1992)

*Secrets of the Pulse: The Ancient
Art of Ayurvedic Pulse Diagnosis*
Dr. Vasant Dattatray Lad (The
Ayurvedic Press, 2nd edition, 2006)

*Ayurvedic Healing:
A Comprehensive Guide*
Dr. David Frawley (Lotus Press,
2nd edition, 2001)

*The Tibetan Book of the Living
and Dying*
Sogyal Rinpoche
(Rider, revised edition, 2002)

*The Complete Book of Ayurvedic
Home Remedies*
Vasant Lad (Piatkus, 2006)

*Ayurveda and Life Impressions
Bodywork: Seeking Our Healing
Memories*
Donald vanHowten (Lotus Press, 1997)

The Complete Yoga Course
Howard Kent (Headline Books, 1993)

Addresses

The Ayurvedic Institute
Box 23445, Albuquerque, New Mexico
87192-1445, USA
www.ayurveda.com
Director: Dr. Vasant Lad
Offers a school, private consultations
and panchakarma; a herb department.

PICTURE CREDITS

Alamy/Caro 63; /Dinodia Photos 95; /Andreas von Einsiedel 31 below right; /foodfolio 165; /Tom Mackie 30 below left; /Jochen Tack 123 below; /Maximilian Weinzierl 167.

Fotolia/Alithenake 163 centre; /Aniuszka 27 Image 6 (used throughout); /berc 85; /Buriy 163 below; /byheaven 97; /Constantinos 162; /detailblick 171; /fkruger 147; /fmonkey 158 below centre; /Furret 155; /gavran333 158 below left; /Angelo Giampiccolo 2; /Scott Harms 159 above centre; /Jiri Hera 13; /ivan kmit 61; /jeehyun 159 below right; /Ekaterina Lin 158 below right; /lunamarina 14; /Maridav 67; /Monkey Business 23 centre below, 27 Image 4 (used throughout), 27 Image 5 (used throughout); /Swapan 158 above right; /tfazevedo 159 above right, 159 below left; /Vidady 159 below centre; /Krzysztof Wiktor 107; /Oleg Zhukov 55 right.

Getty Images/Ursula Alter 50; /BLOOM image 64; /Burke/Triolo Productions 123 above; /Digital Vision 11; /Dinodia Photos 129; /Fabrice Lerouge 118; /Ericka McConnell 109; /Tom Merton 86; /my second last dream 82; /Michael Paul 192; /Matthew Wakem 119; /Dougal Waters 7.

Glow Images/Eye Ubiquitous 71.
Image Source 120 above; /Carlos Hernandez 120 below.
Narratives/Martin Hahn 91.
Octopus Publishing Group/Frazer Cunningham 46, 47.
Science Photo Library/CNRI 22.
SuperStock/Westend61 163 above; /Yuri Arcurs Media/SuperFusion 121.
Thinkstock/Brand X Pictures 111 Centre Left, 149; /Design Pics 27 Image 1 (used throughout), 31 above right; /Digital Vision 39; /Eyecandy Images 90; /Goodshoot 175; /Hemera 23 below, 23 above, 30 above right, 55 centre, 160; /iStockphoto 23 centre above, 23 centre, 27 Image 2 (used throughout), 29 left, 29 centre, 29 right, 31 above left, 31 centre right below, 51, 53, 54 left, 54 centre, 54 right, 55 left, 111 below right, 111 above right, 111 above left, 133, 152; /Jupiterimages 42; /Photos.com 31 centre left above; /Martin Poole 93; /Kraig Scarbinsky 115; /Stockbyte 27 Image 3 (used throughout), 30 above left; /TongRo Images 111 centre right; /Wavebreak Media 125; /Zoonar 161.
Wellcome Library, London 187.